A Publication of
the Council on Foundations

The Council on Foundations is a nonprofit membership organization for grant-makers. Founded in 1949, the council's mission is to promote and strengthen organized philanthropy. The council represents grantmakers, their concerns, and their interests to public policymakers, the media, and the general public. Membership includes over 1,300 independent, operating, community, public and company-sponsored foundations, corporate giving programs, trust companies, and international foundations. Members of the council represent more than $95 billion in assets and contributed $5.5 billion in 1992 for programs in such fields as education, social welfare, health, science and research, environment, the arts, urban planning and economic development, religious charity, and international development. Through their subscription to a set of principles and practices for effective grantmaking, council members provide leadership in the area of public accountability for the field of philanthropy.

Programs. Council programs help members achieve their charitable goals and foster a broad public understanding of philanthropy and its impact within society. The council provides education and professional development opportunities for grantmakers through workshops, conferences, publications, and other information and technical assistance. The council also has programs in government relations, communications and public affairs, research, special support services, and special initiatives to promote the growth of organized philanthropy.

Meetings. The council sponsors an annual conference to focus on current global political, economic, and social issues confronting the United States and the world and their implications for organized philanthropy. Other educational programs and seminars held throughout the year concentrate on specific program issues, tax and regulatory policies, management and administrative practices, communications, and other areas.

Publications. The council publishes *Foundation News,* a bimonthly magazine featuring coverage of the nonprofit sector and current philanthropic issues and activities. The council also publishes a biweekly newsletter, resources for grantmakers, and other periodic surveys, reports, and studies on issues related to grantmaking.

COUNCIL ON FOUNDATIONS
1828 L STREET NW WASHINGTON, DC 20036-5168
(202) 466-6512 · FAX (202) 785-3926

EVALUATION
for
FOUNDATIONS

Council on Foundations

EVALUATION
for
FOUNDATIONS

Concepts, Cases,
Guidelines,
and Resources

Jossey-Bass Publishers · San Francisco

Substantial discounts on bulk quantities of Jossey-Bass books are available to corporations, professional associations, and other organizations. For details and discount information, contact the special sales department at Jossey-Bass Inc., Publishers. (415) 433-1740; Fax (415) 433-0499.

For sales outside the United States, contact Maxwell Macmillan International Publishing Group, 866 Third Avenue, New York, New York 10022.

Manufactured in the United States of America

The paper used in this book is acid-free and meets the State of California requirements for recycled paper (50 percent recycled waste, including 10 percent postconsumer waste), which are the strictest guidelines for recycled paper currently in use in the United States.

10% POST
CONSUMER
WASTE

The ink in this book is either soy- or vegetable-based and during the printing process emits fewer than half the volatile organic compounds (VOCs) emitted by petroleum-based ink.

Library of Congress Cataloging-in-Publication Data

Council on Foundations.
  Evaluation for foundations : concepts, cases, guidelines, and resources / Council on Foundations. — 1st ed.
    p.   cm. — (The Jossey-Bass nonprofit sector series)
  Includes bibliographical references (p.   ) and index.
  ISBN 1-55542-541-0 (alk. paper)
    1. Endowments — United States — Evaluation.   2. Nonprofit organizations — United States — Evaluation.   3. Charitable uses, trusts, and foundations — United States — Evaluation.   I. Title. II. Series.
HV97.A3C68   1993
361.7'632'0973 — dc20   92-44466
                                                                      CIP

FIRST EDITION
HB Printing   10 9 8 7 6 5 4 3 2 1   *Code 9344*

The Jossey-Bass
Nonprofit Sector Series

Contents

Contents

Preface

Evaluation is commonly thought of as a good thing — a way of understanding something, improving it, or avoiding future trouble with it. In parts of our lives we routinely rely on evaluation processes for important guidance — for example, trial by jury, school accreditation, or a physician's periodic physical examination.

For many years, evaluation of process and product in grantmaking programs has seemed especially worthy of encouragement. Observers of the grantmaking process have maintained that both grantmakers and grantees would do better work if they tried more frequently and more systematically to assess what their grant-financed activity was accomplishing and how it might be made more effective.

Background

The Council on Foundations, a leading professional association in philanthropy with more than a thousand foundation and corporate members, regularly polls those members to inquire what aspects of grantmaking and administration should receive greater attention in the council's conferences and educational programs. *Evaluation for Foundations* came about because during the 1980s, one of the most frequent suggestions was that the council should provide more information and guidance about evaluation.

In considering this advice, the council's Research Committee noted that it was unlikely that more than one hundred U.S. foundation and corporate giving programs were pursuing serious or sustained evaluation of their own programs or of grantee projects. Furthermore, the committee was unable to identify more than thirty corporate and foundation program officers who felt sufficiently comfortable in their knowledge of evaluation practices to volunteer specific training or consultation to others.

Why does such a large gap exist between the perceived need for evaluation in grantmaking, which is high, and its actual performance, which is infrequent? One answer is that "evaluation" has almost as many meanings as there are people talking about the subject, and these multiple meanings may lead to confusion about its feasibility. Ideally, a grants officer or project manager should be aware of the major evaluation-strategy choices — and the main advantages and pitfalls of each — before trying to organize a specific evaluation in an organization. Until now a simple yet reliable orientation for such persons has not been generally available.

Another reason for the gap between opinion and practice is the commonsense awareness on the part of foundation officers and organizational managers that any tool can be misused. Badly designed or executed, evaluation may merely generate make-work, may be used to assign or shift blame for failure, or may become an excuse to prematurely end programs that should have been continued. In practice, fear that evaluation will be done foolishly often leads either to avoiding it or to designing it for minimum effort — and minimum significance.

Purpose of the Book

The Research Committee of the Council on Foundations believes that many forms of grantmaking evaluation have useful potential, that increasing numbers of foundation and corporate grantmakers can learn to be effective organizers and users of evaluation, and that the rising national interest in evaluation in many areas is not a short-term fad. Therefore, they determined that the most helpful first contribution they could make to stimulate more and better evaluation would be to commission a readable, practical, and reasonably comprehensive book that would orient grantmakers, and perhaps grantees, to different kinds of grant evaluation work and to the strengths and weaknesses of each kind. With this initial exposure, many corporate and foundation program officers will be better equipped to take their confident, successful first steps into program or project evaluation.

Scope and Treatment

Evaluation for Foundations is not a textbook on evaluation study designs. Nor does it explain general statistical or observational methods — for example, how to estimate whether an experimental group is performing significantly differently from a control group or how to inhibit interviewer bias from contaminating evaluations based mainly on interviews. This technical information is readily available elsewhere. The case studies are not intended to be exhaustive critiques of any single foundation or government evaluation effort.

Instead, the book provides a framework for thinking about the practicality and desirability of evaluation and supplies real-life examples of ways in which evaluations have been conceived and carried out. Moreover, many evaluation texts are written from the standpoint of either government-sponsored social programs or particular service programs. This book, however, is attuned to the particular needs, perspectives, and constraints of a philanthropic foundation interested in the evaluation of its grants, its programs, and its own operating practices.

Audience

The main audience for *Evaluation for Foundations* is corporate and foundation program officers at both large and smaller foundations who are relatively inexperienced at evaluation work but sense its possible advantages. Foundation officers with little formal training in evaluation are introduced to specialized vocabulary and information that can help them shop intelligently among evaluation professionals for the most effective and economical consulting help available. The book will also be useful to trustees and staff in grantmaking organizations that are considering launching or revising a general strategy of evaluation. Other audiences will include foundation applicants and grantees and professional independent program evaluators and consultants.

Overview of the Contents

Part One of *Evaluation for Foundations,* written by Barbara H. Kehrer, introduces the reader to the issues that foundation administrators should consider before beginning a program of purposeful evaluation. Chapter One discusses the choices that must be made if an evaluation is to have a clear direction and purpose; Chapter Two offers practical advice for initiating and implementing an evaluation.

Part Two presents nine case studies that describe how real foundations, facing real evaluation choices, made those choices, how the evaluations evolved, and how results were reported and used. The cases represent a broad cross-section of projects, ranging from low-income housing to education and the arts and initiated by both large and not-so-large corporations and foundations. Chapter Three examines the Meyer Memorial Trust's evaluation of its request-for-proposal process for projects to help the elderly maintain independence. Chapter Four looks at the L. J. and Mary C. Skaggs Foundation's evaluation of grants made to two fine arts organizations for the purpose of establishing new sources of income.

Chapter Five covers an evaluation of a program developed by the Winthrop Rockefeller Foundation to help at-risk students in the Arkansas public shools. Chapter Six focuses on the evaluation conducted by the Cities in Schools (CIS) program in New York City to examine the effectiveness of using existing city services to staff the CIS program. The results of the Technology for Literacy Project, funded primarily by the F. R. Bigelow Foundation and The Saint Paul Foundation, are the subject of the evaluation studied in Chapter Seven. The role of the Lilly Endowment's National Youthworker Education Project in making youth organizations more relevant to contemporary needs is the topic of the evaluation presented in Chapter Eight.

Chapter Nine analyzes the evaluation initiated by the William Penn Foundation to produce yearly feedback about the Career/Vocational Exploration Program in Philadelphia. Chapter Ten examines an evaluation of the Gautreaux Program's progress in improving housing and living conditions for inner-city public housing residents in Chicago. The final case study, presented in Chapter Eleven, covers the W. K. Kellogg Foundation's methods of evaluating clusters of grants.

Important concepts drawn from all nine case studies are presented in the Conclusion in the form of thirty-five keys to effective evaluation. Robert Matthews Johnson is the author of Part Two and the Conclusion.

Resource A defines commonly employed evaluation approaches and methods, and Resource B is an annotated bibliography of further reading in the form of evaluation texts, evaluation manuals developed by various foundations, reports about individual evaluations, and works that offer specific perspectives on evaluation. It also lists selected professional journals in the field. Both resources were written by Jan Corey Arnett.

St. Paul, Minnesota Humphrey Doermann
February 1993 President, Bush Foundation
  Past chair, board of directors,
  Council on Foundations

Acknowledgments

Evaluation for Foundations is the product of the labors of many
talented people who willingly contributed their expertise and
encouragement, from the project's inception to the delivery of
the final draft. Elizabeth Boris, then the Council on Foundations' vice president for research, and Humphrey Doermann,
who chaired the council's Research Committee, first came to
me with the idea for the book in 1985. They were invaluable
in marshaling resources and support from council members.

In 1989, Boris and staff member Deborah Brody worked
with the Research Committee and its new chair, Sara Engle-
hardt, to identify the general scope and content of the book.
They appointed an advisory committee, chaired by Charles Bonjean, an educator and expert in evaluation and vice president
of the Hogg Foundation for Mental Health. Joining the council
in 1990 as director of research, Judith Kroll assumed oversight
of the project.

Together, the Advisory Committee and staff developed an
outline for the book and identified its potential audience. They
ultimately decided that the book should have several authors

with different types of knowledge, experiences, and orientations. Jan Corey Arnett, Robert Matthews Johnson, and Barbara H. Kehrer proved to be outstanding choices.

Advisory Committee members Janet Carter, Marion Faldet, Suzanne Fuert, Jean Hart, Dana Phillips, Ronald Richards, and Susan Wisely played key roles in developing the book's organization and identifying the materials that would become its unique and central feature—the case studies. Carter and Faldet deserve special thanks for their creativity, attention to detail, and valuable suggestions throughout the process. In addition, thanks go to three external reviewers (who were "anonymous" at the time) for lending their expertise in evaluating the manuscript: Ralph E. Culler, executive associate of the Hogg Foundation for Mental Health; William E. Bickel, senior scientist at the Learning Research and Development Center at the University of Pittsburg; and Kirke Wilson, executive director of the Rosenberg Foundation.

There is a saying that anything assigned to a committee or a group can be done better by one person. However, thanks to Elizabeth Boris's leadership during the early stages of the project and Judith Kroll's organizational skills and willingness to listen to everyone during the later stages, the collective method proved the most effective approach to producing this book.

Thanks are due also to Charles Bonjean for his diligent supervision, suggestions, and advice. The energy, enthusiasm, and diverse talents of the many contributors to this project made the endeavor a rewarding one for all involved.

Washington, D.C.   James A. Joseph
February 1993   President, Council on Foundations

Contributors

Jan Corey Arnett is a communications and evaluation professional who consults under the company name In Layman's Terms. She is also the information services coordinator for Starr Commonwealth, which has campuses in Albion and Detroit, Michigan, and Columbus and Van Wert, Ohio. She received her B.A. degree (1974) in English from Albion College and her M.A. degree (1987) in management from Nazareth College and has undertaken graduate study in evaluation at the University of Illinois, Chicago. She chairs the American Evaluation Association's Topical Interest Group on Evaluation in Nonprofits and Foundations. As a member of the evaluation staff of the W. K. Kellogg Foundation, Arnett wrote an evaluation manual for staff and grantees.

Robert Matthews Johnson is a consultant and writer in philanthropy. He received his A.B. degree (1947) from Harvard University. For nearly thirty years, he has served as foundation executive, grantmaker, and consultant to foundations and other nonprofit organizations. As executive director of the Wieboldt Foundation from 1966 to 1983, Johnson helped the foundation establish many of the principles associated with the funding of community groups. He was later staff consultant to the Chicago Community Trust. His book *The First Charity* (1988) explores the links between foundations and local community organizations that build community participation and develop leadership in addressing major community issues. Johnson is also author of numerous articles for *Foundation News,* beginning with his "Between Grants" columns in the early 1970s. On the national level, Johnson has participated actively in the Council on Foundations and the National Network of Grantmakers. His interest in evaluation began during the early 1960s when, as consultant to the U.S. Department of Justice, he assessed the impact of major demonstration programs funded by the national Juvenile Delinquency and Youth Development Program.

Barbara H. Kehrer is vice president of research and evaluation with the Henry J. Kaiser Family Foundation. She received her B.A. degree (1963) in economics from Barnard College and her M.A. (1964) and Ph.D. (1969) degrees in economics from Yale University. Before joining Kaiser in 1984, Kehrer was senior program officer at the Robert Wood Johnson Foundation from 1982 to 1984, senior researcher at Mathematica Policy Research from 1975 to 1982, and director of the American Medical Association's Department of Economic Research from 1971 to 1975. Her primary research activities have been in health manpower, health policy, and health program evaluation. At the Kaiser Family Foundation, she has been responsible for developing and monitoring a wide variety of evaluations of the foundation's programs, ranging from major evaluation projects employing outside consultants to small-scale postgrant assessments carried out by staff.

EVALUATION
for
FOUNDATIONS

PART ONE

Introduction and Overview
of Evaluation

Barbara H. Kehrer

Did the project work? Did it do what it was supposed to do? Who was helped? Who wasn't helped? How can the successes and failures be explained? Did the project make a difference? Were the results worth the investment?

These are the kinds of questions evaluations answer: questions about attainment of goals and objectives; questions about implementation, feasibility, effectiveness, and cost; and questions about quality, utility, acceptability, and value. The answers are then used to make decisions and judgments about future programs and projects. Evaluations may also be used to make decisions and judgments about a past program or project — was it a good idea after all? — or about the past performance of a grantee.

Some grantmakers have consciously built formal evaluations into their regular activities, but they are in the minority. Many more foundations want to develop an evaluation capacity but are not sure how to go about it. However, sometimes without even realizing it, many foundations engage in various in-

1

formal evaluations, and could expand those activities gradually, once they identify the activities as likely starting points for fuller evaluation programs.

Good evaluation is systematic, disciplined inquiry. Beyond that, what evaluation is and does varies enormously. An evaluation can entail a site visit by a solo consultant, a phone survey by a student intern, or rigorous scientific research conducted by a team of academics. It can cost a few hundred dollars or several millions. Sometimes it can cost more than the program being evaluated. It can be conducted by foundation staff, grantee staff, outside consultants, or by another independent grantee or contractor. It can serve the interests of the foundation that sponsors it, of grantees, policymakers, practitioners, and social scientists.

Part One will introduce the reader to the issues a foundation that is beginning purposeful evaluation should consider and will provide guidance for developing an evaluation plan appropriate to a particular purpose and for interpreting the evaluation results.

Evaluation doesn't come in a neatly tied package that grantmakers can choose to buy or not to buy. Staff members charged with responsibility for evaluation must choose the pieces that should be in the package. They cannot delegate the decisions to others whose preferences and values may be different. They must make the choices themselves or risk finding the results to be of little use and interest and end up regretting the expense. They do not have to be experts in evaluation in order to make intelligent decisions about it. But they should be knowledgeable enough about the options to make informed choices among them.

Chapter One describes the important choices that should be considered in making decisions about evaluation. It lists different reasons foundations choose to explain their support of evaluation activities, explains why there can be no simple evaluation cookbook for foundations, and introduces standard evaluation terminology, which highlights the kinds of choices available to foundations thinking about evaluation. The chapter concludes with some thoughts about overcoming the resistance to evaluation often encountered within foundations.

The presentation of choices continues in Chapter Two, with a discussion of the practice-oriented, or operational, decisions and choices that foundations must make as they move further into the evaluation arena.

1

Understanding Evaluation:
Uses, Choices, and Methods

Foundations exist to spend philanthropic dollars in ways that benefit others. The essence of foundation life is making choices among competing requests for those dollars. It often happens that meritorious requests must be turned down because resources are limited and other requests are more compelling. Evaluation uses resources that otherwise could be spent to benefit people directly. Why should foundations choose to spend scarce philanthropic dollars to support evaluation?

Reasons for Evaluation

The answer is that evaluation helps programs or projects already supported by the foundation to serve their target populations better, points the way to developing or improving services to benefit people other than those directly served by the foundation's grants, and makes the foundation a better grantmaker.

To be more specific, there are at least seven reasons for a foundation to allocate resources to evaluation.

To Be Accountable as a Public Trust

Evaluation can help a foundation find out whether its grants and programs were implemented as planned and whether grantee and foundation objectives were met, not met, or even exceeded, and why.

To Assist Grantees to Improve

Evaluation can provide feedback to grantees to help them improve their performance. In this way, it serves as a program planning and management tool and amplifies the impact of a foundation's grants.

To Improve a Foundation's Grantmaking

Evaluation can also be a useful foundation management tool. Feedback on grants and programs helps a foundation track the progress and accomplishments of its projects and identify problems and aid in their timely resolution. Information about factors that contribute to successful grants and programs helps a foundation to design more effective grants and programs in the future. A foundation also might use evaluation to improve its own operating practices and choice of program areas by finding out what others think of them.

To Assess the Quality or Impact of Funded Programs

Foundations may support evaluations to find out whether and how an innovative program works. Foundations may also support evaluations to obtain a measure of the foundations' contributions to such goals as helping people, changing policy, and increasing knowledge.

To Plan and Implement New Programs

A foundation may undertake a pilot project with an accompanying evaluation in order to assess feasibility and guide the design of a larger program. Or it may conduct an evaluation to examine the nature and extent of a problem that it is considering as the focus of a new program. Reassessments of the needs being addressed by foundation programs help a foundation decide which areas should have priority in funding.

To Disseminate Innovative Programs

Foundations have ambitious goals but limited resources. Often these goals can be attained only if other organizations join in the effort. Evaluations can provide the information needed to persuade other organizations of the worth of the effort. A foundation also may evaluate as a leveraging device, to provide answers to questions that matter to other organizations (for instance, government agencies) whose activities the foundation wishes to influence.

To Increase the State of Knowledge

Evaluations that assess the impact of new interventions or programs can contribute to the attainment of a foundation's mission and the public good by identifying more effective means for addressing social problems and by increasing the state of knowledge about what approaches work best for what groups and why. Evaluations may also increase the understanding of social problems and help in devising solutions. In such ways, a foundation's combined investment in a program and its evaluation can contribute in an enduring way to the well-being of individuals and groups beyond those who participated in the program.

Table 1.1 is a guide to the reasons to evaluate that will be represented in the nine case studies in Part Two. The case studies will also further illustrate the benefits that evaluations can provide to their sponsoring foundations.

Despite valid reasons to support evaluation, it remains true that money spent on evaluation is money no longer available to spend on direct-service programs. A foundation's values and philosophy must come into play when making decisions

Table 1.1. Case Study Reasons to Evaluate.

Case Study	Reasons for Evaluation
The Meyer Memorial Trust request-for-proposal program (Chapter Three)	Improve grantee programs, improve grantmaking
L. J. and Mary C. Skaggs Foundation program for arts organizations (Chapter Four)	Be accountable, improve grantmaking
Winthrop Rockefeller Foundation at-risk youth program (Chapter Five)	Improve grantee programs, disseminate successful programs
Cities in Schools program (Chapter Six)	Increase the state of knowledge
Technology for Literacy Project (Chapter Seven)	Be accountable, improve grantee programs, improve grantmaking, assess quality or impact of grants/programs
Lilly Endowment youthworker project (Chapter Eight)	Be accountable, improve grantmaking, assess quality or impact of grants/programs, increase the state of knowledge
William Penn Foundation career/vocational program (Chapter Nine)	Be accountable, improve grantee programs, improve grantmaking
Gautreaux program (Chapter Ten)	Increase the state of knowledge
W. K. Kellogg Foundation grants (Chapter Eleven)	Be accountable, improve grantee programs, improve grantmaking, assess quality or impact of grants/programs, plan new programs, disseminate successful programs

about evaluation. A decision to evaluate reflects a value set that assigns a relatively higher weight to the future than the present, since many of the benefits of evaluation take time to be realized. A decision to evaluate also reflects a value set that emphasizes learning and showing others what works, in contrast to doing things that benefit people directly and immediately. Evaluations sometimes don't work as expected, despite all efforts to make them excellent, so supporting evaluation also demonstrates a willingness to take risks.

One cannot say that the values that support evaluation are right or wrong, only that they are different from values that do not support evaluation. It is the intention of this book to provide arguments and information to support the utility of evaluation as a foundation activity and to aid foundations new to the field to use the tools of evaluation effectively within the foundations' own contexts.

The material that follows in this chapter and the next discusses the major areas in which evaluation choices must be made. Evaluations can be looked at from the point of view of their subjects, their technical methods, their timing, and their many various purposes.

Three Categories of Evaluation Subjects

Evaluations come in many shapes and sizes. This variety results from the diversity of the subjects of evaluation and the multiplicity of acceptable approaches available to evaluate a given grant, project, or program. The subjects of foundation evaluations can be categorized by target, activity, and size.

Targets

The continuum of targets for foundation evaluation comprises proposals, individual grants, projects supported by others, clusters of related grants, program components, entire program areas, and a foundation's own operating practices. Evaluations of different types of targets can be complementary and useful. However, not many foundations are likely to be willing to spend the money it would take to do every kind of evaluation possible. A foundation should consider how its missions, program areas, number and types of grants funded, and so on, can benefit from the various types of evaluation in order to establish priorities among possible targets.

Activities

Foundation grants support disparate activities, including — but not limited to — direct services to people, education and training,

leadership development, institution building, technical assistance, research, evaluation, performing arts, advocacy, and information dissemination (for example, conferences, books, media
projects). The nature of an activity will often be more amena-
ble to some evaluation approaches than to others.

Sizes

Foundation grants, projects, and programs vary greatly in size,
from hundreds to millions of dollars. Although this book does not
recommend using a fixed percentage to determine how much to
spend on a particular evaluation (more on this topic later), it is
sensible to take account of the amount the foundation has invested
in a project when deciding how much to spend on its evaluation.

Evaluation Approaches and Methods

One of the greatest challenges encountered in thinking about
evaluation is that there usually is more than one acceptable way
to evaluate a given grant, project, or program.
    The form that an evaluation takes and the products that
it yields will depend on choices made about the following issues:

- The purposes of the evaluation
- The target audiences for the evaluation
- The evaluation questions to be answered
- The kinds of information needed
- The evaluation methods to be used
- The qualifications and experience of the person or group
  conducting the evaluation
- How much to spend

Purposes and Priorities

Seven different reasons were given for foundations to spend resources on evaluation, but a foundation should not expect that
every evaluation will satisfy all these needs. This means that a foundation must identify its greatest needs and the ways it, or others,
will use evaluation results, and then use this information to set

evaluation priorities. Most foundations would probably assign a high priority to the accountability purpose and to improving their abilities as grantmakers. Beyond this, the reasons for supporting evaluation that will be important to a particular foundation will depend on the foundation's own goals and programs.

For example, a community foundation whose primary interest lies in providing start-up support for new services or in enhancing the capacity of existing agencies to serve their target populations is likely to support evaluations designed to improve grantee performance. A national foundation providing support to a multisite demonstration program is likely to be interested in evaluations that can be used to diffuse new program ideas and increase the state of knowledge. A foundation that supports basic scientific research may want to assess the technical quality of its grantees' work and the impact of its funded research on the field.

The Audience

Possible audiences for evaluation findings include foundation trustees and staff, grantees (including program staff, management, and boards of directors), other program funders, policymakers, the field at large (program planners, researchers, and so forth), and the general public. At the time of deciding whether and how an evaluation ought to be undertaken, a foundation should also decide upon its desired audience for the evaluation findings. The information needs of various groups can be very different, and the costs of obtaining certain kinds of information—notably, the kinds of information provided by scientifically rigorous evaluation—can be very high. Foundations will be wise to take into account the kinds of information that will be convincing and useful to the target audiences.

Evaluation Questions

The evaluation literature distinguishes several types of evaluations by the nature of the questions they attempt to answer. Many evaluation projects will involve more than one of these types.

Needs Assessments. These evaluations verify and map the extent of a problem. They answer questions about the number and characteristics of the individuals or institutions who would constitute the targets of a program to address the problem. Needs assessments can help design a new program or justify continuation of an existing program.

Monitoring. Monitoring activities produce regular, ongoing information that answers questions about whether a program or project is being implemented as planned, and identifies problems and facilitates their resolution in a timely way.

Formative Evaluations. These evaluations answer questions about how to improve and refine a developing or ongoing program. Formative evaluation usually is undertaken during the initial, or design, phase of a project. However, it also can be helpful for assessing the ongoing activities of an established program. Formative evaluation may include process and impact studies. Typically, the findings from formative evaluations are provided as feedback to the programs evaluated.

Process Evaluations. Studies of this kind are directed toward understanding and documenting program implementation. They answer questions about the types and quantities of services delivered, the beneficiaries of those services, the resources used to deliver the services, the practical problems encountered, and the ways such problems were resolved. Information from process evaluations is useful for understanding how program impact and outcome were achieved and for program replication. Process evaluations are usually undertaken for projects that are innovative service delivery models, where the technology and the feasibility of implementation are not well known in advance.

Impact or Outcome Evaluations. These evaluations assess the effectiveness of a program in producing change. They focus on the difficult questions of what happened to program participants and how much of a difference the program made. Impact or outcome evaluations are undertaken when it is important to know how well a grantee's or foundation's objectives for a program were met, or when a program is an innovative model whose effectiveness has not yet been demonstrated. (Some evaluators make distinctions between "impact" and "outcome," but these distinctions are not consistent. For the purposes of this book, the terms are treated as interchangeable.)

Summative Evaluations. Summative evaluations answer questions about program quality and impact for the purposes of accountability and decision making. They are conducted at a project's or program's end and usually include a synthesis of process and impact or outcome evaluation components.

Kinds of Information Needed

Once a foundation knows which questions it wants an evaluation to address, the next step is to decide what kinds of information are needed to answer those questions. The first decision is whether informal expert judgment or formal data or both will be needed. Using *expert judgment* means, simply, bringing the attention of knowledgeable people to bear on a project, program, or activity, to assess its organization, content, quality, progress, and/or accomplishments in the light of their special knowledge. *Data* means information collected systematically. Data can be quantitative (numerical, categorical, objective) or qualitative (descriptive, perceptive, subjective). Further, either sort of data can be primary (collected specifically for purposes of the evaluation) or secondary (collected previously for another purpose). Data can be obtained in the form of records (that is, documents), interviews, surveys, or observation. Most evaluations make use of more than one kind of data.

Evaluation Methods

Some primary evaluation methods presented in greater detail in Resource A are introduced briefly here in the context of evaluation choices.

    Expert peer review is associated with *judgment-based* information. The peer may be an individual or a committee. The review may consist of reading documents (desk review) or site visits and interviews with project staff, participants or others, or both. The benefits of this approach are that it can be done quickly and at low cost. The hazard of the approach is that it depends totally on the knowledge, experience, and viewpoints of the experts chosen, and so runs the risk of being biased.

Data-based evaluation uses other methods. A *descriptive analysis,* for example, uses descriptive statistics (such as means and medians, and frequency distributions) to characterize a program, its participants, and attributes of the relevant social, political, or economic environment for the purpose of understanding how and why a program works. A *case study* makes extensive use of descriptive analytic methods.

A *comparison-group design* is called for when it is important to measure effects and to attribute those effects to a project or program. In such designs, a group of people or institutions who receive an innovative treatment or participate in a new program are compared with a similar group who do not receive the treatment or participate in the program. Differences in prespecified measures of impact or outcome between the two groups are attributed to the intervention.

Comparison-group designs include the *randomized controlled experiment,* in which subjects are randomly assigned to experimental or control groups, and the *quasi-experiment* in which program participants are compared with nonparticipants selected to be as similar as possible to the treatment group (for instance, students in another high school, residents of an adjacent county). Sometimes the treatment group itself, analyzed before the program begins, can be its own comparison group. However, this *pre-post design* is often thought to be a weak one because factors external to the program could be responsible for changes that occur.

Comparison-group designs are examples of evaluations that use quantitative methods. Quantitative methods are also associated with deductive analysis, meaning that relationships between variables are specified or hypothesized beforehand and statistical tests are used to determine whether the data conform to those relationships and to measure the strength of the relationships. To use quantitative methods, it is necessary to specify, in advance of data collection, a program's objectives, its important features, and the characteristics of the population to be served, and how all of these will be measured.

In contrast, qualitative methods are called for when what is desired is to obtain greater understanding of a program as it really functions, the real-life context in which it operates, how it was designed and implemented, what it means to the individuals involved in making it work and to the individuals served, and how it accomplishes its objectives. Qualitative methods have been called *naturalistic* because the researcher seeks to understand a phenomenon in its naturally occurring state. Qualitative methods are usually associated with inductive analysis, in that general patterns are derived from direct detailed observations without specifying the expectations for those patterns in advance (Patton, 1990a).

The case studies in Part Two contain many examples of the use of the concepts and methods described in the last few pages. Table 1.2 provides a guide to these real-life examples, naming the major concepts and methods illustrated by each case.

Who Conducts the Evaluation?

Evaluation activities may be conducted by the program itself (the grantee), foundation staff, one or more outside experts, an independent grantee or contractor, or a combination of these (for example, a grantee may subcontract with an outside evaluation group or a site-visit team may consist of foundation staff and outside experts).

As will be discussed in greater detail in Chapter Two, the choice of people to carry out an evaluation should depend on the purpose of the evaluation, the target audience, the evaluation questions, the information needed, the methods to be used, the availability of potential evaluators, and the importance of objectivity.

How Much to Spend

The cost of an evaluation project can range from a few hundred dollars for an expert-judgment assessment of a completed research

Table 1.2. Case Study Evaluation Concepts and Methods.

Case Study	Evaluation Concepts and Methods Used
The Meyer Memorial Trust request-for-proposal program (Chapter Three)	Process and formative evaluation; expert judgment; interviews, survey, and site visits
L. J. and Mary C. Skaggs Foundation program for arts organizations (Chapter Four)	Process, impact/outcome, and summative evaluation; case studies; expert judgment; interviews
Winthrop Rockefeller Foundation at-risk youth program (Chapter Five)	Formative evaluation
Cities in Schools program (Chapter Six)	Formative and impact/outcome evaluation; comparison-group design; quantitative and qualitative data; interviews and surveys
Technology for Literacy Project (Chapter Seven)	Formative, process, impact/outcome, and summative evaluation; comparison-group design; case studies; quantitative and qualitative data; participant observation, interviews, and surveys
Lilly Endowment youthworker project (Chapter Eight)	Descriptive impact/outcome evaluation; case studies; qualitative data; interviews and surveys
William Penn Foundation career/vocational program (Chapter Nine)	Descriptive, formative, process, and summative evaluation; quantitative and qualitative data; interviews and surveys
Gautreaux program (Chapter Ten)	Impact/outcome evaluation; comparison-group design; quantitative and qualitative data; interviews, surveys, and records data
W. K. Kellogg Foundation grants (Chapter Eleven)	Formative evaluation; interviews and surveys; site visits

grant to a few million dollars for a randomized controlled experiment of an innovative service program at multiple sites. Between these extremes, many kinds of evaluations can be conducted for under $10,000: a visiting-committee expert review involving travel to several program sites; a descriptive study of program clients' characteristics, use of services and satisfaction; a telephone survey of grantees; or a study of the number of publications yielded by a research program. A descriptive evaluation of a program that entails primary data collection at one site might range from $10,000 to $50,000. Process and impact evaluations of programs in more than one community requiring data collection from individuals at two or more points in time might cost from $100,000 to $300,000.

Examples of factors that increase costs are the following:

- A desire to attribute causal impact to the program, which means using a comparison-group design (and hence more data collection)
- Programs that target whole communities rather than specific groups of individuals
- Multisite rather than single-site programs
- Programs that try to make relatively small reductions in problems, so that evidence of impact is hard to discern
- A need to collect primary data, when suitable records or published statistics are not available
- Designs that require data collection in person
- Designs that require collecting data at multiple points in time
- A need for data that must be collected through highly technical procedures such as drawing blood or by highly trained personnel such as physicians

Overcoming Resistance to Evaluation

Although the idea that evaluation is important is generally accepted to be true in theory, many foundation people are not convinced that evaluation is useful or practical for them in particular. One reason foundation staff may resist evaluation is that much of the excitement of foundation work comes from the creative activities of grantmaking. In contrast, evaluation diverts staff energies away from making new grants and may even yield information that could reflect negatively on staff judgment. Further, foundations typically try to keep their staffs small, so adding or increasing evaluation functions can be a burden on already pressed staff. Much of the success of a foundation's evaluation strategy hinges on there being a clear understanding among staff of the evaluation's purposes, processes, and priorities.

Other concerns may be that evaluation is a burden on grantees and may interfere with the projects themselves; that evaluation is costly and its benefits not apparent; that evaluations often take too long, can be too academic, and are not practical enough; that an emphasis on evaluation might lead to decisions on grant proposals being made on the basis of how easy or difficult they will be to evaluate rather than on merit; and that outside evaluators might not understand the foundation's or grantee's values. Finally, grantees might naturally feel anxious about the prospect of being judged inadequate in some way. This could lead to grantee hostility toward the evaluators.

The latter two concerns are more likely to occur when a foundation imposes outside evaluations on grantees than when the grantee initiates the idea of the evaluation and it is conducted for the grantee rather than for the foundation. Thus, one way of overcoming or avoiding grantees' resistance to evaluation is for foundations to encourage grantees to build evaluation components into projects where appropriate, and to help them to do so when they need help, perhaps by suggesting evaluation resources whom the grantees could consult.

In cases where a foundation has good reasons for commissioning an outside evaluation, foundation staff responsible for evaluation should be sensitive to the legitimate concerns of grantees and should devise evaluation strategies that are practical and responsive to real needs for information, that do not impose a superfluous burden on staff or grantees, that are cost-effective in their use of foundation funds, and that, to the extent possible, are responsive to grantees' information needs and priorities.

In the long run, evaluation will have to prove its value to each particular foundation in terms that are meaningful to that foundation and to the stakeholders whose needs and interests the foundation strives to serve. If resistance to evaluation is overcome, it is usually because a foundation's trustees, staff, and stakeholders perceive the results of foundation-funded evaluations to be useful. If resistance continues, or even grows, over time, it is usually because the evaluation strategy itself is in need of evaluation to make it more useful and interesting to its intended audiences.

Three Principles

Finally, paying close attention to three basic principles as one chooses among the various options for evaluation can make evaluation a positive experience for all involved.

- An evaluation should be cost-effective and not unnecessarily elaborate. Development of an evaluation plan should begin with an assessment of the minimum level of evaluation needed to satisfy the foundation's needs and objectives. There should be clear justification for undertaking any evaluation greater than this level.
- The evaluation plan selected for a particular purpose should be credible to the target audience for the evaluation.
- An evaluation plan should also be appropriate to the project being evaluated. For example, an evaluation should seek to discover only those effects that can be expected to occur in the time period within which the results are needed.

In short, evaluations should be cost-effective, credible, and appropriate. Evaluations planned with these principles in mind are more likely to be favorably received.

2

Getting Started
on Evaluation

Chapter One considered the reasons foundations support, or resist, evaluation, and the many choices a foundation must make when it undertakes evaluation. This chapter examines practical considerations in developing an evaluation strategy and in making the kinds of choices described earlier.

Routine Evaluation Activities

Many foundations are already doing some evaluation in the course of carrying out routine proposal review and grant monitoring. They are in an excellent position to gradually expand their evaluation activities. Green and Lewis define evaluation as the "comparison of an object of interest against a standard of acceptability" (1986, p. 171), and this is the kind of comparison involved in the methodical assessment of proposals and systematic grant monitoring. Thus, these activities can be seen as already existing components for a foundation's evaluation portfolio.

Proposal Evaluation

This evaluation activity, which falls into the category of the expert peer review, is carried out by staff and consultants, based on review of documents, site visits, and discussions with applicants. The reviewers assess the need for the project, the appropriateness of the objectives, the feasibility of the implementation strategy, the qualifications of the applicant institution and project team, the adequacy of the proposed timetable and budget, the likelihood of raising additional funds if required, the potential contributions or impact of the project, the potential problems and risks, and the rationale for funding by the foundation.

When reviewers' comments are provided as feedback to the applicant, proposal evaluation can serve a useful formative function. This feedback can help applicants improve the design and potential for success of projects ultimately funded by the foundation. Feedback also can benefit applicants who are turned down by the foundation if it helps them improve project plans or understand how to write a more compelling proposal.

If a project is funded, a written critical analysis of the proposal, together with a clear written statement of the foundation's expectations for the project and the rationale for funding, can serve as the baseline for the postgrant assessment described in a later section.

Grant Monitoring

Grant monitoring refers to the tracking of grant progress through regular interim reports and a final report from the grantee, the reviewing of these reports by responsible foundation staff, and other communications between foundation staff and the grantee. Monitoring should alert the foundation to important changes in project objectives or implementation strategy at an early date and should be helpful in identifying problems and facilitating their timely resolution. If monitoring is to be useful for problem identification and resolution, a reasonable reporting period is every six months.

Monitoring reports also can provide the foundation (and the grantee) with basic process indicators of the grantee's success in accomplishing measurable objectives. To ensure that monitoring reports are as informative and useful as possible, it is a good idea for foundation staff to talk with each grantee at the outset to agree upon the measures of success for the project and to make sure that the grantee will be able to collect the requisite data. Some foundations have developed guidelines that tell grantees what topics their reports should cover. It may turn out that additional funds will be required or that the grantee will need technical assistance to set up a data collection system. If the monitoring process is important enough to warrant the additional expense, the foundation may decide to increase its support of the project.

Postgrant Assessment

If grant monitoring ends with the responsible program officer reading a final report and filing it away, the foundation will lose a valuable opportunity to reflect and learn. A foundation wishing to maximize the learning opportunity from its grants will build on its grant monitoring capabilities and conduct postgrant assessments. These may be considered a form of summative evaluation.

In a postgrant assessment, the program officer or a consultant reviews the grantee's reports and other deliverables and possibly makes a brief site visit in order to assess the grantee's performance and accomplishments relative to original expectations; reconsiders the adequacy of the original plans, budget, and timetable; reflects on what made the project successful or not; comments on the project's potential lasting impact, if any; identifies benefits to the foundation and lessons learned; and recommends whether the foundation should provide future support to the project team, to the grantee institution, or to other similar projects.

John Nason summed up the high worth of this evaluation activity when he wrote, "Foundations do not have profit and loss statements to tell them how well they are doing. Only a postgrant assessment of the results will reveal the foundation's hits, runs, and errors. Failures need to be studied as well as successes. Postgrant evaluation is expensive in time and money. But uninformed grantmaking is more so" (1989, p. 92).

A further benefit is that foundations can add the postgrant assessment — either written or oral — to their evaluation repertoire with relatively little additional expenditure. The written critical analysis suggested as a part of the proposal evaluation at the outset of the funding process will facilitate preparing the postgrant assessment at the end. Grantee report guidelines that specify the information needed will also make it easier to prepare postgrant assessments.

Beyond Monitoring

Suppose a foundation's staff currently conduct methodical monitoring and prepare postgrant assessments on those grants that offer learning opportunities. When will this monitoring suffice as evaluation and when is evaluation beyond monitoring called for? Considerations to weigh in making this decision include:

- The importance of the questions that monitoring cannot answer
- The adequacy and practicality of the evaluation options available to provide answers to those questions
- The potential impact of the evaluation results for the foundation, its grantees, and the field
- The cost of the evaluation options
- The competing opportunities for the available funds

When Monitoring Is Enough

For many grants, evaluation beyond routine monitoring is not recommended, because either the monitoring itself satisfies the foundation's evaluation questions or the ability to learn from further evaluation is minimal. For other grants, limited resources will suggest that further evaluation would not be cost-effective.

Because so many evaluation choices reflect strategies, values, and priorities, which vary among foundations, it is impossible to list types of grants for which evaluation beyond monitoring would never be advisable. However, for most foundations, grants unlikely to warrant evaluation beyond monitoring, even if resources were unlimited, include contributions to the general support of grantmaker organizations; endowments; good citizenship grants (for instance, a contribution to a community Christmas-giving campaign); small contributions to very large undertakings; grants intended to yield tangible products (the purchase of equipment, for example) the results of which will be self-evident; start-up funding to help establish a program already demonstrated to work, where the foundation only needs to know the program is in place; general support grants for programs that are not innovative models; small feasibility studies; and planning grants that are expected to result in another proposal to the foundation.

When Evaluation Beyond Monitoring Is Desirable

The factors that signal that further evaluation may be in order include the importance to a foundation of the project, grant, or program that would be evaluated; the characteristics of the project, grant, or program that make it a good subject for evaluation; and the potential contributions of the evaluation.

Sometimes the reason for deciding to evaluate derives from the foundation's perspective:

- When the grant represents a sizable investment for the foundation
- When the project has great salience for the foundation's programs or larger goals
- When foundation staff have been especially proactive in designing and initiating the project
- When the foundation will be asked to renew funding for the project and wants to know more about the project's effectiveness and future potential than it can glean from monitoring
- When the information obtained from monitoring will not be sufficient to satisfy the foundation's accountability needs

Sometimes the main signal that evaluation would be a good idea comes from the characteristics of the project or grant that would be evaluated:

- When the project has potential to be a model and evaluation can be a tool of dissemination
- When the project has potential to have a measurable impact on a target group of people or institutions
- When the design of the project is such that a credible evaluation is feasible (that is, if important effects can be measured within a reasonable period of time)
- When the grant can be grouped with similar other grants to form a cluster, so that the grants can be evaluated together
- When the grant or project is especially risky or controversial
- When the project, once in progress, experiences problems that could compromise its performance

Finally, the potential utility of an evaluation is indicated:

- When evaluation could improve the performance of the project
- When evaluation would enhance the impact of the project
- When evaluation results have potential to influence policymakers in the public or private sector
- When evaluation will yield information that will make an independent contribution to the attainment of the foundation's goals

Although all these conditions are useful, they are not sufficient for a foundation to decide whether to evaluate a particular grant. The foundation also needs to examine the range of options available for evaluation, the potential value of each option, and the cost of each.

Matching Evaluation Approaches to Types of Projects

A number of the choices posed in Chapter One are constrained by the nature of the grant or project to be evaluated. This section describes evaluation options available for different types of grants or projects.

Research and Evaluation Grants

The state-of-the-art evaluation for a research and evaluation grant is expert peer review, in which one or a few outside experts are invited to evaluate a final report and/or other products of the grant (manuscripts, publications, and the like), with respect to their technical merits and potential contributions to the relevant fields. A site visit typically is unnecessary.

Other approaches for evaluating the impacts or outcomes of research and evaluation grants focus on the publications produced by the grants. For example, it is possible to compile lists of publications resulting from the grants; obtain peer reviews of the technical quality and impact of selected books and articles produced by the grants; or conduct a study of citations of publications resulting from the grants. These approaches are particularly suitable for evaluating grant clusters. The citation study can be especially useful when a foundation has made several grants intended to advance the state of the art or to influence other research in a particular field. However, such a study can take place only after sufficient time has passed — probably at least five years — for the results to be published and for subsequent research citing those publications to be published as well.

Still another approach is to survey the principal investigators from a cluster of grants to find out whether and how the research funded by a foundation led to other research projects and to identify other long-term results of the work. Such a survey could be conducted by mail (with an introductory letter from the foundation's president or executive director to encourage a high response rate) or by telephone.

Dissemination Grants

For many dissemination grants, evaluation beyond monitoring is not necessary, as the product of the grant (for example, a book, a video, a conference agenda and list of attendees) should be self-evident, and the grantee's own monitoring reports should provide any other needed information. Published book reviews can be assembled without the foundation's having to commission its own peer reviews.

However, sometimes evaluations can be helpful. In the case of a conference grant, it can be useful for the grantee to survey the participants' reactions to the conference agenda, setting, and arrangements. Such a descriptive evaluation can help both the grantee and the foundation plan better conferences, in addition to providing measures of the project's success from the attendees' standpoint. Publication and media projects can benefit from evaluations designed to show whether the project reached its intended audience, how it was received, and whether it was more successful with some groups than with others and why.

Advocacy Grants

Advocacy grants may be suitable subjects for a wider variety of evaluation options. Formative evaluation (for instance, holding focus groups to react to preliminary drafts of materials) can be an aid to refining the action plan and the materials to be used. Process evaluation is appropriate to document the activities pursued and barriers encountered, and how they were overcome. Summative evaluation, using descriptive analysis of qualitative and quantitative data, can examine the extent to which the grant's objectives were achieved.

One possible evaluation approach here is to interview *key influentials,* individuals in the field, whose expert judgments could be combined to arrive at an overall assessment of the grant's accomplishments. Another approach is to examine changes in the frequency and content of media coverage of the issue of interest, though it typically would not be possible to attribute such changes unreservedly to the grant in question. Still another approach is to monitor legislative or administrative actions of government agencies that might be expected to be informed by advocacy initiatives and publicity.

Direct-Service and Education and Training Grants

The greatest range of options and the greatest potential for spending on evaluation, and hence the most difficult decisions about how to evaluate, arise with grants for direct services to people and grants for educational or training programs. Formative evaluation can be helpful in improving a new program just getting started. Process evaluation, to document how a model program was implemented, is important for future replications. Process evaluation can also complement a grant-monitoring system, by providing information that demonstrates an intervention is working as planned.

Impact or outcome evaluation can provide bottom-line information about program results, showing whether the program is more successful with certain groups than others and whether it is cost-effective. Because direct-service and education grants are designed to affect individuals, evaluating long-term effectiveness usually requires collecting before-and-after data from those individuals. Data collection at intermediate times may also be desirable, to understand the rate at which change occurs. Similar data must be obtained from appropriate comparison groups in order to attribute effects to the intervention. Also, enough time must have elapsed for the hoped-for effects to occur. These are some of the reasons that evaluations of such projects can be expensive.

But not all impact or outcome evaluations of direct-service or education and training programs need be expensive. Depending on the level of evidence or the degree of scientific rigor that the audience for an evaluation will find satisfactory, less expensive evaluation alternatives can be considered.

For example, data can be collected from intermediate targets of a program: teachers rather than students or health-care providers rather than patients. Informed judgment can be substituted for objective data about program effectiveness. The data needs for the evaluation may be satisfied by routine records kept by the program (test scores, dropout rates, births to teen mothers). If the program's effects are expected to become evident relatively quickly after the intervention, a pre-post design may be sufficient and no other comparison group may be required. Sometimes, readily available national or regional statistics can be used instead of primary data collected from carefully chosen comparison groups. If shorter-term impacts that are credible indicators of program success can be identified, the duration of an evaluation can be reduced.

Finally, a summative evaluation can pull together all the findings of the process and impact or outcome evaluations and can report on the feasibility of implementing the program and its results, make suggestions for program improvement or for policy changes, compare the program with similar other efforts in the field, and present issues to be considered in program replication.

Evaluating the Foundation

In addition to evaluating its grants and programs, a foundation may wish to evaluate its own performance, including operating practices and grantmaking style. Evaluation questions can ask how the foundation is viewed by its constituencies, the extent to which grant applicants were satisfied with their treatment by foundation staff, and the degree to which grantees feel their foundation grants helped them accomplish their goals. Such evaluations can be carried out through descriptive surveys or interview techniques, possibly by an outside agency to ensure confidentiality of responses and objectivity in interpreting the results.

Another option is to commission an expert assessment of the foundation's choice of funding programs and priorities (for example, Patton, 1990b; Krasney, 1991). Such an evaluation may be undertaken every five years or so, in an ongoing effort to bring objective outside opinion to bear on the choices made by foundation trustees and staff. The assessment can be based on review of documents, site visits, and interviews with trustees, staff, grantees, other professionals, and the public.

An expert assessment can be beneficial in confirming that the foundation is embarked on a constructive course, suggesting ways to change programs or priorities to better accomplish the foundation's goals, or signaling that the time has come to shift priorities to other issues. It should be remembered, though, that this type of assessment depends on the expertise, experiences, interests, and values of the outside reviewers. These reviewers must be chosen carefully, and trustees and staff should be clear at the outset about how they will use reviewers' recommendations, otherwise the evaluation could generate as much consternation as assistance.

Organizing for Evaluation

Once a foundation has determined what it would like to evaluate and has some ideas about the kinds of evaluation that would be useful, its next set of decisions will concern resource allocation. These decisions include who will conduct its evaluations, what its internal staff needs will be to carry out evaluation-related activities, and how much to budget for them.

Who Should Conduct an Evaluation?

As noted in Chapter One, evaluation activities may be conducted by foundation staff, grantees, or outside evaluators. What considerations should be taken into account in choosing among these three sources?

Foundation Staff as Evaluators

Most of the time, foundation staff perform routine grant monitoring, although some foundations use consultants to review grantees' final reports and some organize formal site visits by staff and outside experts to evaluate grantee performance. A useful adjunct to routine grant monitoring by staff can be the postgrant assessment described earlier.

Sometimes staff undertake a small evaluation project, such as a mail survey of grantees, possibly in collaboration with a local consultant or with the assistance of a student intern or a research assistant. As a rule, foundations do not hire staff to carry out evaluations that require major data collection and research.

However, foundation staff can play a significant role in the design of a major evaluation by specifying the evaluation's purpose, the target audience, the key questions to be answered, and the methods that would provide the kinds of information desired, and by monitoring the evaluation's progress.

Grantees as Evaluators

Grantees' various reports can provide useful evaluation information. Progress reports can contain process information on project implementation, services provided, and people served. As noted earlier, with some forethought, grantees can arrange to collect the necessary information from their routine record systems.

Grantees' final reports can take the form of summative evaluations based on judgment and information from program records, in which they describe how projects were implemented and the extent to which their original objectives were attained. As previously mentioned, some foundations provide guidelines to help their grantees organize their reports in the ways that will be most informative and useful to the foundation.

Sometimes grantees build, or can be assisted to build, an evaluation component into their project workplans, covering both process and impact questions and carried out by program staff themselves (sometimes a staff person is hired specifically to carry out the evaluation function) or by consultants under subcontract. These evaluations can often satisfy a foundation's needs for evaluative information. However, the foundation should recognize its own role as an important stakeholder in the evaluation and should make sure that its information needs will be met by the built-in evaluation.

A significant role for a grantee — as the actual evaluator, as the immediate client for the evaluation, or as an active partner — is desirable when the purpose of the evaluation emphasizes using the results to improve program performance, when the key evaluation questions concern how well the program has accomplished its original objectives, when the grantee is an important audience for the evaluation results, and when the grantee's cooperation is needed for data collection.

Outside Evaluators

The design requirements of a complex evaluation (for instance, one requiring random assignment, a comparison group at another site, sophisticated measurement methods, or in-depth case studies) may require more technical expertise, more research capacity, and more dedicated staff than either the foundation or the grantee can reasonably be expected to provide. It then becomes appropriate to look to an outside individual or group to conduct the evaluation.

A related consideration is generalizability. If a purpose of the evaluation is to inform the field, it may be important to use a design that will yield results that can be compared with results from evaluations of other programs or with statistics from national surveys. In such cases, outside evaluators familiar with such studies and surveys may be best qualified to conduct the evaluation.

Another consideration is the need for objectivity. If the purpose of an evaluation is to learn about the effectiveness of a new model, and if its target audiences are scientists and policy-makers, the results may carry more weight with those audiences if the evaluation is conducted by an impartial outsider rather than by the staff who are conducting the program being evaluated or by a subcontractor to the grantee.

Sometimes multiple grants are evaluated at the same time as part of an overall program evaluation. In such cases, it may be most acceptable and practical to have the evaluation performed by a neutral third party.

Table 2.1 summarizes the types of evaluators selected for the evaluations presented in the case studies in Part Two.

Staffing and Budgeting

Two key questions for foundations new to evaluation are how to staff and how much to budget for evaluation.

Staffing

Staff responsibility for evaluation is demanding, especially when an evaluation project is funded directly by the foundation. To be effectively proactive in selecting an evaluation approach and an evaluator, responsible foundation staff must have detailed

Table 2.1. The Case Study Evaluators.

Case Study	Type of Evaluator
The Meyer Memorial Trust request-for-proposal program (Chapter Three)	Two-part outside evaluation: (1) independent consultant, (2) committee of experts
L. J. and Mary C. Skaggs Foundation program for arts organizations (Chapter Four)	Outside evaluation: university-based consultant and graduate student
Winthrop Rockefeller Foundation at-risk youth program (Chapter Five)	Grantee staff guided by university-based consultant and foundation program officer
Cities in Schools program (Chapter Six)	Two-part outside evaluation: (1) independent consultant assisted by another adult and student interviewers; (2) two independent consultants
Technology for Literacy Project (Chapter Seven)	Outside evaluation: two university-based consultants and a graduate student
Lilly Endowment youthworker project (Chapter Eight)	Two outside evaluations: (1) independent consultant, followed by (2) university-based researcher
William Penn Foundation career/vocational program (Chapter Nine)	Foundation staff assisted by a graduate student
Gautreaux program (Chapter Ten)	Outside evaluation: university-based research team
W. K. Kellogg Foundation grants (Chapter Eleven)	Collaborative evaluation: coordinated by a university-based department of education with active participation of grantees

knowledge of both the program being evaluated and the desired design and implementation strategy of the evaluation. Even when an evaluation is built into the project being evaluated, foundation staff should know enough to feel comfortable that the evaluation will provide the information needed.

Monitoring evaluation projects requires continued attention for unanticipated problems. The program itself may not be implemented as originally planned, for example, expected access to data for the evaluation may not materialize, or the information needs of the evaluation audiences may change. To ensure that evaluation results will be as useful to the target audiences as planned, responsible foundation staff should stay closely informed about the evaluation's status and be proactive when changes call for adjustments in the evaluation. Outside or grantee evaluators should be able to call on their foundation contact for advice and guidance when either problems or new opportunities arise.

Specialists or Generalists? A foundation's major staffing decision is whether there should be specialized evaluation staff who design, monitor, and advise on the foundation's evaluation activities or whether the management of evaluation should be a responsibility of all staff. Again, although there is no single right approach, there are considerations that can aid a foundation in making this decision.

The more that evaluation activities fall into the expert judgment category, the less necessary it is to employ specialized in-house staff, because no technical methodology is involved. The more that evaluation activities require scientific research, the more useful it is to employ specialist staff who are conversant in the scientific methods used and who can accurately assess the evaluation work.

The more proactive foundation staff are in developing a foundation's funded projects, the more appropriate it may be to assign the evaluation function to other staff. The reason for this is that program officers may become too invested in their projects to be objective about evaluation.

The more that evaluations are built into a foundation's grants, the less it needs its own specialized evaluation staff, while the more that a foundation uses outside evaluators, the more it needs its own specialized evaluation staff. When evaluations are built-in, their design can be reviewed by consultants as part of the proposal review process, if necessary, and the responsibility for ensuring that the evaluation is carried out properly belongs to the grantee. When a foundation uses outside evaluators, foundation staff typically outline the evaluation design, solicit proposals, negotiate with potential evaluators, and monitor the evaluation project. This requires evaluation expertise.

For a foundation wanting to increase its evaluation activities, the existing staff's capability and interest in handling evaluation functions will bear on whether new specialists should be hired. Over time, as the evaluation function takes shape, and especially if the foundation opts for data-based evaluations, it may be desirable to have one staff member take the lead in directing the foundation's evaluation activities, allowing that person to develop expertise that will benefit the foundation's evaluation enterprise.

On the other hand, some foundations believe that it is important for program staff to be generalists, able to handle evaluation functions as well as their other program responsibilities.

Even when staff specialists are hired, it is a good idea for them to involve the program staff responsible for the projects being evaluated in the development of the evaluation plan, and to keep the program staff informed of evaluation results as they come in. In this way, evaluation staff can benefit from program staff's knowledge of the project, and program staff are more likely to be receptive to the evaluation findings because their concerns and interests have been taken into account.

Number of Staff. If evaluation specialists are hired, how many are needed? Here a more definite answer is possible. It seems safe to say that only the very largest foundations (more than $500 million in assets) would require more than one full-time evaluation staff person. (This assumes that routine monitoring functions would not be assigned to the evaluation specialists.) For smaller foundations, one full-time evaluation professional should suffice, and this individual should be able to perform other foundation functions as well.

Recruiting. When an evaluation staff person is recruited, ideally his or her qualifications and credentials will include practical experience in conducting evaluations. Alternatively, a local graduate student who is completing his or her thesis and has close ties to faculty advisors who are experienced in evaluation may be recruited. Foundations should be aware that, although there are a number of academic programs in evaluation, many practicing evaluators' formal training is in a specific social science (such as sociology, psychology, anthropology, or economics) or subject area (such as public health, education, or social work) rather than in evaluation methodology. In addition, individuals from different fields tend to favor different evaluation approaches, so a foundation hiring evaluation staff would be well advised to look for a good match between its own evaluation preferences and the background and orientation of its new hires.

Finally, local evaluators — both academic and nonacademic — can be asked for advice (this is also a good occasion for the foundation to introduce itself to these local resources and increase its community network). A regional association of grantmakers can be asked for a reference to another foundation already embarked on evaluation activities. These sources can help foundation staff write the job description, and local evaluators may be willing to interview potential candidates for the foundation.

Budgeting

The question of how to budget for evaluations is as critical a resource allocation issue as how to staff the evaluation. It would be easy if there were a formula — such as a fixed percentage of the amount of a grant — that could tell a foundation how much to spend on a particular evaluation. However, as already noted, the cost of an evaluation depends heavily on the nature of the project to be evaluated. Further, a foundation's more costly projects need not be more expensive to evaluate than their less costly ones, even though the foundation may be willing to spend more on the project in which it has invested heavily. Finally, some grants or programs may be more worthy of evaluation than others because they offer a greater opportunity to learn or to influence the field.

As a general principle, then, the amount spent on an evaluation should be reasonable relative to the amount spent on the project being evaluated and, most important, relative to the potential value of the evaluation.

A variation on this rule of thumb occurs when a foundation supports the evaluation of a program in which it has made no investment (the evaluations described in Chapters Six and Ten are examples). In such cases, the foundation's interest typically reflects the potential contribution that the evaluation can make to the foundation's mission or program goals, and the amount spent should reflect the intrinsic value of the evaluation from the foundation's perspective, just as would be the case with the amount allocated to any other kind of grant.

Although a foundation should avoid using a fixed percentage formula when funding a particular evaluation, it is appropriate for a foundation to decide how much it is willing to spend on evaluation as a whole. This sum could well be a percentage of the grants budget, and should be determined only after the foundation has reflected on its values and priorities and assessed how evaluation can contribute to its overall goals and objectives. In developing a total evaluation budget, the foundation should also assess the types of grants and projects it would like to evaluate, consider the kinds of evaluation approaches that would satisfy the needs of those interested in the results, and inform itself about the likely costs of particular types of evaluations.

Whether or not a foundation establishes an overall budget, it will benefit from gathering information about typical evaluation costs. One useful method of doing this is to meet with some local evaluators to discuss possible projects and their associated costs. Another approach is to contact other foundations that already conduct evaluations and to obtain copies of their evaluation reports and find out what these evaluations cost.

A foundation may be wise to begin with a few selected evaluation projects and an overall budget for evaluation. Staff and trustees can then allocate the available funds among the selected projects according to their expected value and cost. Or a few ad hoc evaluation projects can be funded based on the same criteria. If the results prove valuable, the foundation can then increase its evaluation activities.

Finding and Using Outside Evaluators

In this section, we provide some introductory advice about finding outside evaluators and how to use them in ways that are likely to result in a gratifying experience for those concerned. This discussion may be useful to grantees looking for external evaluators as well as to foundations.

Who is Right Depends on the Kind of Evaluation

Outside evaluators may be university faculty members — sometimes assisted by graduate students — student interns working under the direction of foundation staff, solo private consultants, nonprofit research organizations, and for-profit contract research firms (the latter two may range from very small to large).

Expert-judgment evaluations are often conducted by academics or individual consultants on a per diem. To locate an appropriate academic for such an assignment, ask the chair of a relevant department at a local university for a reference to one or more faculty members. A review of pertinent scholarly literature can also produce a list of experts who could be commissioned to conduct a review. Some academics have little practical experience and a person with more field experience may be needed. Most foundation staff are well acquainted with local experts who can be asked to serve as ad hoc consultants on a review assignment. Another approach is to network with knowledgeable counterparts in the foundation world or in government to find the right expert reviewers.

Small evaluations, such as an evaluation of a local single-site service or educational program or a telephone survey of grantees, usually can be handled by one or two academics with the support of a few research assistants, or by a small consulting firm. Alternatively, a foundation staff member can direct student interns in carrying out these small projects.

Evaluations that are themselves major research projects, especially those entailing primary data collection at more than one site, normally are not one- or two-person undertakings. They usually require a team to design the research and data-collection, actually collect the data, and analyze it. Such projects may be conducted by academic-based groups or by applied research organizations, which may be either nonprofits or for-profits. Many evaluation groups serve national markets. If the project being evaluated is located at a distance from the foundation, it may be worthwhile to seek out such a national group. Again, reviews of the literature and networking with colleagues are good ways to identify potential resources.

Hiring Them

Individual outside evaluators may be hired by a foundation or grantee on a per diem or on a retainer for a fixed period of time to perform a specified scope of work. Team projects ordinarily are funded through a separate grant or contract from the foundation or through a subcontract from the grantee institution.

Using Them

A clear understanding of what the evaluation is to encompass is important if the evaluation experience is to be a happy and productive one for both the foundation and the outside evaluator. A good way to assure this is to put the requirements in writing. For evaluations carried out by individuals on a per diem or retainer, foundation staff, possibly with the evaluator's assistance, can prepare a letter of agreement setting out the foundation's expectations for the evaluation.

For evaluations funded through a grant or contract, it is recommended that the evaluator prepare a complete written proposal describing the objectives and implementation plan for the project. The proposal should specify the purposes of the evaluation, target audience(s), evaluation questions, evaluation design, data sources, data collection plan (including plans to ensure confidentiality of personal or proprietary data), analysis plan, all the deliverables the foundation will receive, dissemination plan, workplan and timetable, and staffing. It should also include a line-item budget, and a description of the evaluating institution's capabilities, and the qualifications and experience of the project team.

In addition, the proposal should include a description of the program to be evaluated that demonstrates the evaluator's understanding of the rationale both for the program and for the evaluation. When an evaluation will be complex, it is helpful for foundation staff to begin the process with a formal proposal solicitation that describes the program to be evaluated and lays out the foundation's priorities and ideas for the evaluation.

Grantee Involvement

Involving a grantee as much as is appropriate and feasible in all phases of an outside evaluation is also recommended. Because it is essential to obtain the grantee's agreement to cooperate with the evaluation, it is best if a foundation informs the grantee of its intention to have an outside evaluation before the project to be evaluated is even funded.

A high degree of grantee familiarity and comfort with the evaluation plans and the evaluator both facilitates the evaluation's implementation and enhances the acceptability and practical utility of its findings. A foundation should consider involving the grantee as much as possible in selecting the evaluator and designing the evaluation questions. (Ask the grantee, What would you most like to find out about the program from the evaluation?) If evaluation proposals are solicited, consider asking the grantee's project director to participate in the proposal review, although this is less feasible when multiple projects are to be evaluated together.

It is helpful for the responsible foundation staff person to introduce the evaluator to the project staff in an initial meeting. If a meeting in person is infeasible, a personal letter from foundation staff to the grantee should describe the purpose of the evaluation and the role of the evaluator, request the grantee's cooperation with the evaluation, and offer to answer questions or help to resolve any problems that might arise.

Once the evaluation is underway, it is wise to keep the grantee informed about its progress and interim findings. Depending upon their nature, either the full reports or executive summaries should be shared with the grantee. Such feedback can do more than simply satisfy the grantee's curiosity and allay concerns about what might be happening; it can provide the grantee with detailed insights into how its program can be improved. The grantee should also be a target audience for the final report as well as any other evaluation products. If evaluation findings are announced in a public forum, invite the grantee to attend as an active participant.

Reporting and Disseminating Results

Unless the evaluation project is very brief, no one wants to wait until the end to learn what the evaluators found. Interim reports on progress and findings from the evaluation are important to keep the foundation and the grantee informed. Moreover, reading such reports sometimes triggers suggestions for additional questions or topics to be covered; therefore, a schedule for regular reports should be built into the evaluation workplan. At the end, the foundation should expect to receive a complete report on the evaluation methods and findings, accompanied by an executive summary.

When audiences other than a foundation and its grantee are expected to be interested in an evaluation's results, a dissemination plan should be drawn up to target appropriate publication vehicles and to make sure that enough time is allotted to the preparation of manuscripts and to the presentation of findings at professional meetings. Many evaluators are eager to publicize their work among their peers, so this requirement is unlikely to pose a problem when outside evaluators are used. Nonetheless, sometimes the foundation may need to encourage evaluators to broaden their dissemination sights.

Many foundations have developed periodic newsletters or special publications to communicate results of their grants to such audiences as policymakers, practitioners, and a foundation's particular constituencies. Some hold press conferences or convene meetings of interested persons to present study results.

A foundation's board of trustees is a special audience for evaluation results. Often the responsibility for communicating evaluation findings to this audience falls to foundation staff, who should be able to synthesize technical material and highlight its policy significance in terms that are appealing to their board.

During dissemination, evaluators and staff must continue to protect confidential information and ensure that each respondent's identity cannot be linked to his or her data in any report of findings. In addition, when dissemination activities include audiences beyond the foundation and the grantee, steps should be taken to avoid releasing information that could be embarrassing or detrimental to the grantee or viewed as a breach of trust. (The case study in Chapter Four illustrates how this can happen.) Responsible foundation staff, sensitive to the harm that dissemination of evaluation results could do to a program, should work with the evaluator to protect the program's identity appropriately when important lessons learned are shared with a broader audience.

Suggestions for Getting Started

Foundations that are new to evaluation should avoid trying to do everything at once. Rather than thinking about how to evaluate every new grant or project, it is better to begin slowly with one or two evaluation projects, both to get some experience and to discover what is truly most important for a foundation to learn.

Another suggestion is to take some time to look at evaluations carried out by or for other foundations to get a taste of what is possible. The examples in Part Two are an ideal starting point for this investigation.

Sometimes grantees will have included evaluation components in projects that have been completed. Revisiting the evaluation components of their reports with a more critical eye may reveal existing evaluating capabilities close to hand. A further suggestion is to ask a consultant to review these reports and help foundation staff understand what was helpful about them and how they could have been improved.

A final recommendation for doing evaluation is not to *overdo* it. As stated earlier, a foundation should know who has a valid interest in evaluation results and what kinds of evidence will be credible to these people. A foundation should avoid evaluations that are more elaborate than necessary. And a foundation should never spend more money on evaluation than it believes the results will be worth.

PART TWO

Nine Case Studies
of Foundation Evaluations

Robert Matthews Johnson

The nine case studies in Part Two provide specific examples of evaluation processes from conception through implementation to final reports and the use of the findings. Most of the evaluations described were initiated by foundations. Meyer in Oregon, Skaggs in California, Winthrop Rockefeller in Arkansas, St. Paul in Minnesota, William Penn in Philadelphia, Lilly in Indiana, and Kellogg in Michigan, all saw the need to take a more deliberate step in investigating the consequences of their grantmaking. The clearest exception is the Gautreaux program, where the evaluative research model was put together by two Chicago-based agencies and Northwestern University. The other exception is the Cities in Schools program in New York City. Cities in Schools had developed a habit of evaluation nationally and joined readily with its two evaluation-funding sources in New York to move the evaluation process ahead there.

But even when it has been foundations that have taken the lead, grantees — whether school personnel in Arkansas, the Technology for Literacy Center in St. Paul, or job-finding agencies in Philadelphia — have been intimately involved. Their role needs to be emphasized: most of the time in these evaluations, grantees are essential partners in the process, and the case studies reflect their participation.

The focus of evaluation varies. For the Meyer Memorial Trust, the foundation's own request-for-proposals process gets principal attention. For the others, evaluation focuses primarily on work they have funded in the field, but there is almost always serious consideration also given to underlying designs and strategies, grantmaking programs and particular roles played by the foundations — for example, thought is given to the active program involvement of the William Penn and Winthrop Rockefeller foundations, the cluster style of grantmaking at the W.K. Kellogg Foundation, the choice of a "temporary systems" approach at the Lilly Endowment, and two contrasting ways for grantees to invest venture capital at the L. J. and Mary C. Skaggs Foundation.

These case studies place a great deal of emphasis on using evaluation results. There is an obvious prejudice against letting reports pile up on the shelf. Probably the most frequent usefulness seen in the studies is the value of formative evaluation in providing timely feedback to both grantees and grantors, so that current work in the field can be made more effective. The description of an evaluator at work with a program team at the Technology for Literacy Center in St. Paul, the story of every teacher becoming an evaluator in the Winthrop Rockefeller program in Arkansas, and the special approach Kellogg is developing with its clusters of grantees show three very different instances of this direct applicability of results.

Other evaluations, especially those undertaken by Lilly and Skaggs, are more after the fact and exclusively summative, examining what happened in order to inform future practice and policy decisions. The agencies involved in the Gautreaux program in Chicago and the Cities in Schools program in New York, have made a significant use of evaluation to help programs have an impact on public policy. The usefulness of an evaluation report in raising money to continue a program is evident in cases such as William Penn's summer youth employment program and the Cities in Schools program.

For the foundations specifically, these evaluations have also been useful in helping determine whether grantmaking decisions were wise ones. Without such information, philanthropy flies blind. Through evaluation, basic grantmaking strategies are tested, and improvements are suggested. The Meyer case study, especially, shows a foundation taking an evaluation to heart and making important changes.

With respect to methodology, most evaluation approaches and techniques are represented here. The evaluation designs in the cases of Cities in Schools, Technology for Literacy, Lilly's youthworker education program, William Penn's summer youth employment activity, and the Gautreaux program have produced considerable quantitative results — some through quite sophisticated methods, others more informal. But there is as much or more emphasis on qualitative findings, perhaps reflecting the evaluation mood of the day. The Meyer, Winthrop Rockefeller, Skaggs, and Kellogg foundations, at least in the evaluation processes described here, are not looking so much for numbers as they are for intuitive insights into what is actually happening in grantees' programs and their own grantmaking processes.

Time frames vary considerably among these examples. Some evaluations are content to slice through a program at a particular moment and describe only what was going on then. However, repeated studies of this kind, such as William Penn's annual evaluations and those developing at Cities in Schools, can fine-tune an ongoing program and show some trends in its experience. Other evaluations described here give longitudinal views over time, such as Kellogg's persistent attention to its clusters, the Gautreaux program's monitoring of family experiences through the years, Skaggs's comparative histories of two grantees, and the fortuitous follow-up study that enabled the Lilly evaluation to consider change.

Costs also differ widely. The Skaggs Foundation's evaluation came in at about $1,000. Others cost $6,050, $14,000, $18,000, and $45,000, and a couple — Gautreaux's and Kellogg's — began to add up to hundreds of thousands of dollars. These costs should not be given too much importance, however. The case studies show basic principles, skills, and experiences that many evaluations will share, regardless of cost, and lessons that will be useful to staff and members of the board of directors in big foundations or small.

The discussion of the evaluation process for each case study also looks at many practical details of carrying out an evaluation and reporting its findings. To give the reader a feeling for the different ways the process can evolve, the discussion usually looks at the sequences of program and evaluation events, who is responsible for what, how necessary data are collected under different circumstances, how reports are organized and delivered, and other details that show both the potentialities and limits of various techniques and concepts. Examples of evaluation findings are included to provide a view of the different kinds of results that the various evaluations produce and, most importantly, to create a context in which to illustrate the strengths and weaknesses of each evaluation. Some readers, indeed, may also find the evaluation conclusions interesting in themselves, for what they reveal about the virtues and problems of grantmaking.

Each case study is introduced with a fact sheet listing of some of its basic characteristics, including its stakeholders. *Stakeholders* is a common evaluation term, but it is defined differently in different places. Ultimately, all clients and consumers of nonprofit enterprise have a stake in the evaluation of important programs affecting them, but unless they're lucky enough to be included in a sample somewhere, they don't even know an evaluation is going on. So here, the stakeholders are the relevant organizations — and their staffs and boards — that have been involved in the evaluation process to such an extent that they feel a sense of ownership. They are called stakeholders because they have participated in initiating, planning, interpreting, or using the evaluation as well as, perhaps, in the data gathering itself. This definition is convenient because it emphasizes that the people who are the target audiences for the results of an evaluation do indeed need to be involved as stakeholders.

The nine cases were selected by the Evaluation Handbook Advisory Committee of the Council on Foundations. With help from the council staff and its consultants, committee members searched for candidates through extensive contacts with foundations, regional grantmaking associations, evaluation centers, and any other sources suggested. Well over a hundred possible evaluation projects were considered. These nine were selected on the basis of what they as a group could show about a variety of evaluation values, methods, results, uses, surprises, and problems. The thirty-five keys to effective evaluating that appear in the Conclusion come directly from the experiences described in these nine studies.

None of these evaluations is without flaws, as the foundations and grantees involved are the first to acknowledge. As a whole, the cases do not exemplify some of the more ambitious, broader opportunities in evaluation that are catalogued elsewhere in this book. These are pragmatic, hands-on evaluations, designed to answer the forthright pragmatic questions today's foundation staffs and boards ask themselves — and are asked by others. It is instructive to apply the test of asking, What would the programs funded and the foundations' grantmaking practices be like without these evaluations? In each of the nine cases, a fair answer to that question is that the program and the grantmaking would have had much less chance of benefiting society. Taken as a whole, the cases show how evaluation improves the quality of our contributions and reduces the two cardinal risks of philanthropy — the risk of wasting money and the risk of doing more harm than good. Conversely, evaluation improves the value received from philanthropic contributions.

3

Assessing Grantmaking Effectiveness at a Foundation: Evaluating a Request-for-Proposal Program at the Meyer Memorial Trust

Site: Five states in the Northwest U.S.
Date: 1988.
Underlying program: A request-for-proposals (RFP)
                          program in the field of services
                          for the aging, conducted by the
                          Meyer Memorial Trust, Port-
                          land, Oregon.
Evaluation purpose: To examine the RFP process—
                          for the benefit of both this partic-
                          ular program and the planning of
                          other programs—and to review
                          the initial productivity of pro-
                          gram grants.
Evaluation initiator: The trust.
Stakeholder: The trust.
Evaluators: An expert team consisting of
                          Lyle M. Nelson, professor emeri-
                          tus of communications, Stanford
                          University; Leo T. Hegstrom,

Evaluators, Cont'd.:   recently retired director of the
                          Oregon Department of Human
                          Resources; and Clara Pratt,
                          professor of family and life
                          studies, Oregon State University.
                          The team members based their
                          assessment on their own inquiries
                          and on materials provided by
                          trust staff and consultants, partic-
                          ularly Mary Radtke Klein's
                          report on a telephone survey of
                          grantees.

Information sources: Grantees and the trust staff.

Evaluation methods: Personal interviews and site vis-
                          its, telephone survey, discussions
                          with trust staff, and expert judg-
                          ment. (Exemplifies process and
                          formative evaluation.)

Evaluation cost: $18,000.

Paid by: The trust.

Program cost: $7,120,000 among fifty-seven
                          grantees over four years.

Source of program funds: The trust.

Reports: Memoranda and a meeting with
                          trustees to discuss findings and
                          recommendations.

"Cluster" has become a busy word in philanthropy, as foundations think increasingly in terms of clusters of grants. Some
clusters are grants to organizations that have responded to specific requests-for-proposals (RFPs). Others are related grants
initiated by foundations themselves. Still others are grants in
response to similar or related applications that, for one reason
or another, have come in at about the same time. Some clusters
are highly specialized, funding sharply focused work. Others
are specific only to a broad field of interest.

This first case study falls about in the middle of all such
cluster characteristics. It describes an evaluation of an RFP pro-

gram with a well-articulated sense of direction and an ambition to have an impact in the field. However, while some foundations prefer to design aggressive RFPs, the Meyer Memorial Trust has been determined to maintain a generally responsive stance, leaving initiative and choice in the hands of prospective grantees as much as possible.

The Meyer Memorial Trust of Portland, Oregon, has now undertaken four RFP programs, and its responsive approach has become clear. In the words of Charles S. Rooks, the trust's executive director, "Our role is to make known our presence and the general interests we have, and to invite the community to bring ideas to us, with the promise that we will do the best we can to fund some of the best ones. We wouldn't feel comfortable with the type of requests-for-proposals that are like asking for bids on a contract. It's not that we're passive, because we are strongly encouraging people to come to us. But we haven't adopted a set of specifications to push on the community. We're content with being responsive, investing in other people's ideas."

The trust began making grants in 1982, and within a year, it had initiated two RFP programs — one in higher education and one in library management. Although Rooks reports that the trust was "hasty in getting them going so soon" and that he was dissatisfied with both, several grants to programs to encourage coordination among groups of libraries seem to warrant evaluation, and Rooks will soon propose that the trust have someone look closely at these grants "to see if some of the good ideas have taken root."

The Program to Be Evaluated

The third RFP, announced in early 1984, was designed to initiate projects concerning aging and independence. The trust was convinced that our society needed to "develop more ways to maintain and prolong the independence [of older citizens] and enhance their quality of life." The RFP program was organized because few proposals were being presented in this area of concern. The criteria of the RFP were broad. The announcement showed interest in stimulating easier access to existing

services; asked for new ways of providing services, particularly
in the "least intensive and intrusive manner and settings"; and
called for special attention to three "underserved and/or little
understood" populations: elderly who were isolated because of
where they lived or because poverty or frailty inhibited mobility, minority elders, and the very old. Care providers could be
family, other "formal or informal" services, or institutions, with
emphasis again on those arrangements that "directly encourage
and enable independence." Moreover, the trust would "encourage projects that include productive roles for senior citizens"
themselves and would "emphasize support to model projects,
the results of which can be disseminated to other communities."
The trust also announced that "an important consideration in
selecting grantees" would be the "plans and potential of the
project to instruct others in how to provide more efficient and
helpful services."

The Meyer Trust normally limits its grants to Oregon
and that part of Washington state that lies within the Portland
metropolitan area. However, to cast a broader net, this RFP
was open to applicants in Alaska, Idaho, Montana, Oregon,
and the entire state of Washington.

During the next four years, 427 proposals were received
and fifty-seven grants, totalling $7,120,000, were made. The
largest grants were for $556,000 and $359,000. Nine others were
for more than $200,000, sixteen were for between $100,000 and
$200,000, and the rest ranged down to less than $10,000. Virtually all of the large grants were multiyear commitments. The
small grants were unusual for an RFP program, but the trust
found itself in an unusual bind. In a manner befitting the trust's
philosophy of responsiveness, the board and staff found that
many of the more modest proposals coming in were fresh, attractive, and fundable. Under ordinary circumstances, those they
liked that didn't measure up to all the RFP's guidelines could
have been taken out of the RFP category and handled under
the trust's regular grantmaking program. But most of these particular proposals came from outside the regular program's geographic limits. To qualify for support, they had to be kept in
the RFP group, along with the larger grants.

Grantees included ten universities and colleges and a broad variety of private and public agencies and organizations, about a third of which focused exclusively on senior citizens. The other two-thirds were community centers and health, mental health and family service agencies, plus unpredictable applicants, such as a science center interested in adding seniors to its docent team and a cable television access agency wanting to recruit senior volunteers and expand senior audiences.

The Evaluation

The board of trustees called for an evaluation of the RFP program in early 1987, before the planned release of an announcement of an RFP for a second cycle of grants. Because few of the projects funded in the first cycle had been completed by that time, it was too soon to make judgments about the ultimate merits and worth of most of them, but at least the trust could get an idea of the directions in which the grantees were moving and the problems they were having. There had been some discomfort on the board, both with the commitment to the RFP in the first place and with the way the staff had to take such an active role in the management of the process. It was hoped that the evaluation would either lead to a well-informed decision to discontinue the RFP or help relieve the trustees' discomfort and bring them to a fuller acceptance of the mechanics of the program. The cost of the evaluation was to be about $18,000.

The trust had not had much experience in evaluation work. In his message in the trust's 1987–88 annual report, Executive Director Rooks confessed: "Like many foundations, the Fred Meyer Charitable Trust [as it was known then] has been so busy making grants that we have found little time to stand back and take a hard look at how well we are accomplishing our goals." In a more recent conversation, Rooks challenged the conventional wisdom that says RFP programs always deserve evaluation more than some of the individual grants in a foundation's regular program. He feels the principle for all programs is the same: "If part of what you are funding is intended to have a wider influence towards change and progress, there is a special

need for evaluation, to see whether that part works or not and
actually does anyone any good." Marty Lemke, the trust's senior
program officer responsible for the RFP program and its evaluation, does think that RFPs always carry a certain special
responsibility. She says, "Just the formal public statement of
an RFP puts the onus on us to evaluate."

Preparation for Evaluation

As the staff and trustees worked on designing the evaluation,
they developed the following questions that they wanted the evaluation to answer: How successful were the individual projects?
What kind of overall impact was the program having? Should
we continue it? What improvements could we make?

The decision was made to appoint an evaluation team of
individuals known to the trust but remote from any involvement in the field of aging within the RFP's territory. The team
consisted of Lyle M. Nelson, professor emeritus of communications at Stanford University, a member of the William and
Flora Hewlett Foundation board of directors, and a frequent
consultant to the Meyer Memorial Trust; Leo T. Hegstrom,
recently retired director of the Oregon Department of Human
Resources; and Clara Pratt, professor of family and life studies
at Oregon State University. Professor Pratt agreed to serve when
a gerontologist from out of state had to cancel at the last minute.
Although she was certainly not remote from any involvement
in the aging field regionally, she played a strong, professional
role on the team.

The charge given to the team was very general and open.
The trust believed that if the RFP program was to be broadly
responsive, the team had to be free to look at it from any perspectives it saw fit. In addition, the work-in-progress status of
the program at the time was emphasized. The evaluation would
be more of a review or a "taking stock" than an analysis of results.

Trust staff developed materials for the team. They wrote
summaries of the fifty-seven grants, and commissioned and
received two papers by gerontologists, on issues in an aging society. One was written from a national viewpoint, and the other
(by Clara Pratt) focused on the Northwest.

The trust also hired Mary Radtke Klein, an independent consultant in Portland with a background in aging and a reputation as a good interviewer, to conduct telephone interviews with all fifty-seven grantees and prepare a memo on each project that would give further insight into the RFP experience and assess where it stood at that moment. This was done just before the evaluation team was to meet, so the information would be fresh. Averaging six calls a day, from twenty to forty-five minutes each, Klein completed the interviews in two weeks. Most of the calls were made from the trust office, with a secretary helping to set up telephone appointments. Although she had the staff report and the grantee's application and interim reports at hand before each call, Klein believes that two weeks was too short a period to study and work effectively with the materials. As a result, she says, the calls became "open ended. . . . For better or worse, I couldn't pin people down much about whether or not they were doing exactly what they had said they were going to do. That meant the best information I got was probably the surprises — the outcomes and learnings so far that no one expected."

Klein wrote one- to two-page "impact statements" on each grantee's program, organized under the four topic headings of outcomes, funding (prospects for funding after the trust grant), dissemination, and comments. She also had been asked to share her impressions on the program as a whole following these telephone interviews, and she was eager to do so, because she felt she had "formed some overall opinions and wanted to explore some patterns." In her report, "Enhancing the Impact of Grantmaking," she admired some of the more successful projects without, however, naming them, spoke of promising new connections being made in the field across disciplines and between seniors and useful resources, and remarked that the "projects which serve minority elders have increased the sensitivity of the system and ultimately will force its expansion" (Klein, 1988).

She used the example of mental health services to raise the question of whether the trust might take a more active role in helping its grantees move ahead from small model projects to changes that would benefit seniors generally. She felt there had been few mental health services available to seniors in the

past and little attention from mental health resources to the needs
of seniors and of the organizations working with them. However, she said, "some of the trust projects [that deal with mental
health among the aging] have already shown striking results. . . .
The initial outcomes provide the experience necessary to break
down long standing stereotypes and myths. . . . By identifying
a specific need and seeding the region with demonstrations, the
trust has created an opportunity to incubate information and
set the stage for social and policy change. Whether or not there
is a long range impact may depend, in part, on the role the trust
chooses to take."

Klein then discussed four barriers she had heard about
repeatedly in her telephone interviews — "barriers that will limit
the impact of these projects unless strategies for change are actively pursued."

1. System overload: Klein called this "a major barrier," say-
    ing that "the current human services system has little room
    for a good new idea. . . . Staff time is at such a premium
    in human services, there is no slack. . . . Unless an idea
    or activity will immediately save time or money, it cannot
    be incorporated."
2. Lack of continued funding: "In many projects," said Klein,
    "it appeared that program development took significantly
    more time than anticipated and that the complex work of
    putting together continued funding was only beginning as
    the end of the grant period approached. Some of these prob-
    lems may result from a lack of a requirement that grantees
    have a formal workplan for the development of continued
    funding. In other cases, the person responsible . . . was not
    very sophisticated."
3. Ineffectual dissemination: Klein reported that "most grant-
    ees never request sufficient funds to 'market' their products,
    models, or findings. The need for change, the significant
    investment of the trust and the fine work of some of the
    grantees deserve better opportunities for exposure and im-
    pact. . . . Once the trust knows that it has fueled a bright
    light . . . it should not allow it to remain hidden under a
    bushel."

4. Inadequate strategies for replication: Klein acknowledged that replication is a difficult goal, but cited the ways that a few funded projects had succeeded in having such an impact by working with industry, by sending the right expert witnesses to see policymakers, and especially, by organizing informed grass-roots constituencies. She pointed out that "the fine results of many of these [Meyer] grants may never find their way into social policy unless grass roots advocacy and self help groups are given the support they need to carry the ball."

Klein's report then talked about ways the trust might "increase the impact of the work it funds." Some suggestions were to strengthen applications and support grantees by referring them to one another and bringing them together, by helping them gain access to management assistance and literature in the field, by helping them develop realistic financial plans, and by encouraging better evaluation work.

Klein also suggested strategies for the trust's own program activity, so that the trust might engage in "more aggressive examination of outcomes and active pursuit of long term impacts." These strategies include assessment of a grant's potential: "By the halfway point in the grant, program officers might begin to ask not only what has been accomplished but also what the long term effect is likely to be." Then, Klein continued, the trust should implement "proactive strategies" on a carefully selected basis: "Observations in this review indicate that grantees are limited in the impact they can achieve within the scope of their individual grants. . . . A short list of best prospects should be pursued aggressively, with the intent of refining ideas, disseminating concepts, and supporting the elements necessary to change public and private policy." Klein's examples of possible roles for the trust included encouraging or sponsoring conferences to refine ideas and develop impact strategies, and making supplementary grants to support dissemination, replication, and advocacy.

Klein's report and her impact statements for each grant, the staff's grant summaries, the gerontologists' papers, and other selected background material were sent to the team members in advance of their visit.

The Evaluation Team at Work

Two members of the team, Lyle Nelson and Leo Hegstrom, came to Portland two days ahead of time to conduct on-site interviews with grantees whose work especially interested them. Foundation staff made the appointments for them. Although there were only half a dozen such site visits, they were credited later with having greatly enriched the evaluation. Executive Director Rooks believes that the site visits gave the team "a much deeper understanding and appreciation of what the RFP program was all about. . . . The projects then made more sense. . . . On one hand, [the team was] able to see much more about grant-making from the trust's point of view; on the other hand, they had a chance to look at the trust from the grantees' perspective."

Hegstrom, perhaps owing to his background in public agency leadership, had always insisted on the importance of professional control of services, but at the evaluation meetings, he reported that he "couldn't believe what [he] was seeing" during site visits with respect to the effective use of volunteers. Later, someone said Hegstrom really became converted to voluntarism because of this exposure.

All three members of the team met with Charles Rooks and Marty Lemke. Clara Pratt remembers that she asked the staff if the real question being put to the team was whether the RFP program should be continued. Although the staff assured them that there were other considerations, the members of the team heard enough confirmation that the program was in jeopardy to make Pratt especially concerned, and she admits that "for someone like me, in the field, once that issue was raised at a foundation that plays an extremely important role in aging, it tended to blow everything else out of perspective."

Nelson, Hegstrom, and Pratt's intensive two-day schedule of working together began with a meeting among themselves for part of the first morning. Then they met at the trust offices with six grantees of their own choosing. The grantees talked among themselves as well as with the team, and these exchanges among the grantees were especially memorable for the team. As Clara Pratt reports, "The way they interacted together about common problems and issues gave us a much better feeling for them as people."

In the late afternoon, the team members met by themselves again, and then had dinner with the trustees and staff. After another meeting among themselves early the second morning, the team members presented an oral report to the board of trustees, at a special meeting which lasted most of the rest of the day. Rooks remembers it as good discussion with everyone sharing views and reactions, and Pratt admires the trustees for having been "genuinely open. . . . There was nothing hidden or out of scope." According to Program Officer Lemke, the team members were critical of several ways in which the RFP program had been run, "but they made a strong concluding argument for continuing the program. They told us, 'You've got something valuable here, and there is a great deal left to be done.'"

Nelson, Hegstrom, and Pratt's written report, delivered to the trust just ten days later, was in two parts: a seven-page "Evaluation Report" (Hegstrom, 1988), which combined findings and several recommendations, and a five-page summary of the recommendations (Nelson, 1988) that had been presented at the board meeting. The covering memo stated that the team hoped the recommendations would help the trust build on "an already strong program. . . . Unsaid, but fundamental to the recommendations, is our conclusion that the program is basically sound and one in which the trust has provided leadership worthy of national recognition. [The program] has gained the trust almost universal respect and appreciation among the social agencies involved."

Evaluation Findings

The team's findings can be organized into seven interrelated topics.

The Trust's Grantmaking Style Is Reactive

The team's report said, "Even though the Aging and Independence Program was a special program distinguished from general purpose grants, it relied almost entirely on the imagination of the grantseeking organizations."

The Aging and Independence Program Lacks Direction

Because the RFP's scope was so broad and inclusive, and because the trust had not organized the grants into orderly categories, the team felt the projects funded "have much merit but in the aggregate lack a sense of direction or substantial impact." This made it "difficult to generalize about the program." However, the team also said that this lack of direction was perhaps understandable at the beginning of the program, to keep the "options open while testing the waters."

Minimal Replication

The team remarked that "very little information is available about the extent of replication that actually has taken place, but probably it is minimal."

Insufficient Marketing

A question the team repeatedly raised was why the trust didn't "capitalize on its successes by marketing the product," so that good ideas could be "adopted by other communities or be incorporated into public programming." Team members said of this missed opportunity, "The projects [funded] can be likened to research and development in business, [which warrant] further investment in project evaluation and selective marketing of those services or products proven most effective."

Insufficient Evidence to Evaluate Impact

The team saw as missing the first ingredient essential to marketing: "factual information about the condition of the people served, and what happened to them." Showing some frustration, the team said it was all well and good that the grantees had met their objectives in that they had done "the specific tasks or activities that were intended to be carried out," but in trying to go the next step, the team too often found it "impossible to determine . . . what impact or results [the projects have] had upon the independence or quality of life of the elderly who were served." As a consequence, any decision that a project should be replicated or should influence public policy would have to be based on nothing more than "a leap of faith."

Trust Staff Have Little Marketing Time

Recognizing that many of the grantees lacked the "internal sophistication" to plan effective marketing, the team thought the trust's staff might take a more active marketing role, but the team found that this was unrealistic at the moment: "Staff of the trust are almost totally consumed with processing the large volume of grant proposals and reports. . . . Relatively little time is available to monitor or evaluate projects, let alone getting involved with the design of project proposals. The staffing situation appears to be a product of the broad scope of the program [and of the] philosophy of the least intrusive relationship with grantees, and a conscious effort to keep administrative costs to a minimum."

Many Projects Are Overoptimistic

The team found that many of the fifty-seven projects did not have "a realistic basis for their optimism about future funding," and that too much time was being lost by grantees "before devoting serious attention to efforts to find ongoing funding." Again, the team traced this problem back to the trust's grantmaking style: "The trust inquires into the plans of the grantees for long term funding, but does not appear to make a critical analysis of the potential for success."

Evaluation Recommendations

Nelson, Hegstrom, and Pratt's recommendations were divided into three categories: recommendations to improve the overall program, to maximize the investment, and to improve procedures.

Program Recommendations

The team's major recommendation was to narrow the RFP's scope, so its energy would be concentrated and, it was hoped, more aggregate impact gained. Specifically, the team said, "the trust should now limit the scope of its program to those projects that preserve and expand independence." This would mean cutting out the more general category of "enhancing the quality of life." The team observed that "social services can be a 'bottomless pit' unless there is some focus or direction. . . . Trust funds and staff time are limited. . . . Unless the focus is narrowed, the trust is faced with handling a huge volume of grant requests which reduces the intensity with which individual proposals can be analyzed. The diverse nature of the proposals further compounds the difficulty of evaluating. . . . As a result, the trust is in less control of its destiny than it would be if it were more definitive of what it wanted to finance."

Recommendations to Maximize the Investment

These recommendations were all concerned with marketing. The team built on their own findings and frustrations and on Mary Klein's conclusions to formulate their strongest challenges to the Meyer trustees.

They said first that "the trust should earmark a significant portion of its Aging and Independence Program budget for 'marketing' and replicating the most successful and most promising of the projects it has supported, [because] it is not enough to have successful projects and to expect word somehow to get around." The team also pointed out that "there is no point in 'reinventing the wheel' when a comparatively small investment of funds will provide others with a model upon which to build." They stated: "If the trust is to have a significant impact, . . . it will have to alter its course of investing almost exclusively in new developmental projects. Some portion of its funding should be devoted to marketing the most promising projects and financing their replication in new locations." The team specified an action the trustees could take as part of this marketing effort: "we recommend the trust sponsor meetings and workshops that bring grantees together, as well as provide firsthand information to policymakers and agencies or groups that have an interest in the kind of successful programs stimulated by the trust."

Finally, Nelson, Hegstrom, and Pratt made note of how these and other recommendations would require considerable staff or consultant attention and time not presently available at the trust. And they were forthright about the policy implications of their recommendations, saying: "The trust's reactive mode of operation is appropriate if the board of trustees is satisfied with the results it is achieving through its grants. However, if the board has doubts or concern about the product it is getting for the amount being invested, . . . the board needs to reexamine the principles that set the present style of operation of the trust."

Procedural Recommendations

In suggesting procedural changes, the team called especially for "a more specific set of requirements that must be met by applicants," including the collection of better data on people to be served and more explicit information about expected outcomes.

The team suggested that the trust pay more attention to questions about future funding, not only for the projects themselves, but also for the replications or large-scale changes in practice they might lead to. And the team offered specific procedures. For example, they said: "Where future public funding is expected to be a major source of on-going support, a firm letter which establishes the possibility of such funding, as well as merely interest in the project, should be required." The team also suggested that "the trust should conduct a cost analysis of each proposal, separating development costs from service delivery costs. [On the basis of such information], the trust should critically analyze the realistic feasibility of the project, particularly its potential for future funding." And they stated that, "the trust should not create a demand for services for which there is little or no reasonable chance of funding . . . in the future."

To facilitate the program's impact on public policy and replication, the team also encouraged funding for "quantitative research on selected projects with potential for replication." Specifically, "the trust ought to consider investing in some longitudinal studies. [For example], better information is needed about the duration of the effect of service to keep elderly persons in

their own homes. Hopefully, through such information some
measure could be made of the length of time their independence
was prolonged, and some assessment could be made of the
cost/benefit of the service."

The team recommended that the trust help its grantees
in both the areas of future funding and evaluation by providing them with "training and technical assistance on fund development and monitoring. This training should be conducted during the first year of each project."

Evaluation Consequences for the Program

Nelson, Hegstrom, and Pratt's evaluation report provoked a
great deal of useful conversation among the staff and trustees.
The recommendations that stimulated the most discussion, and
still do, were those calling for the trust to become more proactive in its work with grantees, in order to see that successful
projects would be effectively marketed.

On one level, the trust felt that the evaluation team un-
derestimated how close the staff was to its applicants and grantees, and how often the staff worked informally to see that proposals reflected solid marketing plans and that grantees had the
right opportunities to carry out such plans. On another level,
the board and staff said the findings about being responsive and
reactive were certainly not news. They acknowledged that the
board members' conservative strain often made them uncomfortable with roles such as advocacy, influencing public policy,
telling grantees what to do, and having a staff large enough to
give program officers time to be entrepreneurs. As Executive
Director Rooks says, "It's no accident that we are reactive and
nonintrusive; the trust has been deliberately organized that way."
The trust was not established to be a public interest agency press-
ing hard on favorite causes, and it would be difficult for the trust
to go as far in this direction as the team recommended.

Program Continuation

The major operational consequence of the evaluation was that
the board of trustees decided to continue the Aging and Indepen-

dence RFP program. Furthermore, Rooks's letter in the trust's first annual report to follow the evaluation included impressive evidence of the trust's acceptance of the principle that, if it were going to continue activist programs such as RFPs, there would have to be more consideration given to assuring that its bright lights were not allowed to "remain hidden under a bushel," as Mary Klein had suggested was happening. Rooks quoted Klein's eloquent paragraph about system overload as at least one reason why it was so difficult to get institutions and agencies to accommodate new ideas. However, he also accepted that the trust had a responsibility here. He wrote, "Without an aggressive and effective method of 'marketing' their achievements, most projects cannot have much influence beyond their own locale. [Therefore], we will give more support to disseminating information about outstanding programs. . . . We will be interested in a variety of methods by which noteworthy lessons can be transferred to other agencies and public policy makers. . . . The trust will provide funding for the kind of [evaluation] studies needed to test and measure the results of our grants. . . . We will demand from applicants more realistic consideration of other funding sources and from grantees more specific plans and timetables for obtaining such support."

Response to Recommendations

The evaluation report's recommendations about narrowing the focus of the RFP met with considerable resistance at the trust. Perhaps the evaluators and the staff and trustees had different assumptions about what can be expected in response to an RFP. Rooks and his staff felt their experience in looking for and reviewing applications had made them appreciate how easy it is to exaggerate an RFP's potential. It is tempting to assume that there are a great many wonderful people out there just itching to have you fund their new landmark, history-making projects that focus on some narrowly defined field and have an approach that coincides with your own sense of strategy. The reality, says Charles Rooks, is that you have to be grateful that there are any high-quality applications at all:

There are a relatively small number of organizations in our region that have the capacity and sufficient motivation at the moment to develop the kind
of project we want to fund. The danger in pursuing the assumption that there are a lot of them out
there is that, when all the fine proposals don't come
in, you will go out and find people and push money
on them. In our experience, that doesn't work. You
can certainly encourage people, but when you make
the grant you've got to be responding to what they
are able and willing to do at the time.

Many of our best grants in this program
wouldn't have been made if the RFP hadn't been
so broad, inviting organizations with such a variety of projects to apply. There are lots of grants that
aren't in any predictable narrow focus but have
ended up to be just as good or better a use of our
dollars as would have happened otherwise.

As an example of the advantages of being broadly responsive, Rooks cites the efforts funded under the RFP to work on
problems of alcoholism and drug abuse among seniors. Before
the RFP, there had been little public or agency recognition of the
effect of alcoholism on many seniors' abilities to cope, and the
trust had not anticipated proposals addressing this problem.
But some relatively modest applications came in, grants were
made, and projects brought service agencies together, encouraged them to become more effectively aware of the problem,
raised some issues and ideas, and placed responsibilities where
they needed to be placed to help seniors.

The evaluation team had also stressed the need for as-
surances from applicants that projects started up with trust funding would, if successful, be likely to be picked up by other sources
of funding, largely public. As mentioned earlier, the team went
so far as to suggest that the trust should require a "firm letter"
from the prospective funding agency, on the grounds that this
procedure would help the trust anticipate others' acceptance of
both a project's merits and its cost. However, in his message

in the annual report, Rooks challenged the team's point of view. He stated: "Few enterprising ventures would be funded without taking risks in this area." He also stated a belief that "there may be occasions when the cost seems too high because our society has not yet acknowledged the value of a particular service," and he concluded: "Just as we wish to avoid 'hot house' projects that can never be replicated, we also want to avoid imprisonment in the status quo because of an unwillingness to challenge current views of what is humane and appropriate for this country."

Acceptance of Recommendations

Although the trust clearly did not accept the evaluation recommendations unreservedly, the new guidelines for the next round of the RFP, which were circulated in draft form among the evaluation team members for comment, showed considerable influence from Nelson, Hegstrom, and Pratt's recommendations and Mary Klein's observations. Without sharply narrowing the scope of the RFP, the guidelines now began with a more direct, clear statement about "independence" as the key topic for the program: "Ways must be found to prevent [older citizens'] unnecessary institutionalization. [Our discussions and experience so far] clearly indicate that the elderly have the potential for extended independence when given support."

The guidelines now also made explicit the desire to fund replications: "The trust will emphasize support for . . . model projects . . . and projects that implement activities which have been demonstrated elsewhere to be especially effective." The guidelines also were more specific about future funding considerations and the need for serious provisions for monitoring and evaluation. In addition, apart from the published guidelines, Executive Director Rooks and Program Officer Lemke say that, since the evaluation findings and recommendations, they have made it a practice to ask applicants for clearer statements about constituencies and intended outcomes, and they repeat this information about objectives back to grantees as part of the grant letter. Lemke reports that, in those cases where marketing will be essential, evaluation has been promoted to "an outcome in itself," rather than an afterthought.

As for the trust's own involvement in marketing, the most direct indication of the evaluation's influence has been a series of all-day forums, or "briefings," that bring leaders of four or five of the trust's projects together with fifty to seventy-five key advocates for seniors, top professional people, key legislators, and agency representatives—individuals who can give grantees access and ideas for future directions. One forum examined the use of volunteers, another discussed mental health and aging, and the third is just now being planned. Lemke can point to several developments for which these forums have been at least partially responsible, including changes in state funding, replications initiated, and new legislation considered.

Because the forums have featured groups of grantees and have had multiple consequences among important people, they have been an efficient use of staff time for marketing. "Still, Lemke reports that "they have been enormously time-consuming." Therefore, most of the trust's efforts to increase the impact of funded projects will rely on grantees themselves and consultants hired to work on specific opportunities. Since the evaluation, especially, the trust has been giving grantees money to attend conferences or to organize meetings with agencies and public officials. These funds are supplied either as part of the original grants or in response to special requests. To increase the number of meetings of the forum type, the trust hopes to take advantage of a variety of outside opportunities, such as the annual meetings on aging conducted by Oregon State University.

The next step in evaluating the RFP program will be to bring in a consultant to update Mary Klein's reports on individual grantees and add reports on the newer grantees. "Then," says Rooks, "based on what we learn from that process and our own contacts with grantees, we will select a few we would like to look at in a much more systematic way."

Impact on Other Trust Programs

How long the RFP program on aging should continue is again being considered by the board of trustees. Meanwhile, a new

RFP, announced in 1987 and entitled *Preserving the Future: Support for Children at Risk,* is well underway. The evaluation of the Aging and Independence Program has influenced this new RFP. "We went to school on that one," says Marty Lemke. She and Charles Rooks believe that the guidelines for the new RFP are clearer about what the RFP is for and what the trust wants in proposals because the evaluation team's recommendations are reflected in the new RFP announcement. As for more deliberate efforts to see that funded projects have a better chance to influence public policy and gain replication, the staff this time began early to call meetings of grantees in order to exchange information and plan strategies. The trust has been encouraging applicants to include in their budgets provisions for travel and conferences and for organizing their own forums of the type the trust pulled together for the RFP program on aging. The trust has also urged some grantees to hire evaluation consultants at the beginning of their funded projects.

As they did following the evaluation of the program on aging, the staff and trustees have been looking for outside arrangements that might help projects in the new program have an influence in the right places. Oregon has a statewide alliance of child advocacy organizations, and projects funded by the trust's RFP have been well represented as model programs at alliance meetings. The trust has also been exploring the possibilities of a university-based center that could collect and disseminate information about the status of promising efforts in the field of support for at-risk children.

Lemke also reports that the trust is planning to bring in a team to evaluate the Children at Risk RFP and that this evaluation will be different from the Aging and Independence Program evaluation in some ways, based on what the trust learned from that evaluation: "The team will be here for a longer time, or maybe two times, with time between for reflection and staff work. It will be much more structured in terms of what we ask them to find out; we will ask them to help us make those decisions ahead of time. We will involve our grantees more. With some experience behind us now, we will be able to plan better about who needs to be on the team and how they will work together. And we will give them more information before they come, not only about the individual grants but what [the grants] look like as a whole."

Despite some new ways of doing things, Rooks points out that the trust's "emphasis on responsiveness hasn't changed." He feels that the Children at Risk RFP "is no more narrowly focused than the aging one. We expected to refine the scope as time went along, but we find again that the region doesn't work that way." Like the projects on aging, the projects for at-risk children show a lot of diversity, and there are many small grants.

Rooks adds, however, that the first evaluation's finding that a "lack of direction" was inhibiting successful marketing did persuade trust staff to categorize the new projects into three areas: the few truly "exemplary" projects that are right on target for the RFP's stated purposes of broadly influencing policies and practices, the "good solid local projects" that look as though they will have an impact on their own communities, and the small projects that "don't have all the bells and whistles" and may be on the fringes of the RFP guidelines, "but have some qualities that may evolve into something." These classifications have helped considerably in establishing different project contexts for considering what may need to be done about project evaluation, cost analysis, and marketing.

Rooks emphasizes that the evaluation of the Aging and Independence RFP has had repercussions within the trust that go considerably beyond RFPs themselves: "The very experience of having an external assessment has sharpened our awareness of what has to be done on all our grants — many of which have just as much potential for helping people accomplish something important as the RFP grants do. We tend to think more now about encouraging all our appliants to clarify their objectives. And in our general purpose grantmaking, we spend more time now looking ahead to see what the larger beneficial impacts may be and how they are most likely to happen."

Evaluation Strengths and Weaknesses

The experience with an outside team was a good one. The members of the team were not as much removed from the field of aging locally as they might have been, but they were a team the trust would listen to. For a first evaluation and expert assessment such as this, a team of three seemed to have a more effective voice than one visitor. Because they were well accepted by the trustees, the team did indeed help give the trustees a better understanding of the mechanics of the program.

The main points of the evaluation were strongly expressed and respected, though some of them — about replication, evaluation components, and cost-benefit analysis, for instance — were obviously over-simplified. It may be the nature of team evaluations that even the good ones — or perhaps especially the good ones — tend to view a foundation's work with more alarm than necessary and prescribe with a certain arbitrary self-confidence. The team is challenged to come in and in a ridiculously short time understand all there is to know, come to conclusions, report, and then go riding out of town. It is a tour de force, appreciated by everyone as exactly that. Their conclusions can be nothing but first impressions, and first impressions have the advantage of being uncomplicated by less-obvious influences, as yet unseen and unthought of. It is understood that they are far from being final verdicts on anything. Thus, when these impressions are communicated succinctly and without reservation or apology, they provoke profitable discussion, without anyone feeling too threatened.

The result in this case was a useful confrontation between two philanthropic points of view. The team clearly sensed the lack of what they called marketing, and they challenged the trust to make sure that the best, most promising projects would not die on the demonstration project vine. The trustees and staff answered with the courage of their convictions, but this challenge probably enabled them to define the trust's dedication to responsiveness better than before, and it clearly moved them toward a more active concern with what happens to the good ideas generated by an RFP.

The team's site visits and their meeting with six grantees in the trust's offices provided indispensable insights. There is no other way than direct contact with the grantees for outsiders to gain an understanding of who is getting the money and what they are doing with it. It was interesting to see in the team's report that the team liked the experience of being useful in bringing grantees together and "were surprised how much individual project directors seemed to learn from each other" at the meeting. The team also remarked that all six grantees "expressed appreciation for the opportunity this provided to compare notes, discuss problems, and obtain new information."

Mary Klein's individual write-ups on the fifty-seven projects funded were also helpful, but perhaps the best payoff from her assignment was her report of her overall impressions. Many of the evaluation team's conclusions and the trust's responses showed the influence of the insights she gained, which is a useful reminder that in an evaluation of grants and grantmaking there is no substitute for direct and deep contact with grantees, even if it must be by telephone.

The trust was as nonintrusive into the team's approach as it had been into the lives of its grantees. With minimal instructions from the trust, the team of experts in the social services chose instead to be experts in philanthropy and concentrate on the trust's processes rather than the effect the RFP was having on the field of aging. That was all right as far as it went, but it meant that they reported little about the substance of the programs in which the trust was investing.

They did not highlight projects they might have felt were most promising, remark on issues in aging being raised as a result of the grants, attempt to estimate whether the trust was carrying out its current mission to give priority to special populations, or make even the most tentative identifications of change agents that might be available to turn promising projects into lasting improvements for more people. Discussion of such topics may have happened informally at meetings and in dinner conversations, but there is little recall of such exchanges, and nothing in the written reports that would have helped the trustees gain understanding and enthusiasm for the program content of the projects they were funding. Even Mary Klein's comments avoided any mention of specific grants and projects. Of the four questions asked before the evaluation began, only the two procedural ones about continuing the RFP and making improvements in the method were answered. The two questions about success and impact were not well addressed.

It might be argued that the projects weren't far enough along to show much substance, but no one expected the evaluation to pass final judgments on the projects. Instead, the value of interim process and formative evaluations lies in pointing out midway trends and indications and in suggesting options the foundation may have in meeting emerging program needs. In this case, the evaluation team placed great importance on the general need for more marketing, but they did not document the circumstances in specific funded projects that aroused their conviction about the need for better marketing.

They also did not discuss the RFP's future in the context of specific projects and groups of projects. They did not help the trust begin to envision what might happen if a half dozen of these projects were properly marketed, or what the trust might do in a few specific cases to encourage that to happen. A recommendation means a great deal more and stimulates more realistic discussion when it includes the beginnings of some creative thinking about real situations, based on what the evaluators have seen and learned in their investigations. They do not have to produce well-developed strategies, but rather some clues the foundation and its grantees can use in coming up with ideas of their own.

Even producing these clues is hard work, and perhaps a foundation has to say beforehand that it expects its evaluators to produce on that level of assistance. It also, very likely, has to build more time for the team into the evaluation schedule. The plan for the evaluation of the Meyer trust's RFP about children looks forward to a team staying a little longer, preferably in two visits, so ideas can simmer for awhile in between.

Despite the team's blanket criticism of the lack of evaluation among the projects funded, there were several grantees engaged in respectable monitoring and evaluation work on their own. Mary Klein says she talked about these evaluations with grantees and trust staff, but it was an oddly missing element in her reports on the individual grants. In turn, the team stressed the need for grantee-based evaluation but made no comment about any of the work underway.

In its RFP programs, the Meyer Memorial Trust is trying to combine both a new proactive stance, in which it presses its grantees and others to work for constructive social change, and its traditional reactive stance, in which it supports other people's good ideas and then leaves them alone to work on them. Executive Director Charles Rooks said in a recent annual report that the trust hopes to be both "appropriately modest" and "daring." There will always be tensions between such different approaches to philanthropy, but continuing evaluation work at the trust will help assure that the tensions will be creative ones.

4

Comparative Case Studies: Evaluating Two Grants in a Nonprofit Venture Capital Program

Site:	Two cities in Northern California.
Date:	1989.
Underlying program:	A series of grants by the L. J. and Mary C. Skaggs Foundation, Oakland, California, to enable small arts organizations to develop new sources of income.
Evaluation purpose:	To record and compare the experiences of two grantees in the program and find generalizable particulars in those experiences.
Evaluation initiators:	The lead evaluator and the foundation's program director.
Stakeholders:	The lead evaluator, the foundation, and the program director for this activity.
Evaluators:	Outside evaluators Laura Landy, associate director, Center for

Evaluators, Cont'd.:	Entrepreneurial Studies, New York University, and graduate student Ellen K. Prior.
Information sources:	Grantee staff and board members and foundation staff.
Evaluation method:	Personal interviews, case studies, and expert judgment. (Exemplifies process, impact or outcome, and summative evaluation.)
Evaluation cost:	$1,000 (out-of-pocket expenses only).
Paid by:	The foundation.
Program cost:	$100,000 for each of the two grantees.
Source of program funds:	The foundation.
Report:	A paper written by the evaluators, shared with arts organizations and funding sources, and used as a curricular resource in classes on nonprofit venture creation.

The Program to Be Evaluated

Between 1983 and 1986, the L. J. and Mary C. Skaggs Foundation made a series of special $100,000 grants to six relatively small arts organizations in Northern California. The money had to be used for capital, and was to be invested in "a business, a product line, [or] a promotional strategy" that would generate new streams of income for the organizations.

Jillian Steiner Sandrock, program director for this part of Skaggs's activity at the time, felt that, in those Reagan years, "there was a different set of rules and a different marketplace" for small arts organizations. Costs were up; giving was becoming more problematical. There were challenging new expectations; the best of these organizations would survive on strengths of self-reliance and entrepreneurship.

"We wanted to help these organizations get out of the cycle of living from hand to mouth, asking us and everybody else for so much of their funding year after year," adds Philip Jelley, foundation manager and secretary of the board of this $10,000,000 family foundation in Oakland, California. "For these unproven, start-up arts groups, trying to raise endowment for this purpose is unrealistic. There needed to be some other answers."

The foundation picked its own candidates for the grants and built a lot of technical assistance into the program — how to choose ventures, how to start them, and how to build them into something productive through better marketing, bookkeeping, board training, or whatever seemed necessary. The organizations did not qualify for the first payments on their $100,000 capital grants until they had undergone a year of management development and planning. To a considerable extent, the grants were part of a larger effort by the foundation to help small arts organizations become better organized. The foundation's motive in funding the development of income-producing ventures was as much to stimulate good organizational management as it was to develop alternative resources.

The Evaluation

Jillian Sandrock had attended a Grantsmanship Center workshop on nonprofit entrepreneurship conducted by Laura Landy, now associate director of the Center for Entrepreneurial Studies at New York University and adjunct professor at Columbia University, teaching nonprofit entrepreneurship. Landy became one of the technical assistance resources for the Skaggs Foundation program. As the program developed, she and one of her graduate students at NYU, Ellen K. Prior, became interested in studying the venture projects more closely. At the same time, Sandrock and the foundation wanted an evaluation that would document what they were learning from the experience. The design they all chose together, while certainly not examining the whole program, led to an analysis that offers valuable insights for anyone interested in entrepreneurial development in any nonprofit field. The design also supplies a good model for a sharply focused evaluation of minimal scope and expense that — given evaluators who are knowledgeable in the field and eager to explore — can provide precisely the information and reflection desired.

The evaluation design featured comparative case studies of just two of the projects funded by the grants, concentrating just on the grantees' experiences in developing their ventures. "We decided," says Landy, "to choose the two grantees that had the most intense, varied experiences and examine what they brought to the venture, what they did, and what at least the immediate consequences were."

The Two Grantees' Experiences

Landy and Prior's fifteen-page evaluation report, presented to the Skaggs Foundation in May 1989, began with a narrative section that briefly summarized what happened in each project (Landy and Prior, 1989).

A Dance Company Starts a Coffeehouse. One of the grantees was a modern dance company in a small city south of San Francisco. Highly respected artistically, it was always struggling to raise even its bare-bones $150,000 budget. With consultants provided by the Skaggs Foundation, in anticipation of one of the $100,000 grants, the dance company re-evaluated its goals, by-laws, board and staff roles, budgets and funding strategies and developed some entrepreneurial abilities. According to Sandrock, who was quoted in the report, "It took more than a year to reposition the company and board to the point where the strain of superimposing a business on an already shaky nonprofit would be anything other than a coup de grace. . . . Out of the process emerged a stronger organization and a more focused and committed board, ready to plan for the use of their newfound funds."

Meanwhile, the dance company's board of directors discovered that a local coffeehouse was for sale, and they thought it could become their new fundraising venture under the foundation's grant. Recognizing their primary needs as capital beyond the $100,000 grant and a partner with solid commercial experience, they approached the owner of a successful bookstore next door to the coffeehouse. He became interested, and a partnership was established between the bookstore and a new for-profit subsidiary of the dance company. The evaluation report summarized the new partnership's experience in getting a bank loan, weathering disagreements on the dance company's board, surviving cost overruns in renovating the space, and opening for business in April 1986. The venture began to break even within a few months, and enjoyed a net first year's profit of $20,500. Community relations were good, board member involvement was high. The report concluded that the company "emerged from the experience a more unified, sophisticated organization."

Landy and Prior's updated 1990 version of the report added a note on the loss of the coffeehouse in the 1989 California earthquake. But the evaluators' assessment of the project as an entrepreneurial development activity of a small nonprofit organization remained positive. (Incidentally, there are plans to start the coffeehouse again, with the same partnership arrangements.)

An Opera Company Buys a Theater. The second grantee was a small opera company, again with a distinguished reputation in its specialized field. The evaluation report talked about the quality and success of the company's performances, but also described a weak, divided board and management. As it had with the dance company, the Skaggs Foundation supported considerable technical assistance to strengthen the organization.

From the beginning, the opera company's general manager was convinced that the Skaggs grant should be used to establish a permanent performance space, and that ambition became the focus of the development process. The evaluation report described how a space was chosen and how plans were put together to renovate it, use it as a home for the company's own performances and administrative offices, and also rent it to other organizations. It was expected that this asset would provide considerable savings over time, plus a new source of independent income.

Like the dance company, the opera company founded a new organization to handle its business endeavor. But in this case a decision was made, largely for fundraising reasons, to establish the new organization as a charitable nonprofit agency, with a separate board of directors. The report mentioned how a snag then developed when the company applied for Internal Revenue Service 501(c)3 status. The IRS objected to the purely commercial nature of the new organization as first proposed, and it insisted that several activities to help tenants and other nonprofit groups had to be added to the purpose and program before the theater's nonprofit status could be approved. After the company developed a financial plan, the city approved a loan, with the Skaggs grant as collateral. The lease that was signed appeared to be favorable in recognizing the value of the opera company's renovation work. Other funds were raised, the space was renovated, and in April 1987, the first opera of the company's new season opened in the company's new theater. The evaluators' report described how initial enthusiasm ran high and $245,000 was generated in rental fees and other ancillary income in the first nine months. But it wasn't enough. Operating expenses to manage and maintain the space were over $400,000 for the same period. At that point, the new organization's board of directors closed the theater, laid off the staff, and eventually filed for bankruptcy.

The updated 1990 report indicated that the opera company itself had been reborn, with the same artistic leadership but new administrative management. The $100,000 appeared to be gone, and the company rented more modest space, as it had before. However, even more recent news suggests that the city may return the $100,000 collateral.

Comparing the Two Grantees

Following these narratives, which were a form of process evaluation, the report presented two tables (Tables 4.1 and 4.2), that compared key objective and subjective characteristics of the two organizations. Each characteristic had been documented in the narrative section, although the documentation was often brief and sometimes made its point by implication only. For instance, the characteristic of market research (Table 4.1) was

Table 4.1. Comparison of Two Grantees' Key Objective Characteristics.

Characteristic	Dance Company	Opera Company
Parent legal form	Nonprofit	Nonprofit
Primary activity	Modern dance	Opera
Project commencement	9/85	9/85
Venture description	Coffeehouse	Theater
Relation to nonprofit's mission	Unrelated	Related
Venture opened	4/86	4/87
Venture legal form	For profit	Nonprofit
Partnership	Yes	No
Location	Prime commercial	Struggling tourist
Capital grant investment	$100,000	$100,000
Business plan	No	No
Market research	None	Minimal
Breakeven	Immediately reached	Not reached
Tenure of venture	Open	Closed 1/88

Source: Landy and Prior, 1989. Reprinted with permission.

found to be minimal for the opera company and nonexistent for the dance company. The narrative for the dance company documented the marketing research with this statement: "Coincidentally, a member of the company's board of directors had managed the coffeehouse. . . . He knew that the location had the potential to be profitable." The narrative for the opera company documented that company's market research when it stated that, "with the assistance of a volunteer businessman, the opera conducted a survey of performing arts groups in the Bay Area to identify their interest in renting the space for forthcoming seasons," and the survey showed there was sufficient potential to justify the venture.

Evaluation Findings

Referring to its comparison charts, the report picked out the characteristics which Landy and Prior felt were most critical in influencing the two ventures' respective futures. Two such characteristics were organizational stability and the strength of the board and management. The report observed:

In the development of a successful nonprofit, and
most certainly in a subsidiary activity of a nonprofit,
it is vital that the board participate appropriately. . . .
If the board is actively and positively involved, it
can lead the way, ask probing questions, and raise
needed capital. . . . If the board is resistant or ob-
structionist, it can make the organization retreat
from opportunities and even surrender or collapse
under market pressures. [The dance company] had
the advantage of being "board-driven" by an active
and educated group. . . . Board members provided
volunteer support and became the champions for
the venture project through to implementation. In
contrast, the opera was clearly driven by the general
manager. The opera's board members did not come
together in support of the venture plan.

Table 4.2. Comparison of Two Grantees' Key Subjective Characteristics.

Characteristic	Dance Company	Opera Company
Nonprofit board role prior to venture	Moderate	Weak
Stability prior to venture	Moderate	Weak
Dependence on venture	Helpful	Critical
Venture champion	Board president	General manager
Nonprofit board involvement	Active	Minimal
Nonprofit staff involvement	Minimal	Active
Relationship with Skaggs Foundation	Consultative	Dependent
Prior experience in venture activity	Moderate (board)	None
Use of specialist consultants	Moderate	Minimal
Success of other organizations' ventures at same location	Success	Failure
Local competition	Yes	Yes
Competitive advantages		
Location	Yes	Yes
Price	No	No
Service	No	No
Design	No	No
Promotion	No	No
Current stability of nonprofit	Strong	Weak
Current quality of artistic product	High	High

Source: Landy and Prior, 1989. Reprinted with permission.

The report also compared characteristics that related to the ways the two organizations selected their ventures, and to the attitudes the "venture champions" and others had about the selections. In the case of the opera company, getting a new permanent home for performances was "the personal mission" of the general manager. With little respect for the downside possibilities, he "would do whatever was required to obtain the space, because the space had become the objective." The dance company had been open to selecting a venture from a broader variety of opportunities and had experienced the good fortune of having the coffeehouse become available at the right time. Members of the board had knowledge of the coffeehouse's past and some experience with the local marketplace, but it was still a business deal. Laura Landy and Ellen Prior noted, "There was no personal investment by the dance company in the venture business." While the dance company "actually conducted less formal [market] research than the opera, the market variables were easier to assess and rely upon. The investment had a higher quotient of solid business logic and a much smaller amount of emotion tied to decisions."

Referring to the legal form of the new ventures, Landy and Prior's report pointed out how disastrous it was for the opera when "the design of the activity was molded to fit the requirements of the legal structure rather than vice versa." The service activities it set up to get IRS nonprofit status were "time consuming, costly, and a significant diversion" from the real-estate venture itself, which was obviously going to be difficult enough without such complications.

Evaluators Landy and Prior saw the dance company's venture partner as a decided advantage. They said that someone like the bookstore owner, appropriate to the field of the venture, "can allow nonprofits to exploit opportunities otherwise too intimidating or foreign for the nonprofits to tackle alone." The partnership enabled the dance company to venture into something that was at arm's length from its basic work, so that, as the evaluators pointed out (Table 4.2), the venture was "helpful" to the organization rather than, as was the case for the opera company and its building, "critical" to the nonprofit's well-being.

If a venture were to fail, the risk of it seriously hurting the organization was much less for the dance company. The report warned, however, that the presence of a venture partner "was no panacea," and it listed "issues that must be clarified before an effective alliance is established."

The report briefly discussed the use of the technical assistance consultants by the two organizations, the role of the venture champion (was he or she a "catalyst" or a "maverick"?), the need for clear differentiation between an organization's nonprofit mission and its quest for business profits, and the need, ordinarily, for long-term commitments to venture activities. In the two instances compared in the report, the coffeehouse was highly unusual in making a profit from the start, so it hardly tested the dance company's patience, whereas according to the report, the opera company's theater venture was perhaps closed down prematurely: "A more appropriate action might have been some combination of restructuring the corporation that owned the theater, cutting expenses, investing more cash, and increasing marketing."

Evaluation Recommendations

Landy and Prior concluded their report with two checklists of "lessons" to be learned from the comparison of the grantees' experiences. Both checklists took the form of questions based on the report's previous discussion, and one list was primarily for the "planners" of similar grantmaking programs, the other for "recipients" of such grant funds. Therefore, the lists were cast differently. The first emphasized the major steps that need to be taken. The second emphasized caution and preparation, warning that "organizations [embarking on such ventures] must restrain themselves from being driven by the money. The message is that there is a process that must be undertaken and it should not be rushed to seize an opportunity."

But overall, Landy and Prior's report concluded that there is great potential in funding venture projects, and the report summarized the constructive impact the experience of developing a "creative income-generating activity" can have on the whole operation of a nonprofit grantee by "assessing the stability of the entire organization," clarifying and strengthening roles, gaining new relationships in the community, and of course, producing cash that "supports the organization's mission."

Use of the Evaluation

By the time the report came in, the Skaggs Foundation had stopped making these special grants for the development of income-producing ventures, but Philip Jelley says the report was valuable in "reinforcing" several of the foundation's own evolving convictions:

> We used to focus as much or more on the roles of professional staff when considering applications, rather than boards of directors. This evaluation helped us put more emphasis on the need for strong boards. It also was a good reminder again not to get swept away with rhetoric. We've become more demanding about financial data and realistic planning. Laura Landy used to tell our grantees to go out and get good information and then "believe your data," rather than letting [those data] be overwhelmed by personal prejudices. That applies to us too; this project helped us do a better job of gathering the right facts and figures and then taking them seriously.

The report has had little circulation in the Bay Area because the original version named the two organizations, and there was a reluctance to distribute it broadly. Landy has prepared a new version treating the dance and opera companies anonymously, and there are plans to make copies of this version available. Among the few area grantmakers who have seen the report, there is respect for the way it strikes home about the choices to be made in starting ventures such as those described here. As Susan Clark Silk of the Columbia Foundation in San Francisco points out, "the lesson from these two experi-

ences is contrary to the conventional wisdom," which would ordinarily advise nonprofits to stay close to their own familiar field
when starting an income-producing venture. Here, the organization that followed that advice suffered when the venture turned
out to be a risky dream, tied so closely and emotionally to the
basic program that it jeopardized the opera company's own future. The dance company, on the other hand, picked a project
they could easily think of separately and treat rationally as a
business deal that could win or lose. Failure would not affect
the dance company in any life-threatening way; success would
produce new community relationships as well as new income.
It will not always work out that way, but John Kreidler of the
San Francisco Foundation agrees with Silk that the possibility
"is a useful point to have been made so clearly."

David Knight, a program director and office manager of
the Skaggs Foundation, notes that there have been a few requests
from other foundations around the country for the report and
further information about the special grants program, but not
many. Jillian Sandrock has referred to the report at meetings
of several arts and arts funding groups, including the National
Endowment for the Arts. The principal continuing use of the
evaluation has been at New York University and Columbia
University, where Laura Landy uses the report to good advantage in her classes on nonprofit-venture creation. She is distribut-
ing copies through NYU's network of people interested in the
field and hopes to find a way to make the report more broadly
available to foundations and organizations considering such programs. She comments:

> Case studies are rare and so useful because they
> give you insights about what makes for success and
> failure. In this field it's dangerous to generalize a
> lot about what works and doesn't work; a bunch
> of well-researched and written case studies informs
> you about a wide variety of experiences and encour-
> ages you to begin coming to your own conclusions.
>   A story like the dance company's also helps
> show the self-respect that grows in such an experi-

ence. There is a sense of empowerment for an organization; it's no longer so much just a cash poor, impotent, struggling little agency. It has been through a good process of planning and preparing, and now it's got something new and productive going for it. Its place in the community has changed. We have to have case studies like this evaluation to make that point.

Evaluation Costs

No one involved seems able to estimate the actual cost. The chief evaluator, Laura Landy, was a paid consultant to some of the program's grantees, and she was glad to contribute time in return for having the chance to develop a report that would be useful in her work. Ellen Prior wanted the experience as a student. Both Landy and Philip Jelley say the cost to the foundation was only about $1,000, representing Prior's travel expenses to do the interviewing and a modest contribution to the costs of interpretation and writing time for Landy and Prior.

Evaluation Strengths and Weaknesses

This case study is a useful model for comparative evaluations. As evaluator Landy says, using case study narratives and pointing out the similarities and differences gives us insights and provokes thinking in ways that other approaches probably couldn't.

Moreover, the case study process can be especially educational for the evaluator, the grantees, the foundation, and anyone else participating in gathering information and drawing even tentative lessons from it. Those involved will find they have to pull "the story" together into a coherent whole, and that helps them organize their intelligence about the program experience.

The evaluation raises several useful points about nonprofit entrepreneurship ventures. For example, contrary to wishful thinking, even the best ventures can't be counted on to provide big shares of the total income of organizations; Landy says realistic expectations are usually 15 percent or less. This level of new annual revenue may have all sorts of financial, psychological, and social benefits but will hardly take the place of philanthropic giving.

Another lesson that will already be familiar to many funders appears in the painful narrative about the opera company saddling its venture with costly service capacities just to win nonprofit status for its ancillary corporation. From the beginning, therefore, the new organization's mission was only partly to make a profit to feed income to the opera company. Its mission had to include providing conventional nonprofit service, which ate up money without producing any corresponding income.

The company made this unfortunate choice because it perceived that a nonprofit status for the new organization would be important to the foundations and corporate giving programs with which the company might have a relationship. The company was conforming more to what it felt was expected of it by the funding world than to any IRS regulations. "Nonprofit organizations do this all the time," Landy noted in a recent conversation. "They base crucial decisions on assumptions about funders that aren't necessarily correct." It is hard to read the report without thinking how great it would be if grantmakers could more often sense such predictable assumptions among grantees and help them avoid these errors in the making.

As is the case in several other case studies in this collection, there was a good match between the interests of the foundation and the evaluator — one that went far beyond any notion of immediate payment for services rendered. Laura Landy knew the kind of evaluation that would be valuable for her students and others interested in learning about this field, and the foundation agreed her approach would be appropriate for its needs also.

The study doesn't pretend to be more than it is: a limited assessment of the dynamics of venture development, in the form of two examples described and compared. In subsequent conversations, Landy was the first to insist that this was not an evaluation of the overall program. An overall evaluation, she said, would have examined the technical assistance experiences and how well the venture projects stimulated better management generally, as the foundation had hoped they would. Some reference to the other four projects supported by this grant program would have been important. It also would have been desirable to place these experiences in the context of what is known nationally about alternative income-producing ventures. A longer time frame or a follow-up study would have made possible more conclusive findings and would have enabled the evaluators and the foundation to involve the grantees more in the evaluation and feedback process. These are typical of the sacrifices that must be made when there is an emphasis on narrow focus and economy. Yet, because the purposes of the study were also set at a minimum, the study was a useful one.

An inescapable issue in case study design is the ethical question of how to handle program or project failures. A person reading the second version of the report, with the grantees' identities concealed, would not need much familiarity with the arts scene in the Bay Area to be able to identify the two organizations. Depending on how disastrous and personal the failures are, therefore, it can get very hard for the evaluator to be candid, yet case studies must be candid if they are to be much good. This can be a dilemma for anyone considering this kind of evaluation. One answer, of course, is to keep the report secret, but this prevents any circulation in the field, which limits the report's value. There must be some creative solutions to this problem. Although something might be lost in the process, maybe evaluation reports that are to be publicly released should routinely lift case studies out of their communities into Everytown, U.S.A.

5

Evaluation as a Creative Key
to Institutional Change:
The Winthrop Rockefeller Foundation's
At-Risk Youth Grant Program for Schools

Site:	Ten communities in Arkansas.
Date:	1988–.
Underlying program:	An RFP program of the Winthrop Rockefeller Foundation, Little Rock, Arkansas, to encourage innovations among local school personnel that will help students who show signs of impending failure, and to stimulate similar innovations throughout the state.
Evaluation purpose:	To get teachers, principals, and others to become evaluators, identifying indicators of success with which to measure the effects of their work.
Evaluation initiator:	The foundation.
Stakeholders:	Teachers, principals, and others at grantee schools, and the foundation.

Evaluators:	Grantee personnel, assisted by outside evaluator William Wayson, professor of education, Ohio State University, and foundation senior program officer Jacqueline Cox-New.
Information sources:	Mostly classroom activity of teachers.
Evaluation methods:	Observation, record keeping and self-reporting, and discussion. (Exemplifies formative evaluation.)
Evaluation cost:	Difficult to separate out, since evaluation is an integral part of the program. Estimate of $14,000 includes part of William Wayson's time and expenses and part of conference costs.
Paid by:	The foundation.
Program cost:	$750,000 among ten grantees over three years.
Source of program funds:	The foundation.
Reports:	"Report cards" from school personnel and oral presentations to professional groups and state education authorities by foundation staff. Written reports to follow.

The Program to Be Evaluated

The Winthrop Rockefeller Foundation's At-Risk Youth Grant Program was initiated in early 1988 for Arkansas public schools. The foundation's RFP stated its belief that the "state's future social and economic well-being hinges upon our ability to address the problems of at-risk youth and to help them move into productive lives." Foundation Senior Program Officer Jacqueline Cox-New had led a considerable review of the field and determined that there were "characteristics common to all successful at-risk programs" around the country. In the RFP, the foundation asked that such characteristics be reflected in the proposals. For instance, applications needed to show schoolwide involvement in planning, with an expanded role for teachers and participation from parents and community resources. Projects were to be "mainstream," rather than separate "pull-out" activities, and "student-centered" in addressing those bureaucratic tendencies of schools that in themselves inhibit children from realizing their potential. There was to be promise of leverage to win local and state support for the continuation and expansion of successful projects. Grants were to be a maximum of $30,000 a year for three years.

Thirty-six applications came in during the first cycle, and with the help of a reading panel, eleven finalists were chosen. Each finalist was asked to establish a leadership team — consisting of school personnel and at least one school board member and one parent — and to bring that team in for a half-day meeting with William Wayson, a professor of education at Ohio State University and consultant to the foundation. Wayson's role was to help them clarify goals, firm up strategies and plans, and identify the evaluation's indicators of success. The teams went home with suggestions that they involve their school constituencies in revisions and final drafts before returning the proposals. Five of these first eleven proposals were funded. Two grants were for work in individual schools; three were for plans at selected sites throughout small school districts.

Jackie Cox-New worked with the five grantees on refining their plans and indicators and building a broader sense of ownership among the various constituencies of the initial teams. She brought the teams together for a one-day meeting, encouraging conversations among them about their various plans and situations. Six months into the first year, Wayson came back and spent a day on site with each grantee. The second and final cycle of the RFP brought another thirty applications. Five more grantees were chosen, through the same two-stage process. In total, the foundation had heard from 20 percent of the school districts in Arkansas in the two rounds of applications.

The Evaluation

For an institution such as a public school district to change and progress, the teachers, principals, superintendents, and other school personnel need to feel some personal ownership of whatever processes of change they undertake, be clear about what they are trying to accomplish, and have their own dependable measures of success and failure. How do you realize these requirements? You make everyone an evaluator, and give them an evaluation design that is eminently practical, convenient, and stimulating. In this case, that design featured indicators of success.

Indicators of Success

Following his initial meetings with the grantees, Bill Wayson's major opportunity to discuss indicators of success with them was at the 1990 annual June meeting of the winning school teams. The grantees were well into their projects and they were at the conference to report and refocus. He had one-hour meetings with each team, and then talked with them all together.

He kept asking the same question over and over again in different ways: If you know what you want to do, how will you know if it does any good? What are you looking for that will show you're making progress? What are your three or four best indicators of success for convincing a group of parents that the program works? When school-board members ask hard-nosed, traditional questions about this program of yours, how are you going to tell them it's successful?

He took every opportunity, sometimes with individual teachers and their classroom experience, sometimes with approaches that concerned the whole school. When a principal happened to say, "We're doing some things we're happy with," Wayson's immediate rejoinder was, "What is it you're happiest with, and what are the signs that make you feel that way?" When a team said its school's retention rate (students being held back a year) was too high, Wayson insisted the team members dig around right then for causes ("What's your best guess as to why?"), and told them their planning was blind unless they could figure out some possible causes to investigate. Once they proposed some probable causes, he pursued the indicators of success model, asking them, "What's going to happen in the classroom that will let you feel you are beginning to get on top of some of those things?"

Wayson didn't tolerate jargon or rhetoric in the replies to his questions. Indicators of success had to be observable — not necessarily measurable in numbers but something that could be sensed tangibly. Misty expressions such as "increased self-esteem" were out. Specifics such as "more children raising their hands to respond in class" and "more ways to see that twice as many students get recognition" were in.

Report Cards

For the conference, the teams were asked to bring "report cards" with them, on which they had graded themselves (A, B, C, D, or F) on one or two dozen indicators they had selected as appropriate to their project objectives. They were asked to support these grades with numbers and narratives about specific cases. Exhibit 5.1 is a sample of the grades a school district had given itself on the indicators it had identified for one part of its program.

In a sense, such a style becomes management by objectives, but it is also self-management — not among managers as usual but among the school staff, with attention to specific opportunities in which teachers, principals, and others can take charge.

Exhibit 5.1. "Report Card" for the Goal of More Parent Involvement.

We will see parents in school more often.	A
Parents will start participating in classrooms.	C
More students will turn in lists for family library reading programs.	A
Parents will come in to read with children.	B
We will initiate a program to involve businesses to allow employees time off to work at school.	F
A few parents will come to eat lunch with students.	A

In another sense, this whole process is hardly evaluation, and indeed, Wayson is a consultant in education, not evaluation. Yet basic to what he is urging in education is the practice of evaluating. Using his concentrated focus on identifying and then looking for indicators of success, Wayson uses evaluation as a discipline that pushes people into turning their generalized hopes and plans into an anticipation of concrete results they will be able to see and feel.

Evaluation Consequences

At the 1990 conference, Jackie Cox-New and Bill Wayson told grantees that too many valuable programs get dropped when special grant money runs out or when someone complains about a program for some unpredictable reason. They said they didn't want that to happen here and stressed that the best way to "implant" the work the teams were doing "so it will last" was to make sure that initiatives for change came from joint efforts of teachers, administrators, parents, and others full of enthusiasm for the favorable results that showed up on the report cards. These constituents had to become the people who could tell the members of the school board and the community, "We will all be making a big mistake if the best parts of these programs aren't picked up as an important integral part of quality in the schools."

More recently, Cox-New reports that school experiences are demonstrating the importance of having active teams that include school board members and parents and have contacts with more of the same. She cites the grantees case by case and concludes: "In about half the cases, when programs are criticized for one reason or another, there are constituencies of school board members and parents as well as teachers and principals who know what's happening and have been part of it. They can defend innovation successfully and help it grow. In other cases, important people haven't been brought close enough to understand what teachers are doing. We have lost some good programs when that happens."

Cox-New also describes a new classroom technique that

is encouraging broader participation in several schools. Instead of teachers having the full responsibility of watching for indicators of success, "parents come in, or students get involved, using a simple checklist. They can count as well as anyone how many kids raise their hands during a certain period, or how many discipline referrals there are."

The Winthrop Rockefeller Foundation is now applying the indicators-of-success model to other programs. In its most recent RFP for education minigrants of $2,000 or less, schools were asked to include "a set of Indicators of Success for each project objective." A page of the RFP was devoted to describing what an indicator is, how it can easily be "monitored and documented," and how this process can be combined with narratives about individual examples. Cox-New reports that some proposals came in with indicators that were "right on the money," others needed a second try, and a few applicants just couldn't grasp the concept. Among the grantees, she says, several have volunteered that the exercise "gave them a better idea of how to evaluate what goes on in their classrooms. Teachers say they can really tell now whether what they are doing is making a difference."

The foundation is planning its next RFP program (in a related field of education), and it is building in an indicators-of-success component.

Evaluation Cost

The ten grants in the At-Risk Youth Grant Program, over the initial three-year period, have totalled $750,000. It is difficult to specify the cost of the evaluation, both because the evaluation process is so built into the entire program and also because crucial components such as Cox-New's time are not charged to evaluation. When asked how much the evaluation is costing the foundation, however, she considers the part of Wayson's time and expenses that is especially related to the indicators of success and the report cards, adds a share of the conference costs, and comes up with an estimate of $14,000 for the three years.

Evaluation Strengths and Weaknesses

The idea of evaluation as a decision-making aid that can help empower local school constituencies is well developed and articulated here. There is no reason the same approach will not work in a variety of other fields as well. The concept of indicators of success is a clear, practical way to encourage realistic efforts toward improvements that are expressed in tangible, measurable terms. Indicators can be intimate to a teacher's own processes at the same time as they create a useful context for joint planning and activity throughout a school. The concept also serves the schools well in helping them meet the key criteria set forth by the foundation announcements of the program. In this RFP, the criteria, implementation style, and evaluation design are all compatible.

Students themselves may not often have been directly involved in the planning of the program's funded projects, but indicators such as "more children will read by choice," "more students making positive statements about learning," and "identification and reduction of the practices that push kids out of school" suggest that this evaluation process gets down to the level of benefits to students, the program's ultimate constituencies. As some students now join in keeping track of the indicators, they will very likely contribute reactions and ideas. This matches the RFP criterion that stressed the need for projects to be "student-centered."

The report cards kept by individual staff members and schools as a whole are appropriate measurement devices for the education field. Bill Wayson mentioned several times at the 1990 conference that "teachers, better than anyone else," can value the grades they give themselves as nothing precise or final but just as convenient records for making practical comparisons about results, both over time and among different program components.

The school grantees trust the foundation to keep an equally realistic perspective about the report cards. Wayson and Jackie Cox-New show they take the grades seriously; when they visit a grantee which has given itself a D or an F, they ask, "What are you going to do differently to change that grade?" The school people know, however, that the foundation's personal contact and familiarity with the programs govern grantmaking decisions, not the report cards. They don't seem to be inhibited about giving themselves D's and F's when they feel those grades are warranted.

The report cards, then, are a successful device for providing what every evaluation needs most: efficient, firsthand, and discussable information, by and for the people who really need it.

Much of the consistency in the program's approach is due to the strong match of interests between the foundation program officer in charge and the outside consultant. Although Cox-New and Wayson come from quite different backgrounds and perspectives, they share convictions about how change will come in schools. Their work shows how a medium-size foundation can intervene in a state schooling system with an ambitious, well-focused program that will help some communities directly and also has the potential to contribute to statewide efforts for school reform.

Cox-New found Wayson through a contact she established when she formed an advisory group to help put this RFP program together for the foundation. She wanted to have an "awareness session" about the program with Arkansas school people, and she asked around for suggestions as to who should conduct it. Joan Furst of the National Coalition of Advocates for Students was a member of the advisory group and mentioned Wayson. On the basis of this experience and several conversations with Wayson, Cox-New saw the potential value of having him involved for the life of the program. From Wayson's point of view, the opportunity was an especially attractive one. He felt his trips to Arkansas schools would give him some "real-life stories over time" which would enhance his university work. The three-year-plus nature of the job was also important, since experience had shown him the limitations of short-term assignments, which offer little chance to see change, consequences, and influences.

"Weakness" seems too harsh a category in the case of a new program that is just coming into its own. Cox-New and Wayson are well aware that the program is still new and that there are things they haven't done yet. For instance, there isn't enough connection between the self-evaluation at the schools and the foundation's own evaluation and dissemination processes. It's true that Cox-New and Wayson are using the indicators and report cards, and the wealth of anecdotal material that backs them up, in a formative sense when talking with grantees about their projects. Cox-New also makes periodic reports to the staff and board of the foundation. But it is clear that there is a great deal of important information and experience flowing from the program and that it deserves being reported to others interested in school reform, in Arkansas and elsewhere.

In particular, the work going on in this program makes a strong case for bringing school staffs, parents, and local school board members in on the ground floor of statewide planning for school reform, in a state noted for its recent determination to "restructure" its school systems. That testimony is not being presented yet, which is unfortunate. State legislators and state education leaders can learn a great deal from this program for at-risk youth. The fact that the foundation was aware in the beginning that responses to the RFP were coming in from 20 percent of the school districts in the state shows that the staff and board knew the program could be conspicuous in the real world of Arkansas education. That potential needs to be pursued.

Cox-New is beginning to make presentations about the program to professional groups and education authorities. She and Wayson are keeping memos on all site visits and lessons learned in the program, and they are planning to begin writing a final report shortly. Cox-New adds that the foundation will soon be stepping up its efforts to impact state programs with the indicators-of-success model, especially in instances where the foundation is being asked to contribute funds to match other public and private grants.

There is more turnover in the school teams coming to the conferences than anticipated. In a way, this is fine since it broadens the involvement, but it does jeopardize the model when people do not go home from one meeting full of clear resolve and then come back and report to the next meeting.

Turnover is an inevitable complication, but ways should be found to realize the value of continuity as much as possible.

The ranks of school board members and parents on the teams that meet in local school districts have also suffered attrition. With so much emphasis on seeing that the best new activities stimulated by this program live on and build a creative mood in the schools, board members and parents are important and need to be kept involved.

For a program trying to impose new styles and disciplines in planning, implementing, and evaluating, this one is minimally staffed. Cox-New has given a great deal of time to it, but she has other responsibilities as well. Wayson sees each grantee at brief conferences and one-day site visits just twice a year. In Arkansas, as everywhere, there is intense competition for the time and attention of school personnel. In this particular program, some supplementary assistance from, perhaps, local university faculty and graduate students would help keep attention on the program and begin building a support group for this type of school reform activity throughout the state.

The grants are small in relation to school budgets. They pay only for a little staff time or extra materials or expenses for a special project. Payoff has to come from an impact that starts small and then grows, as the encouragement of invention and the habit of evaluation become more ingrained in school life. Roger Massey, principal of a Dardanelle, Arkansas, elementary school that participates in the program, sums up the value of the RFP this way: "Let's face it. The trouble with most good ideas in education is that we know the only way they are going to get done is if we work harder, and that often isn't very attractive. The way you overcome that problem is to provoke us into taking more of the responsibility for creating or at least accepting the good ideas, so we can set our sights on something we choose, where we can enjoy seeing some tangible results. That's what this business with the indicators of success does for us."

6

Evaluation and School Reform:
Measuring the Impact of the
New York Cities in Schools Program

Site:	New York City.
Date:	1987–.
Underlying program:	Demonstration and advocacy program to develop a model support system for inner-city children who show signs of being potential dropouts, conducted by the New York City unit of the private-sector agency Cities in Schools (CIS).
Evaluation purpose:	To determine the consequences of the program and get information that will help the agency improve and expand it. A secondary purpose was to implement an innovative methodology to be used by the Bruner Foundation in future evaluation grants.
Evaluation initiators:	The agency and two foundations: Bruner Foundation and Primerica

Evaluation initiators, Cont'd.:	(Inc.) Foundation, both in New York.
Stakeholders:	The agency and the two foundations initiating and funding the evaluation.
Evaluators:	Outside consultant Patricia Campbell, Campbell-Kibler Associates, with help from Alyce Hill, former executive director of CIS in New York, and from student interviewers, for one aspect of the evaluation. Outside consultants Bertha Campbell and Kathe Jervis for a second aspect.
Information sources:	Students (directly and through school records), parents, principals, teachers, staff of CIS in New York and city agency staff.
Evaluation methods:	Analysis of participating students' records versus comparison groups, interviews, questionnaires, extensive observations yielding documentary essays. (Exemplifies formative and impact or outcome evaluation.)
Evaluation cost:	$45,000.
Paid by:	Bruner and Primerica (Inc.) foundations.
Program cost:	In the original evaluation year, $1,700,000, of which 86 percent was in-kind contributions from city agencies and the board of education.
Sources of program funds:	New York Human Resources Administration,

Sources of program funds, Cont'd.:   Department of Parks
                                          and Recreation, and
                                          Board of Education, plus
                                          foundations, corporations,
                                          and individual donors.

Reports: Evaluators' reports and
                                          the agency's written and
                                          oral presentations to
                                          funders, cooperating
                                          agencies, the Board of
                                          Education, and other
                                          public policy makers.

The Program to Be Evaluated

"I believe in interagency collaboration. Eventually it's the only way, and there is every chance that Cities in Schools could be the model initiative for making it happen." That's Jill Blair speaking; she is a special assistant in the administration of Joseph Fernandez, the new chancellor of the Board of Education in New York City. She has known the Cities in Schools (CIS) program in New York from previous jobs in which she worked for the city and then as a program officer at the New York Foundation. She is close to at least two active CIS board members. She knows how private sector programs such as this, which depend on cooperation from government agencies, have to get political to survive and make their mark. Fernandez himself came to New York from Miami, where he knew and liked the CIS program in place there. The two are determined to get some things done and maybe—just maybe—they can help this twelve-year-old nationwide agency make its model work for a truly significant number of children in New York City. If they do, evaluation activity will have played an important part. Politics among New York government agencies is like the last minute under the basket in a tight game at Madison Square Garden. It's push and shove up close, elbows and knees in your face, nothing's perfect, but you've got a shot if you have solid information that commands respect for what you are trying to do—the information an evaluation can provide.

Cities in Schools came out of the New York street academies of the 1970s. William Milliken was and still is the leader; he takes it as his personal mission to move the program into as many public school systems across the country as is humanly possible. The program works on three principles: schools are the place to help poor children at risk cope and begin to succeed, the most practical way to provide that help is to get the relevant city agencies to coordinate their support services at the schools, and those services have to be built on personalized, small-scale trusting relationships with students.

Cities in Schools in New York began in 1982. The basic unit of the New York model is a "family" of forty students, two full-time staff members, and part-time tutors and other supplementary aides and volunteers as they are needed and can be recruited. The full-time staff are on loan to CIS from social service agencies, which in New York has meant largely the city's Human Resources Administration (HRA) and Department of Parks and Recreation (DPR). Students are selected for the program because they show the warning signals of potential dropouts: erratic attendance, poor grades and test scores, and evidence of trouble at home. During the 1990 to 1991 period, there were CIS families in seventeen elementary and junior high schools in four of the city's most troubled school districts — East Harlem, the Bronx, and Brooklyn's Bedford-Stuyvesant and Sunset Park/Red Hook.

As of January 1991, there were 1,127 students involved as full-fledged CIS participants in these schools. Program components included counseling, recreation, special events and trips, tutoring, a CIS room for unstructured activity and conversation, and home visits. Each of the two staff members in a family fills a specialist role and also takes a personal caseload of 20 students. Agency cutbacks have sometimes reduced the staffing, but the commitment is that, one way or another, there will always be a caring adult available to spend time with a child.

For every student on the official CIS rolls, there are at least two or three others who get to join in when they ask or when their participation is suggested by teachers, staff, or other students. When a CIS trip relates to the current work of a whole classroom, the whole class is invited.

There is a CIS project director for each of the four districts. Unlike the project staff at the schools, loaned by HRA and DPR, these project directors report directly to a lean CIS headquarters staff headed by Deidre C. Meyerson, who came to the agency after positions as director of a teacher-networking program at the New York City Board of Education and as an NAACP educational consultant.

The 1990–91 budget for CIS in New York is $2,753,218. Eighty-three percent comes from in-kind contributions of personnel and space from HRA, DPR, and the Board of Education, and another 3 percent is in government contracts. That leaves a core operating budget of $434,000 to be raised from corporations, foundations, and individuals. Fourteen percent private-sector money leverages 86 percent in government funds. Donors number more than thirty, the largest grants coming from American Express Company Foundation, Bristol-Myers Fund, Citicorp Foundation, Aaron Diamond Foundation, Exxon Education Foundation, Charles Hayden Foundation, Richard Loundsbery Foundation, Henry Luce Foundation, Manufacturers Hanover Trust Co., Metropolitan Life Foundation, J. P. Morgan & Co., New York Life Foundation, Pfizer Foundation, Time-Warner Inc. Foundation, and two individuals.

The Evaluation

The evaluation was conducted in 1987. Cities in Schools nationally has a tradition of evaluation, and it seemed time to begin the process in New York City. The budget for the evaluation was $45,000, paid for by the Bruner Foundation and the Primerica (Inc.) Foundation. Bruner specializes in funding evaluations, and Primerica is interested in situations where their grants can help good ideas to be picked up and applied in other settings. Both Janet Carter and Miguel Garcia, the respective executive directors of the two foundations, saw CIS as an important, innovative approach to New York school problems that deserved careful evaluation, and Carter was instrumental in initiating the evaluation and selecting the evaluators. The multifaceted evaluation included analysis of student records and test scores in order to compare CIS participants with other students; interviews with students, former students, and school personnel; written responses to questionnaires from teachers and program staff; and an intense observation, interview, and discussion process culminating in three "documentary essays" about three children in the program.

Patricia Campbell, of Campbell-Kibler Associates, was the evaluator in charge of the first three procedures: the analysis, interviews, and questionnaires.

Records Analysis

With considerable difficulty, because of missing school data, Campbell assembled records for 806 students who had been in the CIS program. With the help of the Board of Education's Office of Educational Assessment, she also developed a comparison group of 1,013 other students, randomly selected from among those who had attended the same grades at the same schools as the CIS students. (Records were incomplete for this group also.) Data were obtained in such a way that individual students' identities were not revealed. The two major types of information gathered were attendance records and achievement test scores, which had been chosen as the two most important—but also very different—potential indicators of success for the CIS program. Information was also collected on whether students were still in the school system or had been discharged and on students' "ages in grade," by which the evaluation could determine whether they had been held back a grade or more.

Interviews

For the interviews with students and teachers, Campbell recruited and trained a team of twenty-six fourth to eighth graders, who were CIS participants, to be student evaluators. In the training, the team learned the essentials of the evaluation process, worked with Campbell in designing the interview schedules, and rehearsed through role-playing. These student evaluators asked other students what CIS activities they were involved in, what they liked and didn't like in the program, whether CIS had helped them or "caused them to change," how they got along with CIS staff, and what improvements they would make if they were in charge of CIS. Fifty-six students were interviewed.

When the student evaluators interviewed teachers, they asked them how they would describe CIS, what was best and worst about the program, whether and why they liked having their students in the program, whether they would like to be more involved, and whether having CIS students in their classes interfered with their teaching. Forty teachers were interviewed.

Selection of teachers and students to be interviewed was left up to the student evaluators. After the interviews, they gave Campbell completed questionnaires and then met with her to discuss the results and their own conclusions. She then wrote a summary of this discussion, returning it to the student evaluators for reactions and revisions before it became part of the final evaluation report.

Campbell, with the help of Alyce Hill, former executive director of CIS in New York and now the Eastern Regional Director of the national agency, also interviewed the principals at fifteen of the seventeen schools that had CIS programs. The principals were asked how they would describe CIS; why they chose to have it at their schools; how it was affecting students, teachers and parents; what the strengths and weaknesses were; what changes they would suggest; and what their opinions were about the CIS team concept, quality of the staff, and similar issues.

Campbell and Hill also interviewed the three project directors in the three districts that had CIS programs at the time, and they attempted to find former CIS students for interviews. A sample of 120 former CIS students was selected, but CIS back then had few current addresses for former students, and the Board of Education could not release such information. To get over this hurdle, letters to the parents of these 120 were prepared, asking permission to interview the children and offering to pay the children $5 each, and the school board's Office of Educational Assessment mailed the letters. The office's addresses weren't the best, responses were few, telephone numbers given in replies sometimes didn't work, and the evaluators ended up with only 10 former CIS students to interview.

Questionnaires

In addition, CIS staff were asked to complete a questionnaire and mail it to the evaluators in a stamped reply envelope. The questionnaire had been reviewed in draft form by HRA and DPR (the two city agencies employing the staff members) and then revised. It asked staff members what they felt the roles were of the project directors and the site supervisors (from HRA and DPR), what they felt their own roles were, what their opinions were of various parts of the program, what impact these parts of the program were having on students, whom they would seek out to resolve conflicts or get extra help for a student, what suggestions they had about changes, and so forth. The questionnaire indicated that one of the staff members responding would be selected at random to get a $15 check. Of the thirty-four on staff at the time, eighteen replied, and the other sixteen were reached and interviewed by phone.

A questionnaire for teachers was also prepared, which paralleled the student evaluators' interviews with them. Similar questions were asked, but with specific reference to the teachers' professional relationships with CIS. The questionnaires were delivered through the school mail systems to a selected sample of teachers who had CIS participants in their classrooms. Again, a $15 chance reward was announced and a stamped reply envelope was enclosed. Twenty-three teachers responded. A similar questionnaire was distributed to the eight tutors involved in the program at the time, and all responded.

Patricia Campbell, as an independent consultant, assured principals, CIS staff, and teachers that their interview or questionnaire responses would be confidential. Their names would never be connected to their comments when findings were reported and discussed with the CIS management and board. Questionnaires could be returned with or without names, although of course they had to be signed if the respondent wanted to take a chance on getting the $15 check. Teachers' names had not been included on the forms the student interviewers turned in. Campbell feels it is important to assure confidentiality, but she has found generally that, if the interview or questionnaire process exhibits proper care and respect, anonymity is not as much of an issue affecting response rates and candor as is sometimes assumed.

Documentary Essays

The fourth part of the evaluation, built around the documentary essays, was the responsibility of Bertha Campbell (no relation to Patricia Campbell), a former teacher specializing now in the observing of children in school experiences, and Kathe Jervis, an observer trained in this methodology. Their approach is perhaps best described as "particularistic" evaluation, a term adopted by Robert E. Stake, professor of educational psychology and director of the Center for Instructional Research and Curriculum Evaluation at the University of Illinois (Stake, 1986). This approach requires focusing on a particular person and displaying a great many particulars about the life of that person in the setting in question. The evaluation report (Bruner Foundation and Primerica Foundation, 1988) later described the procedure as it was used in the CIS study. CIS staff at each of three sites chose a student who was active in the program, and then the evaluators spent "over 120 hours of observation, 50 hours of interviewing, and almost 300 hours of charting, analyzing and clarifying data with staff and writing the report." *Charting* is a procedure in which everything that has been observed is noted, so that a set of themes, or "emerging headings," can be identified as the work goes on. A total of thirty interviews were held with all levels of school personnel, other students, and parents. Where possible, CIS staff, teachers, and others in contact with the individual student were asked to help observe and were brought together to discuss the student and the observations.

Evaluation Findings from Comparisons, Interviews, and Questionnaires

Patricia Campbell's best set of attendance records was from the 1986–87 school year, in which she found data for 334 CIS

students and for 551 students from the non-CIS sample. These
two groups of students, in grades three to nine, had mean attendance records of 81 percent and 82 percent respectively, not
a significant difference. Partial data from other years yielded
similar results. The fact that students who had been in the program had just as good attendance records as non-CIS students
was considered an indication of substantial success, since one
of the major criteria in selecting children for the program had
been low attendance and other behavior usually anticipating low
attendance. Annual analyses of attendance that CIS began to
carry out promptly after this first evaluation have confirmed this
early interpretation. In the ensuing four years, CIS students
have been not just even with, but consistently ahead of, the
general New York City school population in attendance. In the
1989–90 school year, CIS students were ahead of the attendance
norms for students as a whole at all the schools with CIS programs, with an average difference of 6.4 percentage points—
91 percent versus 84.6 percent.

Although such monitoring gives CIS the data it needs for
keeping track and measuring one school against another, it will
hardly do justice to the impact of CIS until more revealing comparisons can be made. As CIS Executive Director Meyerson
explains, CIS is increasingly effective at bringing into its program the children who have virtually dropped out of school or
show the strongest signs of doing so. "Elementary and junior
high drop outs," she says, "are such a problem today that the
attendance rates for the students in our program would be well
under 50 percent if CIS weren't here. By helping these students
go from potentially the lowest attendance figures to the highest,
CIS is having a considerable impact on the overall attendance
figures that our present figures don't show well enough." Meyerson needs evaluation data to document her claim.

However, findings from the analysis of achievement test
scores told a different story. Again having to rely on incomplete
data, Patricia Campbell was able to compare the 1983 reading
and math test scores of 209 students who were to become CIS
participants with those of 155 who were not to become CIS participants, and then compare these same students again in 1986.

(Year-to-year comparisons for the groups were not possible because of changes in testing.) In 1983, before the CIS program, the students who were to join the program the next year had reading scores significantly lower ($p = > .05$) than the other students. This was to be expected; the profile of children to be invited into the CIS program certainly included indications of academic difficulties. In 1986, these students still tested significantly lower than non-CIS students. They had not made any progress in closing the gap. In math scores as well, non-CIS students were significantly ahead of CIS students in both 1983 and 1986.

The interviews and responses to the questionnaires revealed a good deal of support for the CIS program. Virtually all of the students interviewed reported that CIS had helped them with personal problems and made them more interested in school, closer to others, and less apt to get into trouble. Most teachers said CIS helped students' attitudes, which they felt led to better work in class. Principals saw CIS as an important addition to the resources they had available for students. In their questionnaire responses, CIS staff said that the program's greatest successes were the friendships the participating students built, both with other children and with adults, and the improvements in attendance. They gave these two outcomes significantly higher response scores than outcomes such as improved academic skills or family life, or better future plans.

The interviews and questionnaires, however, also produced impressive documentation of a major weakness in the organizational structure of CIS. Everyone liked the idea of coordinating agency services at the schools to address problems in a different way. But the responses underscored how far CIS was from being able to display a successful model in which personnel from different agencies and disciplines became an integrated program staff under CIS management. When so-called "CIS staff" on loan from HRA and DPR were asked whom they would go to if they had a problem or needed help with a student, only 8 percent said they would go to their CIS project directors. Instead, most chose their supervisors back at HRA or DPR. The school principals saw the problem clearly. For example, one principal said in his interview, "CIS has the most ridiculous organizational structure here; the program director has only advisory power. [And] the project directors have little role."

Just as the evaluation showed difficulties the city agency employees had in becoming members of a team accountable to CIS, the evaluation activities among teachers with CIS students showed that they also had special problems with the program. Reflecting the concern teachers often have about all such ancillary programs, these New York teachers were critical of the class time lost when CIS pulled students out for other activities, or when students cut classes using CIS as an excuse. Only 48 percent of these teachers saw themselves as members of the CIS teams at their schools, although they had been introduced to the program with that role strongly emphasized by CIS. Even this percentage was probably high, because teachers who were more enthusiastic about CIS were probably more likely to answer the questionnaire and agree to the interviews. Most principals confirmed that teachers and others "needed to be on the team but aren't." Teachers put the blame for lack of communication and cooperation on the CIS staff. Teachers quoted in the evaluation report said such things as: "When [CIS] is involved with such a program they should be involved directly with the classroom teachers on a daily basis," and "[CIS staff] don't speak with me enough to know disciplinary problems I'm having in class. They don't include me in any of their activities."

On the other hand, when teachers and CIS staff were asked to rank and to rate the component parts of the CIS program, the rankings were very similar, and the ratings, surprisingly, were more favorable among the teachers than among the staff.

Patricia Campbell's Recommendations

Patricia Campbell's part of the evaluation report concluded with eight recommendations which referred back to the findings. With respect to the structural problem of "confusion and contradictory roles," she urged that the city agencies find a way to release their personnel to the authority of CIS for designated periods. The other seven recommendations suggested attention to other staffing matters, more work with teachers, a resolution of the conflicting demands of the two indicators of attendance and achievement test scores, the creation of a transition program for CIS participants going on to high school, and the development of an ongoing evaluation plan for CIS. Such a plan, she said, should have as its purpose both "continued program improvement" and the long-term assessment of impact on students.

Evaluation Findings from Observation of Three Students

In the other major part of the evaluation, the particularistic studies, Bertha Campbell and Kathe Jervis produced three essays for the evaluation report, prefaced with a description of the methodology and a brief explanation of the CIS program. Campbell and Jervis described the purpose of what they were doing, outlining a process similar to other formative evaluation methods that work hard to involve the people who can both make the evaluation more accurate and use the results to greatest advantage. CIS staff members were to enter actively into the evaluation work, not only in being interviewed but in reacting to the essays about the three students in draft form, thereby becoming part of the observing and documenting process. The report stated, "Intensive observation, when engaged in by staff, should lead to changes in planning, implementation, and assessment, and those, in turn, make possible richer observations. The process, then, holds the promise of becoming cyclical and of being 'owned' by the staff. . . . The validity of this approach lies in collection of data over time by a variety of people, who share the information and check any differences through further observation and interviewing."

Campbell and Jervis's three essays ranged from four thousand to six thousand words each. The three students were described in detail, in terms of their appearance, their actions, their posture and body language, their classroom behavior vis-à-vis their teachers, their relationships with peers, and their academic abilities and failings. There were also comments and sometimes longer narratives concerning over half-a-dozen specific times when the CIS program touched the life of each of the three — going on a field trip, for example, or relaxing in the unstructured CIS room at school; spending time with a supportive caseworker; joining in picnics, sports, a dance class, or a counseling group; using the lunch program; getting a health check; attending the annual awards ceremony; just meeting and laughing with a CIS staff member; or being the subject of CIS staff work, such as an interview with a parent, without the student being present. In each case there were also references, briefer and less numerous, to weaknesses in CIS services, such as times when there was not enough coordination with a teacher, a CIS room did not have a library, there was not enough food, the tutoring program was not good enough, the awards at the awards ceremony went only to adults, or the evaluator felt the staff had not observed the student closely enough. The essays, however, did not intend to be a record of all CIS activity or a compilation of all the plusses and minuses. They were glimpses of specific children, not CIS. The overall impression one gets from the essays is that the children were getting very little out of their school experiences and had many needs, and that the CIS program, though sometimes disorganized and never enough, was one part of their lives that was from time to time positive.

Campbell and Jervis's section of the evaluation report concluded with remarks titled "What Was Gleaned from the Data." In contrast to the style of the essays, which had been descriptive and matter-of-fact and centered on the children, these concluding remarks were highly judgmental about CIS. For example, the evaluators said that although "originally conceived as a personalized program for young people at risk, CIS has become burdened with accountability. Reports, meetings, schedules and agency mandates have taken precedence over children and their needs. All three schools visited had principals extremely supportive of CIS. But the program is not a part of the school. The teaching and CIS staffs are separate and distinct from each other and their attitudes are often competitive and adversarial."

The strongly worded conclusion stated that the program was failing, partly because of the structural problems in its administration. One could also infer from the evaluator's comments that they believed the people involved in the program didn't have the qualities required to overcome these organizational difficulties.

Campbell and Jervis noted in the report that when an early draft of this section was shared with CIS staff, staff members "recognized themselves in the narrative data" and made it clear that "this was threatening" to them. It became difficult to gain staff cooperation in the particularistic process. The evaluators commented: "Such pressures could be minimized through more of the staff review meetings detailed in the [report's] appendix, but more time would be required. It is now judged that three years would be needed. This study was too short to accomplish as much as it set out to do."

Campbell and Jervis's part of the evaluation report ended with twenty-six briefly stated recommendations, ranging broadly across the scope of CIS activity. They said their recommendations were drawn from both interview data and observations, although they gave no references to specific items in their essays. They listed the first three recommendations separately, suggesting that they were the most important: that the CIS collaborative model should be refined to make it workable, that the program should be expanded to serve older students as a dropout prevention measure, and that more emphasis should be placed on work with parents.

Responsiveness to Evaluation
as a Management Tool

Preliminary evaluation reports were shared with CIS staff and the schools and coordinating public agencies in late 1987. *Final Report: Evaluation of New York Cities in Schools* was issued by the Bruner and Primerica foundations in January 1988. It was shared with funders and with other interested parties on request and was cited in an article about urban schools and the evaluation process that appeared in the *Grantmakers for Children and Youth Report* (Council on Foundations, 1988). It was also the principal reference for a subsequent presentation about CIS at a meeting of Council on Foundations members interested in precollegiate education.

CIS itself made the most direct use of the evaluation findings. Deidre Meyerson and her board and staff have used the evaluation results in four ways.

Feedback to Improve Current Programming

CIS has paid good attention to evaluation findings about certain aspects of current operations. Perhaps the best example of this is the way Meyerson and her staff built their response to three findings into a new activity that addresses three needs identified in the evaluation. First, the participation data and interviews pointed out how graduation from junior high was not going to be a happy occasion for many CIS students because they would lose touch with an important support system. Either there might not be anything similar in the high schools they were going to, or even if there were, students for whom CIS had been a key to relative success in school might no longer be eligible. The evaluation report had recommended a transition program.

Second, the evaluation indicated that the program's tutoring activity was no longer effective. The attempt by some to turn it into a crash course to improve test scores had not worked well, and there was little remaining one-on-one tutoring. And third, there obviously had to be new ways to engage more teachers in the program.

Taking these three findings into account, CIS established Teens, Tutors and Teachers. In this new program, successful former CIS students now in high school are recognized with a status position in which they revisit elementary schools and tutor younger children. The former CIS students receive good training and are supervised by selected classroom teachers. The teachers also work with other teachers to identify students most in need of tutoring. The high school student tutors are paid minimum wage, and the teachers earn the New York City hourly rate for such extra activity.

Other efforts have been made to address the complex issues involved in CIS staff relations with teachers. The agency had its four district project directors, armed with the evaluation findings, work out some changes with their principals. "We weren't asking for more money or time," says Meyerson, "but rather for some arrangements that would give us all better communications." Now the project directors attend all faculty meetings, and CIS staff meet formally every other week with all teachers that have CIS students in their classes. Such moves have helped communication generally, and also have given the project directors a chance to show both staff and teachers that they are in charge of the program in their districts and have something to contribute.

Clarifying Goals and Priorities

The evaluation results highlighted two competing objectives for the CIS program: attendance and academic achievement. After the evaluation clarified the contrast in results for these two indicators of the program's impact, the question became: Which should be valued the most? There had been those who felt CIS's role was to keep the students in school regularly. According to this view, that was challenge enough in districts with high absentee and dropout rates and among the very children predicted to be heading in that direction. CIS should keep many of them in school and let the schools themselves be fully responsible for education once the children were there. Others, however, including some of the foundations and corporations supporting the program, had assumed the bottom line for CIS had to be better school results, measured by reading and math scores. Anything less was an inadequate consequence of little value to the students or the community.

The fact that the CIS program was evidently helping attendance and not helping achievement worked in favor of the view that was more realistic, given that the CIS program at the time had only one academic component, the weak tutoring effort. There had really been little reason to predict that CIS students would quickly start closing any academic gaps between them and their classmates. Over the long haul, it was certainly to be hoped that the nonacademic program benefits would lead to accelerated academic achievement, but educators know from these and other experiences that it is a long haul.

There will always be tensions about the rank and order of purposes at an ambitious agency such as CIS. But since the evaluation, Meyerson doesn't hesitate when she is asked what the program's goal is. It is not short-term academic catch-up. It is to help children with a whole mess of problems begin to handle them, and thereby make school a place where good things happen so children want to be there. Attendance is at least one good indicator of student behavior related to that goal, and this evaluation helped focus attention on improved attendance as a worthwhile, attainable objective for the type of program CIS is presently conducting.

Lynne Weikart, assistant commissioner of the New York State Division of Human Rights, is a board member of CIS in New York. She comments that this evaluation, "like most of them, tells you what you already know. But this one said it better than we had before, and documented it." She reports that the board has continued to use the findings, along with the updates that have come along later, as important materials for strategic planning meetings.

Building Relationships with Other Institutions

CIS has found the evaluation data useful in its complex communication tasks with city agencies, schools, and funding sources. It uses the information effectively in presentations and printed materials. Because the Department of Parks and Recreation recently dropped out of the CIS program when reduced appropriations forced it to use all its personnel at its own facilities, CIS has had to accelerate plans to tap other resources for staffing the school teams. Other city agencies, the city's volunteer corps, private school service agencies, volunteers from church groups, and others constitute a broad variety of prospects who have to be informed and impressed quickly. Being able to start off with the pertinent, dependable information from the evaluation helps CIS do that.

The evaluation also showed the Human Resources Administration how the administrative structural problem was constraining not only the CIS program as a whole but also the effectiveness of HRA personnel at CIS sites. CIS and HRA are establishing closer relationships, and recently, HRA has been able to switch the funding for its part of the program into a new category where federal moneys can be sought directly. This move has allowed the agency to increase its staffing at CIS and may also help it to coordinate the management of that staffing more effectively with the CIS administration.

The evaluation's negative findings certainly bothered some funding sources and other outsiders initially, but in the slightly longer run it seems that these findings were put into proper perspective alongside the indications about the program's merits.

For example, Hildy Simmons, head of the Community Relations and Public Affairs Department of J. P. Morgan & Co., one of the program's donors, says she may not put as much faith in evaluation as some others do, but still, "evaluation in a program like CIS strengthens the case substantially. It shows there is a consistent philosophy worth investing in, and that they are trying to make the most of limited resources. It also shows there will of course be troubles, but what they are doing can make a difference."

Norm Fruchter, consultant to the Aaron Diamond Foundation, gives a good deal of importance to evaluation. The foundation has funded, for instance, the student evaluator work at CIS. He says when he read the CIS evaluation he was much concerned about both the lack of academic acceleration evident in the findings and the "bifurcation" among the city agencies. The report came to him just as he and his board were considering refunding CIS. "We hesitated, and looked closely," he says, but then "we accepted the idea that the level of service and overall strategy was still good," and renewed the grant.

Developing an Ongoing Monitoring and Evaluation Ability

When both the potentials and the demands of good evaluation work became clear through this evaluation experience, CIS began investing in its own monitoring and evaluation capacities for the future. Part of this has meant working with Jill Blair and others at the Board of Education to gain access to data.

CIS is now linked by modem to Board of Education computers and can retrieve records identified by students' ID numbers. When students come into the program, parents are asked to agree that CIS may have access to their children's ID numbers, and therefore to their records, not only while they are in their present school but as long as they are attending New York City schools.

To take advantage of such arrangements, there has to be a capability in-house to keep profiles of all CIS students, each student's activities in the program, staff assignments, contacts with parents, and other program information. Then CIS has to be able to correlate and compare this material, over time, in order to produce monthly analyses that can become basic management tools. A grant from the Charles Hayden Foundation is helping CIS upgrade its system.

There is yet more work to be done. Now that students' performance can be followed into high school, a long-discussed longitudinal study needs funding. As another example, a way needs to be found to measure the impact of the program on attendance more realistically and dramatically. CIS's eagerness to serve all children who need its program prevents it from employing a simple comparison of randomly selected treatment and control groups, but there may be other types of comparison groups that would work. Deidre Meyerson is anxious not to take on such questions "piecemeal," but rather to do as the evaluation report suggested and formulate an evaluation plan for CIS's future.

Patricia Campbell continued to work with CIS in directing the student evaluators each year. The experience these students get in helping the staff develop issues and questions, doing the interviews, analyzing the results, and coming to conclusions and recommendations, has become a valuable part of the CIS program itself, as well as a useful ongoing evaluation resource. A 1990 survey by the students concentrated on the perpetual problem of trying to increase parent involvement in the CIS program. Meyerson says the students' interviews with parents, teachers, principals, and other students produced "some great ideas, different for each school." The project led to the hiring of two part-time parent coordinators at one school as a test. The coordinators make home visits, conduct workshops, have breakfast meetings for groups of parents, recruit volunteers, and pursue problems of attendance and tardiness.

Evaluation Strengths and Weaknesses

This evaluation worked hard for $45,000, looking at CIS from several vantage points and yielding insights about important issues that were clearer than those the agency, its funding sources, and collaborating agencies had before. The quantitative data produced convincing findings about the two major, conflicting indicators of success (attendance and achievement scores), despite the difficulties in finding good historical information. Playing catch-up in evaluation work is expensive and always limited in what can be retrieved from past experience, but Patricia Campbell, CIS, and the Board of Education were able to put together enough data to generate useful results.

Attendance "won" as the more realistic indicator, as judged by both the quantitative data and the interview and questionnaire responses. But it is the way the evaluation stimulated a process of reflecting upon and clarifying goals that is significant here. Inconsistency about purposes happens all the time in nonprofit organizations, especially new ones. Even with the best of strategic planning, program purposes change. If a program taps the vitality of its different communities, and CIS certainly does, the mission statement moves around under pressures from many directions. Yet if the program is to mature and gain understanding and respect, it behooves the board and management to try to stabilize its purposes, at least over the short term. As was the case at CIS, an evaluation project can raise issues about purpose to a more visible level. It can give more accurate, more articulate indications of what a program is actually doing for people than an agency has had before. That consequence provokes a clearer resolve about what the agency can do and wants to do.

The other major finding was the structural problem — the lack of accountability to CIS among the personnel loaned

to it from big bureaucratic city agencies. For some, this was a confirmation of troubles already known, but the evaluation made the troubles more explicit. For instance, numerical measurements — such as how few staff would turn to their project directors in time of need — were new. Interview statements were often strong, such as the principal's remark that the organizational structure was "ridiculous." What was unfortunate was that the evaluation expressed the problem well in lump sum terms, but didn't dig any deeper into its nature in order to find clues to solutions.

Getting disparate agencies to work together is a fundamental part of the CIS plan in New York and everywhere. When it isn't happening right, it's not enough for an evaluation just to point at it generally and say that it has to be fixed. Relationships between CIS and HRA, DPR, and the Board of Education needed to be a topic of the evaluation. What specifically are the handicaps under which CIS operates because of its dependencies on these other agencies? Do some project directors, school administrators, or staff members themselves cope better with these handicaps than others, and if so how? There was an interagency coordinating committee at the program's beginning; what happened to it? Considering the bureaucratic and political factors involved, what alternatives to the present arrangement are suggested? What are the chances that any of these arrangements will help the CIS program grow to where it serves a lot more children?

These and other questions may have seemed beyond the evaluation's scope initially, but when the structural problem appeared so clearly in the early returns, there should have been enough flexibility to give these questions attention. It is important to build flexibility into evaluation plans so that key issues that come along can be addressed. That flexibility comes from clear agreements at the planning stage among the organizations running the program, the evaluators, and the evaluation funding sources, spelling out how such events are to be handled. When the unexpected happens in midprocess, it also takes initiatives by one or more of those involved to identify the new directions needed and how to get there. Janet Carter of the Bruner Foundation believes it is often likely that a funding source can effectively take that initiative, because it is at arm's length from the inhibitions that perhaps have kept the issue in question out of the evaluation in the first place. This distance can allow the foundation to encourage an evaluation that goes "to the heart of what's been discovered, no matter where that leads."

Evaluation inhibitions may come from controversy and factiousness, as Carter's point suggests, but not always. In the case of CIS's evaluation, it was more likely a matter of scope. What may have inhibited this evaluation from coping with the structural issues was that *political* questions were surfacing, whereas those involved thought the evaluation should focus on *professional* questions that reflected educational and social work points of view. If so, that was unfortunate, because CIS has to be a politically sophisticated organization, in tune with the chaotic community context in which it chooses to work. For such agencies, apolitical evaluations have limited usefulness.

Yet apolitical evaluations are the norm. Professionals in the social sciences and social services often seem to regard professional and technical issues and problems — the ones relevant to their own discrete bodies of knowledge — as the most important concerns to address in evaluations. Political issues are seen as messy unprofessional problems that an evaluation perhaps needs to point out and generally complain about, but as far as systematic analysis is concerned, these issues are considered out of scope.

Such a point of view is especially understandable among professional evaluators, who have developed most of their disciplines by evaluating government programs in which the evaluators' assignments do not normally include investigating the programs' political ramifications. In the private sector, on the other hand, there are more organizations like CIS than there used to be, organizations that combine direct service with a determined thrust to change the behavior of public institutions crucial to the lives of the people the organization cares about. Nonpartisan political strategies and issues become central in their work.

The interorganizational problems from which CIS suffers happen all the time in coalitions and projects calling for coordinated efforts. Just as common is the lack of analytical attention to such problems when the projects are evaluated. In illustrating that conventional evaluation practice doesn't offer much help in resolving interagency troubles, the CIS example also illustrates the need for some new unconventional approaches to evaluating the political side of agencies' activities. This task must not be considered irrelevant to scholarly needs or talents; it is just as technically demanding as evaluating service delivery, perhaps considerably more so. It deserves all the academic and professional strengths in psychology, sociology, political science, economics, and anthropology that both professional and academic evaluators can muster.

The CIS study supplies the clearest example of the potential of particularistic evaluation that is to be found among the case studies in this book. The documentary essays on the three students were more ambitious and revealing than the more modest narratives included in several other cases, and the idea of engaging CIS staff in the process of observing and reacting and observing again suggests the strength this method can bring to evaluation work.

But the experience also suggests how much skill, sensitivity, and diplomacy have to be brought to the task. The observing procedure for this evaluation was to focus on the children, not the program. That is the viewpoint called for in the particularistic evaluation discipline. Yet it is the program that is being evaluated, not the children, and somehow the process has to end up with the right ingredients for a bona fide evaluation: sufficient information about what's happening in the program to constitute the raw data of the study and findings based on those data. In the CIS instance, the observers' essays described many contacts between the students and CIS. This was a form of basic information. But it was difficult to see the connections between this information and the observers' conclusions about the CIS program. The conclusions were evidently based more on other interviews and personal reactions than on the observations documented in the essays. The harsh tone of the conclusions led to such feelings of being "threatened" among the CIS staff that the cooperative design of the evaluation process couldn't be achieved. Even if there had been staff willingness to continue cooperating, discussions would have been difficult when the evaluators' findings had so few references back to students' and staff's actual experiences.

But these are not insurmountable problems, and Bertha Campbell and Kathe Jervis supplied enough substance to suggest the clear potential of the particularistic approach. The essays have a vigor never found in a set of attendance percentages. The lively description of a simple, friendly encounter in a school hallway between a young student and a CIS worker shows the warmth of their relationship and underscores how precious it is in a child's life that otherwise has so few respectable satisfactions. At such points, these essays are telling and memorable. One sympathizes with the evaluators' discouragement when they say such projects need three years to do properly. In the interests of having results from this type of evaluation more readily available, one hopes that need not always be the case.

The results of the evaluation displayed the program's major assets and liabilities and encouraged a believable, summative impression that CIS's net worth was valuable to the city. The evaluation compares favorably with evaluations that just report the good news and tone down the bad news with euphemisms and excuses, or just leave it out. Especially among experienced, and hence skeptical, grantmakers, "good-news" evaluations are held suspect and seriously jeopardize the credibility of the organizations that release them.

It is also impressive that the evaluation has led CIS to develop an increasingly capable ongoing evaluation component for itself. There can be hope that CIS will be one of those few agencies that have current, orderly information they can use to tell themselves and others what they are doing. Such intelligence cannot only be used to keep improving a program but also helps an organization deal with the surprises of nonprofit life—a life in which many get disillusioned and reconciled to impassable roadblocks and then, presto, there's a new mayor, a new chancellor, or some other unexpected window of opportunity. The window won't be open long, and there is all kinds of competition. Organizations had better be ready to give it their best effort whenever it happens. There can also be negative surprises, such as the one CIS faced when the Department of Parks and Recreation dropped out of its arrangement with CIS, forcing CIS to introduce itself quickly to other major potential resources of personnel. It is impossible to know everything that might be needed in such circumstances, but one asset that will always be useful is a clear picture of what an organization is doing right now for and to its constituencies. The capacity to present that picture comes from an ongoing evaluation program that grows more able and useful with each working experience. That kind of program is happening at CIS.

The involvement of CIS students themselves in evaluation work has been a contribution to evaluation research methods generally. Patricia Campbell has written professional papers on the experience and spoken about it, assisted by members of her student teams, at social science meetings. CIS is convinced that the students have helped frame better questions, have been good interviewers, and have kept the evaluation process closer to real everyday life in the schools and communities than it would otherwise have been.

There is no reference in the evaluation report to previous evaluations of the Cities in Schools model. Most notably, Charles Murray of the American Institutes for Research conducted an evaluation of CIS in three cities in the late 1970s, and Robert E. Stake (1986) wrote a provocative book about that evaluation. Other CIS projects, notably in Texas, have also been evaluated. The evaluators in New York City were familiar with this material, but there are no signs that it contributed to the CIS evaluation in New York. It is a rare evaluation that has no precedents, and these precedents should be actively sought. They can prevent the time consuming reinvention of various wheels and help predict problems and opportunities.

7

Evaluating a Demonstration Program:
The Technology for Literacy Project

Site:	St. Paul, Minnesota.
Date:	1985–1986.
Underlying program:	A demonstration project in the adult literacy field to develop a new service agency that will show the effectiveness of computer-assisted learning and other innovations, and to encourage and train others to follow.
Evaluation purpose:	To improve the program's operations, to determine their effectiveness, and to be a model for better evaluation practices.
Evaluation initiators:	The organizers of the project, particularly the lead foundations: the F. R. Bigelow Foundation and The Saint Paul Foundation.
Stakeholders:	The lead foundations and other participating foundations, the public school system, and the service

Stakeholders, Cont'd.:	agency established as the center for the project.
Evaluators:	Outside evaluators Michael Quinn Patton, Stacey Stockdill, and Darrell R. Lewis, of the University of Minnesota.
Information sources:	Learners (directly and through program data and tests), tutors, agency staff, grantees of small-grants program, and data from selected other agencies.
Evaluation methods:	Collection and analysis of data on learners and their attendance and performance, pre- and post-testing of a sample of learners, comparisons with a control group and other agencies, focus group interviews, mail question-naires, case studies, and a cost analysis. (Exemplifies formative, process, impact or outcome, and summative evaluation.)
Evaluation cost:	$70,300.
Paid by:	Participating foundations.
Program cost:	$1,300,000 over three years.
Sources of program funds:	Six area foundations and the St. Paul Public Schools.
Reports:	A published report and a follow-up report, distributed to stake-holders and others in the com-munity and nationally who were interested in the field. Also reported orally in conferences and training programs.

The Program to Be Evaluated

There are those who feel adult literacy programs are a poor in-vestment for a foundation searching for the best opportunities for effective grantmaking in education. It is more popular to focus attention on improving school and preschool experiences for children.

There is another point of view, however, that says there is a certain undeniable efficiency in providing the necessary resources for adults who have reached the moment in their lives when they are motivated to learn to read—when a job opportunity requires that they be functionally literate; when they want to read to their children; when they are tired of faking it when confronted with signs, newspapers, and mail; or when they want to join the mainstream of U.S. society. Lou Walker, lead instructor at the Technology for Literacy Center in St. Paul, Minnesota, finds it an especially satisfying field to be in. "You are working," she says, "with people who have just made the decision to get something tremendously important that has been missing in their lives."

The Minnesota State Department of Education estimates that 91 percent of the four hundred thousand functionally illiterate adults in the state have no place to go when they are ready to learn to read. Present literacy programs can handle only 9 percent. In St. Paul itself, available programs can serve only an estimated 6 percent of those in need. How to move that percentage up significantly, how to improve and expand programs already in place and add more, how to make sure these programs attract people and help them build on the enthusiasm of their own first steps—these are the challenges that have been facing a hard core of adult literacy champions in the city and the state for many years.

One of the champions has been Ronald M. Hubbs, retired chairman of the St. Paul Companies, Inc., and former chairman of the F. R. Bigelow Foundation, a private organization that is a client foundation of The Saint Paul Foundation. Hubbs is a Renaissance man who has been involved in a broad range of civic activities. He himself has a library of four thousand books, loves to read, and says he wants to live in "a nation that aspires to maintain a democracy and enjoy the rewards that come to a truly literate society." When he was given the 1988 A. A. Heckman community service award by the Minnesota Council on Foundations, his acceptance speech focused on adult literacy. Ordinarily a calm, conservative gentleman, he talks like a radical on this issue and likes to quote Jonathan Kozol: "We are not one nation indivisible. We are two nations bitterly divided, with liberty for some, illiteracy for others."

In 1983, Hubbs proposed that a key to developing the services necessary to combat illiteracy might be computers. Although software for adult learners was not generally being designed and marketed, Hubbs believed computers would enhance the quality and the appeal of literacy programs and that successes would bring more resources to the field, resulting in a great leap forward in meeting the need. He talked first with Jean Hart, now senior vice president, then educational program officer of The Saint Paul Foundation. Then, with the consulting help of Terilyn C. Turner, director of the ABLE Center in Charlotte, North Carolina — one of the few literacy programs using computers at all — Hart and Hubbs surveyed connections between computers and literacy learning nationally and studied needs and services in the field locally. The results of their exploration led them to establish the Technology for Literacy Project, funded jointly by the F. R. Bigelow Foundation, Cowles Media Foundation, Mardag Foundation, Northwest Area Foundation, The St. Paul Companies, The Saint Paul Foundation, and the St. Paul Public Schools.

Plans for the project called for four components, as cited in the evaluation report (Turner and Stockdill, 1987):

- Direct Service through "establishing a demonstration model that incorporates an educational system using technology."
- Training for "teachers, administrators, graduate students and volunteers to incorporate technology in their programs."
- Research into the "value and applicability of technology in basic literacy instruction."
- Incentive Grants to stimulate "the use of technology by providing incentive grants to existing literacy programs."

A Donor Review Board was established, with representatives from all the contributors. According to the terms of agreement between the F. R. Bigelow Foundation and the public schools, the board's purposes were "to exercise final approval of project policies . . . , resolve any disputes . . . , approve annual budgets . . . , provide a link to various political, business, cultural and religious leaders, [and] make reports from time to time to the . . . funders of the project."

The St. Paul Public Schools were to run the Technology for Literacy Center (TLC) where the direct services, training, research, and technical assistance were to be headquartered. The board of education in St. Paul has several adult literacy instruction sites at public schools and general oversight responsibilities for other community literacy programs that receive state funds through the school system. Incentive grants to other organizations — for hardware, software, and training — were to be made directly by the foundations. Most of the grants turned out to be in the $2,500 to $5,000 range. Funding for the whole project was to be $1,300,000 over three years, three-quarters of it coming from the foundations, one-quarter from the school system.

The TLC opened in May 1985, with Terilyn Turner as its director and a staff of nineteen, plus fifty volunteers. The center displayed several unique characteristics: the extensive use of computers for instruction in both reading and math, a style strongly emphasizing individualized plans for every learner, an attractive storefront location in a shopping mall in a low-income section of St. Paul, a pursuit of outreach and leadership in the field, and a multifaceted evaluation design considerably ahead of anything that had been done before in the field of adult literacy.

It was a busy first year for the center. The goal for the first year was 300 students: actual enrollment was 798.

The Evaluation

The evaluation as a whole was divided into two principal parts. The formative evaluation, starting at the beginning of the program, was to collect data, provide feedback to the project, and keep a "document trail" for all activities. The summative evaluation was to come in later. Using both the formative evaluation's information and the results of its own investigations, the summative evaluation was to assess the merits of the project, largely in terms of whether or not goals had been met. The evaluators had contracts with The Saint Paul Foundation and were paid directly with funds from the supporting foundations.

Formative Evaluation

Stacey Stockdill, then a Ph.D. candidate in educational psychology at the University of Minnesota, was the formative evaluator. She became intimately involved in the development of the center. She attended meetings, she joined in the hard early work, and people were surprised when they heard she wasn't on the staff. In retrospect, she calls herself a participant observer in the evaluation.

The value of Stockdill's work came from the fact that her first priority was always her job of evaluating. Sometimes, however, just the process of meeting an evaluation need directly benefited the program. For instance, the center, like most literacy programs, was using the Test of Adult Basic Education (TABE) to pretest learners and estimate their reading levels. But there were objections to using TABE or any other standardized test to evaluate later student success. The learners— as they are usually called at TLC, instead of students—had different reasons for being at the center, vastly different abilities coming in, and widely diverse ambitions about the skills with which they wanted to leave. Conventional standardized tests couldn't always measure how well these learners were achieving their specific desired skills. To accurately evaluate whether the center was delivering the services the learners wanted, the center needed tests that would show whether or not learners had mastered what they wanted to learn. It was in Stockdill's evaluation interests to see that such mastery testing was realized. Learner success meant center success, and learner-specific mastery tests would be a good quantitative measure of learner success.

Mastery testing was also becoming a program interest of the staff. The task of becoming literate never ends, for any of us. Learners in a literacy program typically never know exactly when they're done; they tend just to drift away when interest wanes. Mastery tests for certain well-defined short-term incremental units of achievement would give them useful indications of completion. With Stockdill's help and encouragement, Claudia Bredemus, the TLC curriculum development director, began to establish blocks of learning, called "modules" and "courses," and tests that would measure completion of these blocks. Through this cooperative endeavor, the project got a useful piece of methodology and Stockdill got the evaluation device she needed.

Formative evaluation is supposed to give an organization new, quick intelligence on how its program is going. Stockdill's activity yields many examples. She was constantly interviewing and surveying learners—when they came in, while they were working, and when they left. Every six months, she gave Director Terilyn Turner a file of verbatim transcripts of these interviews and helped rearrange the information by subject matter. Turner then organized staff meetings around this valuable first-hand material. Stockdill especially credits the way Turner distributed these interview transcripts "in the raw," so that the whole staff could interpret them together, with Stockdill just joining in.

While the staff was busy delivering services, Lead Instructor Walker remembers, Stockdill's focus was where it had to be, "on the impact we were having on the students." Walker says: "It wasn't all rosy. Stacey picked up on student dissatisfaction, things that weren't going right." An example that led to significant program change concerned the system for assigning volunteers to learners. (Volunteer tutors were used particularly with students coming in at the most elementary level—a fourth-grade reading ability or less—where the available computer programs were least effective.) In the spirit of offering flexibility to learners, the original TLC procedure had been to pair up whatever students and volunteers happened to be at the center at the same time, on what Walker now calls "a hit or miss basis." Intake and attendance records showed this procedure wasn't working well. Too many people were coming once and never returning. Stockdill suggested a two-week study of what was happening. The results showed that volunteers were frustrated because they would start with someone and then never see that student again, while students received no promise of continuity and did not connect with a specific volunteer in a way that encouraged a commitment to return. Promptly, Turner and the staff made a radical change, matching volunteers to specific learners and insisting that the pairs work out arrangements for appointments during their first session. Return attendance improved considerably.

Stockdill's formative evaluation work can be broken down into three categories, which are really three levels of formality. One category of the work was the collection of a set of data about learner characteristics, attendance, program activity, and achievement. This was both quantitative — a host of numbers about learners and what they were doing — and qualitative — material from Stockdill's interviews; her questionnaires among students, staff and volunteers; telephone and mail follow-up to students who dropped out; learner activity logs; and case studies. Some qualitative data became quantitative, such as an especially useful chart quantifying the reasons people gave for leaving TLC, assembled after clerical staff searched out former students by telephone. These were all basic data for both formative and summative evaluations. As the formative evaluator, Stockdill reported findings to the staff and to the Donor Review Board. As an "agent" of the summative evaluator, she gathered information, verified it where possible, and kept it for later.

A second category of Stockdill's evaluation work was the pursuit of special investigations on the spur of the moment, ranging from the intervention in volunteer tutor procedures just described to a quick survey among learners about which of three computer station chairs was the best for the center to buy.

The third category comprised Stockdill's unpredictable contributions as a participant observer. For instance, her suggestion at a staff meeting about the center's need for an informal reading space for learners was grounded in both what she was observing and what she was participating in.

Such is the usefulness of formative evaluation done well. The situation was sometimes uncomfortable. Stockdill was not working for TLC. "We knew that whatever we said at meetings went straight to the foundations," says Turner. Walker adds:

"Sometimes we worried about that, but she was still accepted as a member of a trusting staff. She kept in touch, she didn't just sit off in a corner. There was always good communication back and forth about her work and ours."

Of the four components of the overall project, direct services was the focus of most of the formative evaluation. But staff were also asked to keep records of training activity, and Stockdill kept track of the center's efforts to develop research projects. When it came to the incentive grants for encouraging other agencies to use computers, she helped each grantee put together its own evaluation plan, helped design evaluation instruments, and conducted focus group interviews with teachers and students.

Summative Evaluation

Michael Quinn Patton, social scientist at the University of Minnesota, prolific author, speaker, and consultant in evaluation, and past president of the American Evaluation Association, was the summative evaluator for the Technology for Literacy Project. He helped plan the evaluation in 1985 and began his summative work in September 1986, when, according to the evaluation report, "the center's Donor Review Board and staff felt confident that the core elements of the project were in place and that the center had achieved sufficient stability and consistency to be subjected to a formal and independent summative evaluation."

Most summative evaluations that are not in the plans at the beginning of a program lose out on much important early information and must go back and try to reconstruct it. In this case, the formative evaluation activity could be counted on to collect essential information from the beginning. Furthermore, Stockdill worked closely with Patton on the summative evaluation.

Patton's first step was to "validate" the implementation of the program's original plan. He cited this exercise as an "important summative function" because programs often don't follow plans, for better or worse, and evaluations need to take into account the changes and their implications. Patton first looked closely at whether or not the program was reaching the people intended, who were adults of diverse ethnic backgrounds, living in the St. Paul tri-county area, with priority given to those who were poor, those who were English-speaking, and those with reading and math skills below the eighth-grade level. There had also been a desire to bring in a mix of learners, both those who had never before had assistance in adult literacy and those who had previously had some help. Patton examined student records, prepared some tables for the evaluation report, and concluded that the center was reaching its target population. Just in terms of numbers, total learners for both the first and second years had been almost double the original goal.

Continuing his validation, Patton briefly described testing and placement, the instruction program, evaluation and monitoring activity, staffing, hours of operation, and the physical plant. He matched this description to the original plan, and concluded that yes, the center was doing what it had said it was going to do.

In order to measure the effectiveness of the center's direct services, Patton established a sample group of learners, consisting of those who had come into the program during a representative three-month period, from September 1, 1986, to November 30, 1986. To authenticate the sample, he compared its characteristics to the center's data base on all participants. Characteristics included age, gender, race, schooling, reading levels, previous literacy training, and whether or not the learners were on public assistance. On most counts, the summative group was reasonably representative of all TLC learners. There were 165 students in this three-month sample, out of a total of 1,424 participants in the program's first two years.

Although recognizing that standardized achievement tests were not entirely appropriate for these learners, Patton felt he had to rely considerably on the Test of Adult Basic Education tests because they were the only way comparisons could be made with similar data available at other literacy programs. Because learners at the center took the TABE when they first came in, pretest records for the summative sample were routinely in hand. For a posttest, Patton had the TLC staff give the TABE again in April 1987. Fifty of the 165 learners in the sample qualified for this posttest, being active students who had experienced at least twelve hours of instruction since becoming part of the sample. These 50 became, to quote the evaluation report, "the primary focus for measuring achievement outcomes."

Patton searched for a suitable control group with which to compare the summative evaluation sample of 50 learners. As is usually the case in social services, TLC's policy was to serve everyone eligible who came in the door. This ruled out the classic research situation in which program applicants are simply divided randomly into treatment and control groups. Instead, Patton and Stockdill found people who could be a close match to the summative sample. They found such people especially among those who had come to the center but had less than twelve hours of instruction. Groups of 20 and 9 were selected for reading and math comparisons respectively. Patton felt that the people they chose were similar enough to the sample to call them control groups.

The two evaluators and TLC staff also searched for data from other programs with which to compare TLC findings. Although recognizing serious differences in testing practices and types of students, they felt that four other programs across the country, plus some national norms from the literature about literacy programs, lent themselves to comparisons that would, as the evaluation report was to say, "provide another piece of the evaluation mosaic."

Lastly in his set of quantitative approaches, Patton analyzed student records in order to examine two major issues in the TLC experience: attrition and retention, and the question of "completions," including TLC's concept of modules and courses.

The rest of the summative evaluation was handled in a qualitative fashion, producing both numerical findings and text that complemented the quantitative data. Patton conducted three focus group interviews with students, asking how they found out about TLC, what they expected, what difference the experience was going to make in their lives, what problems they had, and what they liked and disliked about the program. Questionnaires, largely about likes and dislikes, were mailed to all learners who registered on two different dates that were picked arbitrarily (an easy sampling method). Case studies were written about

two selected learners. There were also interviews and questionnaires among the staff, and a focus group interview with volunteer tutors. And there was the wealth of material Stockdill and
TLC staff had collected in interviews with learners and those
who had dropped out.

Patton also conducted interviews with the project directors of six agencies that had received incentive grants by the
time of the summative evaluation. His assessment of the program's training component was based on the records kept by
Stockdill and TLC staff and on comments about training activities
that came up in his own staff interviews. For the research component, he was able to report briefly that the formative and summative evaluations of the center were impressive evidence in
themselves of the importance placed on research, but that the
original plans for program-related research had so far not been
realized.

Cost Analysis

Yet one more evaluator was to join the team. At The Saint Paul
Foundation, Jean Hart and others became interested in having
a cost analysis conducted of the center's direct services. They
approached Darrell R. Lewis, an economist and professor of
educational policy and administration at the University of Minnesota. Lewis described a number of different levels of complexity and intelligence they could work on, and from these a
fairly elementary course of action was chosen.

Lewis calls his method in this case a "resource components approach." He listed all the functional activities and services of the center's work, identified and quantified the specific
resources employed within each of the functions and services,
and then put a dollar value on each of these resources. This
may sound like little more than a very precise financial statement using functional accounting, and that is true to an extent,
although there are some different rules. Not only were the costs
of hardware, software, and other educational materials and fur-
nishings annualized over five to ten years, various start-up costs
in administration and training were as well. Some external costs

were also included, such as the foundations' costs in making the grants and, especially in the case of The Saint Paul Foundation, the considerable costs of being directly involved in the project and its evaluation. Volunteer tutor time was given a monetary value, as was maintenance work donated by the school system. All these and the direct costs of operations were allocated to the various functions and services of the center.

Finally, using material from the formative evaluation, Lewis linked student participation and achievement data with the cost figures to get estimated input/output ratios and other findings about the accomplishments of the project compared to its costs.

Evaluation Findings

The TABE pre- and posttest results for the 50 learners in the summative sample were analyzed in three groups: the advanced and basic reading students and the math students. For instance, for the 23 who were in the advanced reading group, having begun at the center with fifth-grade reading levels or better, the test results showed that during an average of 44.5 hours at the center they had gained an average of 1.13 grade levels in comprehension and .79 of a grade level in vocabulary, for a composite gain of .85. The evaluators extrapolated these scores to conclude that these learners had taken, on average, 52.5 hours to advance a full grade level in reading.

For the basic reading group, whose initial reading levels were below fifth-grade standards, the composite gain was .75 of a grade level, which meant they would gain a full grade in 63.2 hours of instruction. For the math group, the composite gain — combining scores for "concepts and problems" and computation — was .72 of a grade level, which would enable them to gain a full grade in an average of 45.4 hours of instruction.

Although these results provided what Patton in his report called "a rough indication of average learner progress at TLC," he asked that the figures be used with caution because the samples were so small and because "there is no average student at TLC." In language lay readers could understand, he explained

how the numbers were typical of a group of people who displayed extraordinary variation in behaviors and test scores rather
than patterns in common. There were high standard deviations,
significant differences between means and medians, ranges of
data that included bizarre extremes, and very little correlation
between hours spent and amount of improvement. Patton supplied several illustrations of this variability, and concluded, "Each
case is relatively unique." But that, he felt, was just the point:
"TLC has created a highly individualized program where learners can proceed at their own pace based on specific needs and
interests. The students come in at very different levels and make
very different gains during their TLC work. [Therefore], one
should expect that there will be tremendous variation in progress."

Comparisons with the control groups in reading and math
showed significant gains in reading comprehension and math
for the summative sample versus no significant gain for the control group. In the vocabulary part of the reading test, however,
the control group made as significant a gain as the summative
group. Therefore, the effectiveness of TLC in helping students
improve their reading comprehension and math skills was confirmed, but it also appeared that TLC was not as effective in
improving vocabulary skills.

Is a control group comparison really necessary in an evaluation such as this, where the time beween pre- and posttests is
short and there is no reason to believe members of a control
group would be acquiring the skills to be tested? When one asks
that question at TLC, the answers are interesting. For instance,
one person in the control group was an alcoholic, drinking heavily at the time of the pretest. He dropped out of the center before receiving any literacy training to speak of, but he had
stopped his drinking before the posttest, and his test scores
showed a three-grade-level improvement. External factors will
often prevent an assumption that those who haven't experienced
a program won't show changes. Organizing and testing a control group doesn't necessarily solve the problem of determining
how much change to attribute to a program, but it helps, even
if only to identify some of the uncertainties.

Comparisons with other literacy programs were limited

to what Patton in his report called "ball park" figures because of differences in the agencies involved and the inadequate evaluation methods of agencies other than TLC. However, TLC performance appeared to be "in the ball park" with the other programs as far as reading progress was concerned, while TLC was doing considerably better than national norms developed in military service and job-training programs where "one hundred hours of instruction per grade-level gain in reading is typical."

A single comparison in math scores was less favorable. ABLE, the program in North Carolina that TLC director Terilyn Turner had come from, was evidently accomplishing one grade level gain in math in an average of 13.7 hours, compared to TLC's 45.4 hours. The tests were not the same and they were administered differently, but the wide disparity deserved attention.

Patton pursued several approaches to questions about the retention and attrition of learners at TLC versus other programs. For instance, he used student records to build an analysis of retention on a quarterly, noncumulative basis. On this basis, TLC retention rates ranged from 44 percent in late 1985 to 65 percent for part of 1986. TLC was again "in the ball park" with much the same averages as the other agencies, and TLC's improvement from the first to the second year was considered an indication of progress.

The summative evaluation report listed the many different responses learners had given when, as part of the formative evaluation, they had been asked why they had left the program, and the report gave a useful interpretation of what these answers had shown: "For many, perhaps most, TLC adults, learning to read is not a straight path of regular hours, steady progress, routine patterns and ever forward movement. It is rather an irregular path crossing valleys, climbing mountains, and often cutting back to an earlier place or going in a circle. These learners encounter frequent obstacles — many minor, some major — which hinder or even stop their progress, sometimes for awhile and sometimes permanently. . . . Many will drop out in the face of these obstacles."

The qualitative part of the summative evaluation — particularly the focus group interviews — yielded many impressive testimonials to the value of becoming a proficient reading adult. Everyone was enthusiastic about what it does for one's life, and most credited TLC with doing a good job. They liked the shopping mall setting, they liked the staff, they appreciated the individualized approach. There were few specific references to computers. Only half of those in the focus groups said they had known before coming that TLC used computers for learning. All of those who commented on the computers and were quoted in the report said they liked learning on them.

Patton found that the training component of the overall program had been broadly defined to include "workshops, student internships, professional networking, and a variety of information dissemination efforts." The report commented briefly on the intern program, which had not grown to the proportions planned, and on the forty-seven workshops held so far to help professionals in the field use computers for instruction. It recorded that there had been 773 TLC responses to requests for information in the first two years and 1,027 visitors. It reported on the national Conference on Adult Literacy and Computers, which the Technology for Literacy Project held in November 1985, just six months after opening the center. Patton said that, although the conference did not result in the immediate action plans for growth in the field that had been hoped for, he saw it as an impressive beginning of discussions about opportunities and issues in the field. He also described a Gannett Foundation [now known as The Freedom Forum] contract under which TLC trained ten "technology consultants" who were then assigned by Gannett to promote technology in literacy programs throughout the country. This contract was obviously a recognition of the center's leadership. The report concluded that all these training activities had been a valuable service but one that had been realized at a high price in the time and energies of a staff already working hard to make the services at the center itself successful.

Cost Analysis Results

In his cost analysis, economist Darrell Lewis produced what was probably the single most useful new, surprising fact of the TLC evaluation. TLC is a technology-based learning center, but Lewis found that labor costs at the center outweighed technology costs by nine to one, and he concluded that "the instructional programs at TLC are still heavily labor intensive. The substitution of capital for labor in the instructional process at TLC does not appear to have resulted in major cost efficiencies."

At TLC, user-friendly computers are a highly visible feature of the instruction program. They are given credit for attracting many students and guiding them through sophisticated, individualized learning programs. Yet with a nine-to-one ratio in favor of human costs, there certainly is no way one can say computers are replacing teachers. The staff have worked hard to find an essential balance between themselves and the computers for successful service. And when the costs are toted up, the machinery is cheap—only 10 percent of the total cost for the agency's direct service, according to Lewis's analysis. The major investment is in people to teach and help.

On the whole, Lewis confirmed the labor intensity that still seemed essential to an adult literacy program, while at the same time he raised the question of whether a greater investment in technology might contribute more to efficiency, so that the center and other programs like it could serve more people. The realistic question for the future, he said, was, "What additional technology might the program adopt as a replacement for some existing labor time and costs?"

Lewis reported that the average cost per instructional hour per student at TLC was approximately $20. He compared this figure to those in recent studies of regular daily public school operations, where costs average $5.50 per hour. He explained the higher TLC level by describing the expensive one-on-one instruction of voluntary students at TLC compared to classroom instruction of children. He also calculated the costs per grade level gained; for all programs at the center, the average per student was $1,060. Such data give planners a conceptual range to work in as they look at the costs of adult literacy programs.

Lewis pointed out that his analysis was not a formal study of costs and benefits. Just in terms of cost inputs, his examination of TLC included some costs to organizations outside TLC but did not consider the opportunity costs to the learners compared with the benefits they derive from the program. Nor, then, did it begin to show costs to the public, or to government, versus the public benefits gained when citizens can read and calculate.

Evaluation Dissemination

The findings of the formative evaluation were reported virtually day-to-day at the center. The first published evaluation report came out in December 1987. Edited by Terilyn Turner and Stacey Stockdill and published by The Saint Paul Foundation, this 177-page book consisted of an introduction by Ronald Hubbs, Turner's description of the program, Stockdill's description of the evaluation plan, the summative evaluation report by Patton with Stockdill's help, the cost analysis by Lewis, and the two case studies.

Seven hundred copies of the report were printed. In addition, a summary of the evaluation was published as part of a conference's proceedings; perhaps 1,000 of these were distributed. Many copies of the published report and the proceedings have been passed out at workshops, presentations to education groups across the country, and national literacy conferences. Turner has mailed materials periodically to fellow professionals in the field, and TLC and The Saint Paul Foundation sent the report to foundations known to have an interest in literacy programs. The rest of the copies have been mailed in response to inquiries. The report is now available through the Educational Research Information Center (ERIC).

Stockdill wrote a follow-up evaluation report in August 1988, under contract with The Saint Paul Foundation. This was at the end of the final year of the three-year grant period. The report (Stockdill, 1988) described some aspects of the project and evaluation in greater detail, brought the data up to date, added five additional case studies, and gave an informative report on the incentive grants program including its "strengths and weaknesses." Stockdill also updated the previous report's evaluation of the project's training component with quotations from providers of literacy services across the state who had attended workshops funded with another grant from the Gannett Foundation. She concluded with some brief references to speculation at the time about what was going to happen to TLC. One hundred copies of her report were printed and distributed to funders and other interested people, mostly nearby. This report is also available through ERIC.

Evaluation Consequences

The constructive day-to-day influence of the formative evaluation on the direct service work at TLC has already been described. There is no question that it helped the center on specific issues and also contributed to the staff's habit of being reflective, looking for ways to improve, and remembering that this was a demonstration project for all the world to watch.

As for the summative evaluation, TLC responded with several specific plans to address issues raised. For instance, the finding that vocabulary learning showed less impressive gains than reading comprehension convinced TLC that it should begin developing its own software for vocabulary building. It has been doing so, under a grant from the U.S. Department of Education.

Terilyn Turner objects when she is asked what TLC got out of the evaluation because, she says, "It's still going on." The staff is confident that there will be an ongoing research and evaluation component, and The Saint Paul Foundation continues to fund Stacey Stockdill's follow-up work and reports, which she shares with TLC. Recently, the center applied to the foundation for funds to replace some computers, and Jean Hart arranged for the most recent evaluation update as part of the foundation's consideration of the computer replacement proposal, as well as a contribution to the foundation's general interest in staying in touch with the field of adult literacy.

Use of the Evaluation in Advocacy

The first cause TLC had to advocate was its own survival. To enable the center to continue beyond the three years of Donor

Advisory Board support, the board and the center entered into negotiations with the Saint Paul Public Schools about the board of education taking over full control and funding of the center. The negotiations produced results: after a year and a half of transition grants that eased the process, the project is now integrated into the public school system. The evaluation played an important role in showing the merits of the program the schools were bringing into the system. Superintendent of Schools David Bennett said at the time of the negotiations that the findings of the evaluation and the qualities of the service it had displayed had "irrevocably changed the manner in which adult literacy will be addressed throughout the Saint Paul School District."

TLC director Turner has moved along with the project. She is currently assistant director for adult literacy and special needs in the community education department of the Saint Paul Public Schools. She will soon be released from other duties to concentrate on implementing the board of education's new Comprehensive Five Year Plan for Adult Literacy in St. Paul. The Technology for Literacy Project evaluation provided the basis for much of what is in this plan. The rationale for the extensive use of computers, the recognition that many adult literacy students need supportive services, and the criteria for the location of a principal literacy center for the schools are cited in the plan as examples of how findings from the formative and summative components of TLC's evaluation informed the plan. As for the practice of evaluation itself, the plan asserts that the public schools must mount "a continuing program of the evaluation procedures which have proven so valuable at the Technology for Literacy Center."

The five-year plan was commissioned by the F. R. Bigelow Foundation. Jean Hart says the foundation would not have been able to make such continuing grants in the field if it were not for the "sophistication and enthusiasm" the evaluation has helped generate among the foundation's staff and board of directors.

Benjamin F. Bryant, supervisor of adult basic education for the school system, points out how the TLC evaluation has stimulated other centers in the city. In one case, instructors were motivated to set up their own evaluation component when they questioned some of the TLC findings and decided to examine the same type of data in their own program. At another center, as their first step in evaluation work, staff members of one of the school system's literacy programs used TLC's methodology to conduct a comparative analysis of learner performances in their own program, at TLC and in a program run by an independent agency.

Advocacy for the broader use of technology and for the general promotion of good literacy instruction has always been seen at TLC as a function carried out through training and conference opportunities. Owing in large part to the Technology for Literacy Project's own conference in 1985, a national Adult Literacy and Technology Conference has been held annually since then. Turner and the rest of the TLC staff use the evaluation findings to good advantage at these and other meetings, and also use such occasions to urge people in the field to adopt better evaluation practices.

The evaluation of the incentive grants showed that they were contributing a good deal to advocacy, especially considering their modest size. By the time of her first follow-up report, Stockdill was able to say that most of the agencies receiving grants had brought computer instruction into their literacy services in ways that seemed successful and permanent and that staff from these agencies were now being called on to give presentations about computer learning at adult literacy conferences.

Turner credits the evaluation for much of the impact the project has had on some important new adult literacy efforts in other parts of the U.S. She cites a new statewide program in California and an innovative new program in Houston as examples.

Evaluation Impact on The Saint Paul Foundation

The TLC evaluation was the most intense, long-lasting evaluation experience The Saint Paul Foundation had been involved in. Jean Hart says, "Stacey Stockdill was virtually on our staff when she was doing the formative evaluation, and we began

to see the value of having someone like that around all the time."
As a result, the foundation entered into an agreement with the
Department of Education at the University of Minnesota whereby
the department selects, through a national search when necessary, a Ph.D. candidate to be a fellow at The Saint Paul Foundation. The first such fellow, Eileen McCormick, came to the
foundation in the fall of 1987, working twenty hours per week.
For the next two years and several months, her tasks included
helping program officers work with applicants to develop evaluation plans, interpret evaluations and other reports from grantees, conduct evaluation interviews of grantees and others in
selected cases, assess special programs such as an emergency
fund and a management assistance fund, and help organizations that ask for advice in setting up their own monitoring and
evaluation arrangements. Her work helped define a comprehensive evaluation program for the foundation and its client
foundations.

      In 1988, the foundation commissioned Stockdill to write an
evaluation manual for its grantees. That publication, *Evaluating
Foundation Programs & Projects,* is now used as the principal reference in the three evaluation workshops the foundation conducts
with new grantees every year. Hart says that the foundation's
comprehensive evaluation program, of which the fellowship,
manual, and workshops are important parts, was largely inspired
by the Technology for Literacy Project evaluation experience.

Evaluation Cost

Jean Hart calculates that payments to evaluators totaled $70,300.
This was considerably more than the $39,000 first budgeted,
largely because of additional time involved in the formative evaluation and because the cost analysis had not been anticipated.
Many of the add-ons for the formative work, also, were expenses
incurred in response to new evaluation chores asked for by Hart
and the Donor Review Board. The board formally approved
all the additional expenses as they were proposed. Not included
in this total were the substantial costs to the center for record
keeping. These were paid through the school system as part of
the center's general operating expenses.

Evaluation Strengths and Weaknesses

In a field where there is little experience with evaluation and virtually no standard practices with which to compare performance, this evaluation nevertheless succeeded in examining TLC's work in a credible fashion. The findings were useful to the agency and its funders and, judging by the number of visitors received and reports requested, to others in the adult literacy field as well.

The formative evaluation was especially notable. Credit goes not only to Stacey Stockdill but to Jean Hart and The Saint Paul Foundation, for continuing to provide support when Stockdill and TLC kept coming back saying Stockdill's work wasn't done, and to Terilyn Turner and the TLC staff for accepting Stockdill as a member of their team. The ongoing feedback was valuable, and more than once the initiatives she took to meet the needs of the evaluation ended up stimulating program improvements.

The cost analysis was a unique enrichment for the evaluation. This approach constitutes a constructive challenge to most evaluators, who tend to come from educational or social service backgrounds and to concentrate on what their peer professionals are accomplishing for clients more than on costs and options. In the adult literacy field, where 91 percent of the people in need can't be served by the present capacity, and where there are no high hopes for major new funding, cost analysis is a useful discipline to have at hand when thinking creatively about how best to reach more people. Since adult literacy is not alone in this regard, obviously cost analysis has broad applicability to nonprofit program evaluation.

When asked how a foundation might find academics like himself to take on such assignments, Darrell Lewis says most universities should have faculty that qualify. He stipulates that candidates should be economists interested in cost analysis, to be found either in economics departments or, like him, attached to other schools, particularly education.

Certainly the way Hart and The Saint Paul Foundation put together the evaluation team of Patton, Stockdill, and Lewis was a strength of this evaluation. It is not often that a foundation organizes an academic team, which shows how remote most foundations are from university resources for evaluation, and vice versa.

Hart says it was partly good luck. But you cannot get lucky unless you actively look for people. The Saint Paul Foundation had deliberately sought out relationships at the University of Minnesota that would give it access to the people it needed. Patton was a known quantity because of his extensive experience in evaluation. The key to success with the other two seemed to be the mutual benefits involved at that particular time. Stockdill was just beginning to establish herself as a professional evaluator, and she enjoyed investing time in this opportunity. Her value was not only her knowledge of evaluation but also her interest in communications (her M.A. was in speech communication), and she talks about ways of working with people that she learned at the university. When senior teachers such as Lou Walker credit Stockdill with being a good communicator, it suggests how important that ability is to formative evaluation.

Hart found Darrell Lewis at a time when his interest and skills in studying the relationships between education and technology were growing. He was able to give her options at different levels of sophistication and cost, and agreed to pursue whatever approach she chose. He also stipulated that he had to be able to use whatever he came up with in his own work in any way he saw fit. He says the project helped him sort out in his own mind the different levels of sophistication on which one could approach this kind of analysis. He uses products of the experience in his classes and has written two journal articles on his TLC methods and findings.

Both of these evaluators, then, had something to gain from the enterprise. Yes, the fact that they had pertinent professional self-interests may have led them to peg their fees a little lower than they might have otherwise, but mutual benefits are far from being solely a budget consideration. Many times, the best people just are not available unless they can see something in the experience to benefit their own professional practice. However, when they do join up, their self-interests will also assure more enthusiasm and staying power. It is smart to look for people who have such self-interests in working with you and who will readily disclose them.

Perhaps the most tangible, immediate evidence of the evaluation's worth was the role it played in the decision of the Saint Paul Public Schools to take full responsibility for the Technology for Literacy Project when the demonstration period ended. Information in the evaluation reports provided the board of education with the confidence in the project it needed to make that decision. That kind of desirable outcome is not the only bottom line for an evaluation, but it's an important one.

Terilyn Turner wrote in her chapter of the evaluation report that she hoped it would help "other literacy projects . . . adopt evaluation and public accountability" as part of their programs. The report did press constructively for new standards by which to evaluate adult literacy instruction. Patton made it clear how seriously he was handicapped in the summative evaluation by a lack of definitions and of consistent practices and by the rudimentary evaluation processes he and the TLC staff found when they looked for programs with which to compare TLC data. His descriptions of the extreme variability among learners' backgrounds, motivations, and performances were also useful in showing the tough conditions under which adult literacy evaluation must function, and in suggesting the directions that need to be taken to overcome these conditions.

The systematic step Patton took to validate the implementation of the program was a good idea that is not often included in evaluations. Even though it was unfortunate that the validation was limited to the direct service part of the overall project, the validation was particularly useful in identifying who was using TLC's services, to see if that constituency matched the population the center had planned to serve.

To an outsider looking at this evaluation, there are things missing. The Technology for Literacy Project's original mission was to demonstrate the value of computers in adult literacy work. Yet the evaluation spent little time and few resources on explicit questions about the impact of computers. Of the major report's eighty-seven-page summative section,

"Reactions to the TLC Computers" receives only a page and a half, and there are few other evaluative references to computers in the balance of the book. It can be said that computers were implied in all the evaluation's investigations, but other innovative features of the program were also influencing the outcomes. Opportunities to compare their various impacts, and to concentrate more attention on the computers, were available.

The subject of advocacy also received little attention. Descriptions of the Technology for Literacy Project have ordinarily begun with alarming figures about how the community, state, and nation need a quantum jump in effective service capacity in adult literacy to address this "economic and social issue of immense magnitude." The purpose of the project was to develop a strong demonstration program that would stimulate the widespread development of quality programs. TLC staff began immediately to conduct training and organize conferences for prospective disciples far beyond St. Paul. The Donor Review Board was to provide, as noted in the agreement with the school system, the "link to various political, business, cultural and religious leaders." Yet the evaluation produced very few findings about the progress of this important work. There were no signs as to whether it was becoming an effective new part of the adult literacy movement.

The reason the use of computers and the progress of advocacy were slighted goes back to the evaluation's relationship to the whole experience of the underlying program. Everyone involved in the evaluation — TLC, funding sources, and evaluators — regards it as a "utilization-focused" evaluation, following principles set forth by Patton in his book *Utilization-Focused Evaluation* (1986). In this approach, there is a great emphasis on assuring that evaluations get used, primarily by the organization whose program is being evaluated. A major strategy prescribed for gaining that assurance is to look to the organization itself for virtually all the initiative in determining what is to be evaluated, on the logical proposition that when the organization prescribes what it wants to know, it will pay attention to the results.

When that strategy is vigorously pursued, as was the case in the Technology for Literacy Project, it becomes difficult after the fact to consider topics that the evaluation did not address. The organization and its founders and funders had decided what they wanted to learn at this point and instructed the evaluators accordingly. Any subsequent discussion of what else might have been examined is likely to be called Monday morning quarterbacking.

The point for others to remember is this: when utilization-focused evaluation concentrates seriously on giving an organization what it wants, it places a heavy responsibility on the organization to prescribe for itself very carefully. The utilization question has to be, What information will be the most *useful* to us?

That question needs to be asked not only when the program begins but also several times later. At the beginning, the answers to the evaluation question need to match up with clear practical program mission statements, or be very explicit as to why they don't. When the question is asked again at later steps, it is especially important to look back over the history of the program so far and see what has changed — in the perceived values, the goals, what people are spending their time doing, what the organizational leaders now think people should be doing, and what the evaluation now needs to find out about the program. Those changes can be the key to learning from the experience and planning for the future. Evaluation is the process of engaging in that learning and applying it to one's work.

Terilyn Turner talks and writes articulately about how this evaluation was and still is a continuing process in the interests of the agency, the funders, the literacy field, and the publics they serve. The conclusion she wrote for her chapter of the evaluation report is a good summary of the value of any evaluation: "It affords an opportunity to reflect upon activities in a systematic way, to tell the center's story to others, and to plan effectively for the future."

8

Helping Established Agencies
Meet Contemporary Needs:
Evaluating the Lilly Endowment's
National Youthworker Education Project

Site:	National.
Date:	1978–1980 and 1986.
Underlying program:	A training program for field personnel of eight national agencies serving young women and girls, to encourage the development of agency programs more relevant to contemporary needs, funded by the Lilly Endowment, Indianapolis, Indiana.
Evaluation purpose:	To assess the effectiveness of the program in stimulating change, and to use that intelligence to guide future grantmaking.
Evaluation initiator:	The foundation.
Stakeholders:	The foundation, the eight national agencies, and the training center for the program (the Center for Youth Development and Research, University of Minnesota).

Evaluators:	Outside consultants Judy Corder-Bolz of the Southwest Educational Development Laboratory, Austin, Texas, with help from an advisory committee of one foundation staff member and two independent consultants; and for the follow-up study, Judith Erickson of the Center for Youth Development and Research.
Information sources:	Youthworkers in local communities and national agency staff.
Evaluation methods:	Personal and telephone interviews, mail questionnaires, and case studies. (Exemplifies descriptive and impact or outcome evaluation.)
Evaluation cost:	$45,000 for the original evaluation, $41,000 for the follow-up study.
Paid by:	The foundation.
Program cost:	$1,661,000 over four years.
Source of program funds:	The foundation.
Reports:	Oral reports in conferences with the eight agencies, a 400-page report for internal use, a 35-page report used as a conference handout, and a 50-page summary report distributed to the agencies and others interested in the field.

The Program to Be Evaluated

Over the past two or three decades, grantmakers have had a penchant for making grants that help nonprofit organizations adjust to changing times. As constituencies change, needs shift, and new issues come along, an established agency that is going to continue to be an important asset in the communities it serves has to adapt. Moreover, it must adapt enthusiastically. If it can show it has the energy and the creative ideas to cope with change, the agency can usually find friends in philanthropy who respect such commitments and want to support them. Or sometimes it is the other way around, with a foundation taking the initiative to seek out the people in a field who have the potential to pull institutions into new positions of usefulness in the contemporary scene.

This study is a good example of a foundation, the Lilly Endowment, taking just that kind of initiative and encouraging attention to new circumstances in a field in which it had an interest. The field was the work of youth organizations, and the foundation's views about the need for change were based on convincing research. The thrust of its initiative would be to urge agencies that worked with girls and young women to accept the findings of that research and use them as clues in the development of new programs befitting the times.

The foundation made two strategic decisions that could be part of anyone's approach to a similar task. First, it decided that the best place to help the agencies begin to address new conditions was not at agency headquarters but in the field, at the agencies' points of community contact. Management would certainly have to be involved and comfortable with the program, but field staff were the best potential agents for change. Second, the foundation recognized the value of promoting a sense of community among the field staff involved, so that each participant could feel the support of others while making personal progress and so that the individual efforts could add up to a powerful overall effort. In this, the foundation was influenced by Matthew B. Miles' concept of "temporary systems" (1964), in which new short-term organizational arrangements are invented to stimulate new thinking in established institutions.

These strategic decisions were the crucial specifications for the program. The rest fell into place once these decisions were made. An intense residential training program was to lead the field staff to new skills and to new insights and motivations about their work. It was also to be a stirring common experience binding the participants together. A follow-up session was to reinforce both their personal growth and sense of community. They could then become models and leaders, generating new vigor among their peers and management.

To conduct such a program, the foundation envisioned a three-way collaboration among the agencies, the foundation itself, and a training base acceptable to the agencies but independent of them and, by reputation, full of clear discernments about contemporary life. An evaluation component was to determine whether the strategic decisions had been good ones.

Initial Research Justifying the Program

The strategic decisions had not been made in a vacuum. The Lilly Endowment's first step towards this program came from the experience of considering a single, relatively limited proposal. In 1973, Camp Fire (at that time, Camp Fire Girls) had asked for research funds to investigate why it was losing its teenagers and what new programs should look like to recapture them. In reviewing this proposal, Lilly came to the conclusion that the problem was endemic to the whole field and that the foundation should work with Camp Fire and seven other major agencies serving girls and young women to mount a broader and deeper assessment. The result became Project Girl, a national study in which 1,000 girls, "representing a mosaic of the different elements in American society," were interviewed about their needs, concerns, and aspirations, and their relationships with service agencies. The research was conducted by the Center for Youth Development and Research at the University of Minnesota under the strong leadership of the center's director, Gisela Konopka. The findings were published as a book (Konopka, 1976).

Toward the conclusion of the research, Konopka and the endowment called together the national executives of the eight major national agencies: American Red Cross, Big Sisters, Camp Fire, Girl Scouts of America, Girls Clubs of America, 4H, National Federation of Settlements, and the YWCA. The agency executives heard the findings straight from the interviewers.

Even though one-third of the girls interviewed had been selected on the basis of their participation in youth organizations, only 15 of the 1,000 said they would rely on a youthworker in a crisis. Such findings indicated that the agencies were irrelevant to the lives of all but a very few adolescent girls. This wasn't entirely news — all the agencies shared Camp Fire's problems — but the sorry picture this survey painted of the agencies' reputations among their assumed constituents drove the point home hard enough to stimulate talk about action. The executives looked to the center and the Lilly Endowment for help in finding solutions. Konopka and Susan Wisely, then a program officer at the endowment, held meetings with each of the national agencies, and it was in these meetings that the idea of a large-scale independent training program for key youthworkers took shape.

The program was named the National Youthworker Education Project (NYEP). The Lilly Endowment was the funder and convenor of the program, the Center for Youth Development and Research at Minnesota was the window to the contemporary world and the trainer, and the eight organizations were to identify and recruit the youthworker participants for the program. "In this way," as the evaluation report was later to say, "the project became the work of three partners whose complementary responsibilities allowed a complex undertaking to move forward most effectively" (Corder-Bolz, 1979).

Beginning in January 1976, virtually every month twenty youthworkers came to the center in Minneapolis for ten days. Sixteen of the youthworkers would be from the eight agencies (two each); four would be from jobs in the juvenile justice system. The curriculum, based directly on the findings of the center's Project Girl research, was ambitious and demanding. Discussions with specialists in fields such as adolescent medicine and abuse patterns in families, presentations by panels of young people, films, videos, and field trips all were designed to help youthworkers gain the understanding necessary to be useful to adolescent girls of the 1970s and 1980s. Small group meetings helped the youthworkers organize and respond to the material and work on their "action plans" — statements youthworkers were asked to write describing something important to focus on when they were back on the job after the training.

By the time the program concluded in mid 1979, 589 youthworkers in twenty-nine groups had come to the center from all over the country, experienced the ten-day training, and taken action plans home to work on. In the original design, each group came together again at the center three months after their initial meeting, to talk about their progress and problems and get a second round of training in certain areas, especially organizational change processes and fundraising. Towards the end of the program, in a move consistent with the temporary systems strategy, the follow-up meeting at the center was changed to a regional meeting of all NYEP alumni in an area, to encourage ongoing regional networking.

The Initial Evaluation

In the summer of 1978, Lilly contracted with Judy Corder-Bolz, a sociologist at the Southwest Educational Development Laboratory in Austin, Texas, to conduct an evaluation of the National Youthworker Education Project. Lilly program officer Susan Wisely had known Corder-Bolz through contacts at Indiana University. Corder-Bolz worked out the evaluation design with an advisory committee consisting of Wisely and two consultants who had carried out evaluation assignments for the foundation's religion division: Barbara Wheeler and Parker Palmer. A summary of the plan, as it was shown in the evaluation reports, appears in Table 8.1. Personal interviews with national agency staff and a survey among the participating youthworkers were to be the major components of the evaluation.

In both the interviews and the survey, questions were structured to cover the four main objectives of NYEP as stated in the 1979 report:

- To increase collaboration among the agencies and between them and the juvenile justice system
- To stimulate change in national and local programming which had become "stagnant"
- To develop an effective training program that would spur agencies to improve their own training work
- To "widen the range" of girls served by the agencies

Table 8.1. NYEP Evaluation Design.

Type of Data	Description of Participants	Purpose
Extended interviews	Staff members of participating national agencies, Lilly Endowment staff, NYEP staff	Assess benefits of NYEP for national agencies and learn what changes NYEP has produced
		Assess NYEP impact on local organizations
Survey questionnaires	All NYEP trainees	Assess participants' views of NYEP impact
Records	Each of the eight participating agencies was asked for:	Assess NYEP impact on participating agencies
	Copy of formal goals and purposes Membership records New training materials New program descriptions Publicity or evaluation relevant to NYEP	
Case studies	Youthworkers and girls in five communities	Highlight NYEP impact on individual youthworkers, on the community, and on young women served by the youthworkers

Source: Corder-Bolz, 1979. Reprinted with permission.

Interviews with National Executives

A team of two or three researchers, usually including Corder-Bolz, visited the national offices of the eight agencies and conducted structured interviews among twenty-nine management staff members, including the chief executive officer in each case. Three Lilly Endowment program officers and six NYEP staff members were also interviewed.

According to Corder-Bolz's 1979 evaluation report, 71 percent of the national agency respondents said that NYEP had been "helpful to them in accomplishing the formal goals and purposes of their organizations." Twenty-four percent answered "maybe" to this question. The evaluation report quoted just three of the answers about overall satisfaction, suggesting that these three were particularly eloquent in representing agencies' favorable views of NYEP. One answer, for example, recalled that the content of NYEP was based on the extensive research called Project Girl.

> So often university research is creative, and yet they don't do anything with it. Dissemination is the really difficult stage, so that something like [NYEP]— where you are able to take that information directly to the workers in the field—is a very far-sighted, a very innovative kind of approach.
>
> In general, I think [it is valuable] to raise people's awareness of the things that are troubling girls and how to deal with those things. But I think the greatest benefit has been that people have a better understanding for the need for collaboration.
>
> From reading the latest reports, the most beneficial aspect seems to be the impact the NYEP has had at the local level, and how it continues to have an impact. There is a participant who has put together a file on all NYEP materials and made it available to her junior high school. Recently the sheriff's department borrowed the file and is turning it into a lending library. That's what I mean. It isn't just something that happens once and that's the end of it, but it's the updates and the follow-up that I think are really very exciting.

When the national agency staff members were asked about negative outcomes, 18 percent reported none, 12 percent criticized the process by which participating youthworkers were selected (which had been the agencies' responsibility), and 12 percent criticized the early training sessions as being too academic and structured. Fifty percent thought the most negative outcome was the frustration being experienced by youthworkers in carrying out their action plans. One person said, "I think many of our staff found brick walls back home to overcome."

In her 1979 report, Corder-Bolz presented more detailed findings from these interviews, organized under four headings corresponding to the four objectives of the National Youthworker Education Project. Here are some examples of those findings:

Collaboration. A breakdown of the overall satisfaction figure of 71 percent showed that national agency staff members valued NYEP's contribution to collaboration activity more than anything else. Answers to related questions, however, indicated they had a hard time giving NYEP credit for this interagency activity. Ninety-one percent affirmed that their agencies had been "part of collaborative efforts," but most of them attributed those activities to their own initiatives rather than any NYEP influence. Although the nine quotations chosen for this section of the report give nine insights into national staff feelings about collaboration, they have little relevance to NYEP; only two even mention the program.

Program Improvements. Fifty-seven percent of the national agency staff members said that NYEP had an impact on program content at the national level. Among the examples cited were an increased emphasis on issues of sexuality, life choice, drugs, career development, and juvenile justice concerns; and the support and reinforcement NYEP supplied for preexisting efforts to develop new programs for young women.

Better Training Programs. When asked whether they could see a ripple effect from the NYEP training on the content of their own agencies' training programs, 50 percent of agency staff answered yes, and 17 percent, no. Eight percent said perhaps, and a full 25 percent didn't know.

More impressively, 78 percent said they were using NYEP alumni as resources for their own training programs. How many of these youthworkers had already been serving as national training program leaders before participating in NYEP is not clear, although one of the quoted responses sums up the process one would hope for: "We've used people who got an idea for something out of their NYEP training, and then they developed it, and then we bring them back in to serve as a resource in the particular area."

Widening the Range of Girls Served. Almost all of the national agency staff reported they were interested in widening the range of young women served, and about half felt they were making progress. The evaluation found it difficult to get any statistical measurement of how much NYEP was responsible. However, the quotes were useful in suggesting how the national staffs felt NYEP had reinforced their own initiatives. For example, one staff member said: "We now serve girls who are underserved. It wasn't that we did not previously serve them. But we're doing a far better job. . . . I don't know that it's changed on the basis of NYEP. I think it was something that was moving there prior to it, but I certainly think that NYEP has helped in terms of having more staff people comfortable with the whole question."

Findings about the results of having juvenile justice system personnel participate in NYEP related to both the purpose of broadening the constituency range and the purpose of collaboration. Project Girl research had shown there was little contact between public and private agency representatives, suggesting private agencies were reluctant to reach out to girls caught in the corrections system. When national staff were asked how they felt about juvenile justice professionals being included in the training, 86 percent responded favorably. However, when they were asked about specific changes that might have come about because these related professionals had been included in the program, the percentage who could identify such changes was much smaller.

Several charts distributed to the eight national agencies indicated how the interviewees at each agency had answered evaluation interview questions. Such charts can be useful to a number of evaluation target audiences, for comparing the observations and attitudes of different groups of evaluation participants.

Mail Survey

Simultaneously with the national agency staff interviews, a survey questionnaire was sent to the 474 youthworkers who had completed the training program by early 1979. The questionnaire was designed by Corder-Bolz and mailed by the Center for Youth Development and Research. The youthworkers were asked to identify themselves in their responses but assured that the center would keep their identities confidential. Returns in the first month totaled 243. A mailed reminder and follow-up phone calls produced another 120 replies, for a total of 363. This 77 percent response was unusually high for this type of survey and seemed evidence in itself of NYEP's considerable impact on those who participated.

The evaluation report listed many of the results of the survey, showing that it had tested program impact in many ways. For example,

- 85 percent of the participating youthworkers rated themselves as being satisfied with the program as a whole, with 58 percent being very satisfied, and the youthworkers were also asked specifically about their satisfaction with the training sessions in Minneapolis and the follow-up meetings.
- Like the national staffs, the youthworkers valued the emphasis on collaboration among agencies, and 60 percent said the frequency with which they worked together with others had increased since their participation in NYEP. Seventy percent said there had been changes in programming at the local level due to NYEP, including expansion, "increased awareness," and more emphasis on the needs of girls. Sixty-five percent cited specific new programs that they felt were stimulated by their involvement in NYEP.
- Forty-five percent had been involving youth more in the planning of programs, and two-thirds of these could confirm that this was due at least in part to NYEP. (The training had strongly recommended youth involvement and had effectively demonstrated it in action.)
- Sixty-seven percent of those currently conducting training were using NYEP training materials and training techniques. Since their involvement in NYEP, 40 percent had conducted training at agencies other than their own. Most of these agencies were ones that had not been part of NYEP. Forty-four percent reported that their agencies were now serving a wider range of young women than in the past, including minorities, the handicapped, and low-income groups. Of these, 49

percent said this was a result of NYEP, 24 percent said it wasn't, and 27 percent said it was difficult to say. When asked what "wider range" meant, the youthworkers gave these descriptions:

Expanded programs that include more women	30%
Inclusion of young women who come through the juvenile justice system	24%
More minority youth	9%
Emotionally disturbed and/or handicapped youth	9%
Young women from low-income backgrounds	8%
More older girls	7%

- Of the juvenile justice system personnel who had participated in NYEP, 75 percent said that they now sought out youth-serving organizations to help youth for whom they were responsible. For their part, 50 percent of the private agency youthworkers had learned "a great deal" about the juvenile justice system while participating in NYEP. Forty-four percent agreed with the statement that, as a result of NYEP, they had changed their impression of people who work in juvenile justice, and 50 percent had changed their impressions of young people caught in the juvenile.justice system.

- The participants reported on the status of their action plans:

Completed their original plans	28%
Still working on their original plans	12%
Working on a modified plan	22%
Working on a new plan	12%
Given up on their plans	12%

- When the 78 percent who reported that they had run into problems trying to carry out their action plans were asked to identify such problems on a checklist, the most often checked were:

Lack of money	14%
Lack of support from co-workers in their own organization	9%

Lack of support from co-workers in
other organizations   8%
Interestingly, the least checked problems
were:
Obstacles imposed by the local agency
board   1%
Obstacles imposed by the national orga-
nization   1%

Case Studies

Five case studies were written, by three writers known to the
evaluation advisory committee — a journalist in the religion field,
a pastor, and a graduate student in theology. A summary report
(Corder-Bolz and Wisely, 1980) says that each case study took
about two days of interviewing plus writing time. Four of the
studies run 1,000 to 1,500 words; one runs 5,000 words.

Although the case studies read more like tributes to outstanding youthworkers and testimonials to NYEP than case
studies, at times they added good insights. A study of a youthworker from a small town in South Dakota described vividly
how she went to NYEP training and found herself surrounded
by people of very different cultures, but was able to translate
much of what she saw and heard into a new awareness of life's
realities in her own hometown. Another study followed a youthworker with an action plan to create an interagency network
back to Denver and described her activities as the networking
project rose and fell. But instead of being an interesting objective case study of the dynamics of an interagency arrangement
and how NYEP had or had not prepared the youthworker to
cope with the problems involved, it was written as a general
tribute to the youthworker for trying to cope.

Confirmation of Program Strategies

Although the evaluation was conducted too early to show
whether NYEP might have long-lasting effects in the field, the
findings suggested that the first strategic decision — to focus on

field staff—had been a sound one. The NYEP alumnae's answers about the program's merit and their own apparent successes back home on the job were positive testimony to both the NYEP program content and its basic concept of training key local youthworkers to push ahead effectively to carry out the changes the program envisioned. When anywhere from one-third to two-thirds of a group point to actual changes in various facets of agency practice that they credit to such a program, it is impressive. The interviews with national agency staff suggested that, compared to the youthworkers, they were more guarded, more apt to reserve credit for their own programs than give it to NYEP. Yet at the same time, they acknowledged the vital role local youthworkers play in making agency services work. The case studies, too, confirmed the vigor of local staff bringing home the message about change and relevance.

The 1980 evaluation report concluded: "This strategy is worth remembering. If one wants to improve local social service institutions, one is well advised to work with people who are directly responsible for those services rather than relying on changes filtering down through national organizations. [However,] in order to reinforce (and sometimes to protect) change at that [local] level, the NYEP staff wisely sought the understanding and support of national executives in the girl-serving agencies."

The second strategic decision had been to encourage the youthworkers to keep in touch with one another after the program and to build an influential community among themselves, so that together they might fulfill the NYEP vision. Although participants were asked whether or not this was happening, none of the evaluation reports gave participants' answers. The reason for the omission was probably not one of avoiding the issue; this soon after the training the informal networking was probably impressive. However, the concept of temporary systems encouraging the youthworkers to join together on behalf of change was an interest of the Lilly Endowment internally, rather than an explicit working principle of this program that needed to be attended to in this evaluation, and that may well be the reason it is not mentioned in the reports.

Evaluation Consequences

The findings were reported to representatives of the eight national agencies at a conference held by the Lilly Endowment in December 1979. At their initial meeting five years before, direct reports from research interviewers had been found to have the most impact on agency executives. Consequently, this conference featured the writers of the case studies, who described what they saw in the field. This firsthand reporting was again effective. As Susan Wisely of Lilly says, the case studies "came alive" at this conference and encouraged an informal exchange among the researchers and people from the agencies and foundation. There were also presentations and handouts about the results of the national agency interviews and the survey among the participating youthworkers. Wisely remembers: "NYEP was seen as a major success, in the new strength and sense of direction it gave to a significant number of youth workers, and the ripple effect when they went back home to work and train in their own communities."

The first written report (Corder-Bolz, 1979) was distributed to agency executives at the conference. Each agency also received a separate tabulation of the data that pertained to its own youthworkers, so it could compare the results with those of all agencies combined. A second summary report (Corder-Bolz and Wisely, 1980) followed. The summary repeated some of the previous report's text but avoided statistics, omitted most of the quotations, and added the case studies plus some general interpretations and observations. The Lilly Endowment mailed copies of the summary report to the national agencies and to the youthworker participants, and has distributed copies on request ever since. Evaluator Corder-Bolz also gave Lilly and the Center for Youth Development and Research a 400-page compilation of evaluation instruments and findings.

It is difficult to separate the impact of the evaluation from the influence of NYEP itself, but it seems clear that the oral and written presentations of the evaluation findings became the medium through which the eight national agencies and others learned about the overall significance of the program. They heard about individual experiences from their own personnel, but that was personal and anecdotal. Karen Bartz was director of research and development on the national staff of Camp Fire during NYEP. She attended the 1979 "report-out meeting," as she calls it, and remembers that the evaluation "reinforced" her feelings about what the Project Girl research and NYEP were trying to tell the national agencies. In her words, "The agencies had been involved in the beginning four years before, but then as time went by it all became pretty mechanical—mostly just choosing who was to go to the training. The evaluation brought us back; it reminded us why we were doing all this. It focused us again on the local level and the issues we had there."

Bartz, now national philanthropic program manager of the Charitable and Crown Investments Department of the Hallmark Corporation in Kansas City, confirms that two years after the end of NYEP, when Camp Fire rewrote its core programs for both junior high and older youth, the individuals leading the process in each case were alumni of NYEP, and the results reflected that program's influence.

At Big Sisters, the merger with Big Brothers soon was the major issue. It was alumni of NYEP who became, as Wisely puts it, the principal "advocates and watchdogs for the girls' half," using NYEP intelligence to push for program content that would make the new joint agency effective for young women.

The Girls Clubs of America saw NYEP and its evaluation as part of its mandate to establish a national center that would focus on research and development in the field, with special emphasis on broadening the constituencies of girls to be served by featuring programs that would be important to more of them.

In addition, other organizations discovered NYEP through its evaluation. Upon reading the findings, Joan Lipsitz of the Center for Early Adolescence saw that she shared the Lilly Endowment's interest in attending to the changing needs of ten- to fifteen-year-old girls and boys. This shared interest led to a number of projects that Lilly values, including an after-school program study, an investigation of the role of churches in meeting the needs of this age group, and the creation of the Lilly Endowment Leadership Education Program, which works in the field of services to young adolescents in Indiana.

At Lilly itself, the evaluation findings became the basis for continuing relationships with the eight national agencies and others. Program officers felt that, unfortunately, the Center for Youth Development and Research, which had been so essential to NYEP, was losing its momentum at the University of Minnesota. The endowment encouraged the Girls Clubs of America to fill a role similar to the center's, and the endowment also supported the development of the Indiana Youth Institute, as an example of possible state and regional arrangements for continuing youthworker in-service training and networking.

More broadly, the NYEP findings had shown Lilly the value of the temporary systems model, and it has used the approach in other fields. In Lilly's Leadership Education Program, the core of that project's temporary systems model has been a group of fifty-three consultant-trainees working with agencies throughout Indiana. In a project to generate new ideas in church ministry for youth, the temporary system was built around a group of faculty members from theological schools. NYEP had been the first of these applications and its evaluation was essential in giving Lilly's staff and board members the confidence they needed to move ahead in other fields.

This was also the first time the endowment had been involved in a program that helped individuals develop action plans for the ideas they were determined to carry out as a result of training and conferring. The evaluation provided a lot of quantitative and qualitative information about the actual usability of action plans, and Lilly has used that intelligence to encourage the effective use of action plans in other programs.

As for evaluation work itself, the endowment concluded that the NYEP evaluation produced real benefits for the investment involved and that it suggested many potential benefits future evaluations could yield. After five more years of nurturing the idea, Lilly established an Office of Evaluation in 1985, with Susan Wisely as its director. Today, the foundation follows a guideline that says it will spend 3 percent of its total grants budget on evaluation. The primary emphasis is on determining the effectiveness of the Lilly grants themselves, but usefulness to grantees and others is always an objective, as Wisely's concluding comments in Lilly's *Evaluation Notebook* indicate: "By imaginatively pursuing answers to telling questions, by searching for patterns among those answers, and by reporting the results economically, an evaluator can distill important insights from an area of foundation work. Both the foundation and the grantee can then use what has been learned to re-order their own procedures and to renew their own internal life. Furthermore, in sharing those lessons in writing and conversation, the foundation and grantee can engage a wider audience in the problems and possibilities at hand. Thus an evaluation is, potentially, the center of a 'continuing education' for all concerned" (Lilly Endowment, 1989).

Certain aspects of the NYEP evaluation were noted at Lilly as particularly effective and then applied in later evaluations. The conferences to report findings to national agency executives, and especially the use of field personnel at those meetings to give firsthand accounts, impressed the foundation as the best way to convey research and evaluation information. Wisely describes how this technique has evolved into a "conversational approach to evaluation," in which relevant people are brought together to discuss findings and next steps to take.

The Follow-Up Study

Probably the Lilly Endowment's major misgiving about the 1978 to 1980 evaluation of the National Youthworkers Education Project was that it took place too early to come to anything but tentative conclusions about the program's impact in the field. So it is no wonder that Susan Wisely was delighted in 1985 to get a letter from Judith B. Erickson at the University of Minnesota Center for Youth Development and Research, saying she was interested in conducting a follow-up study of the NYEP participants. Erickson had been "sharing a storeroom" with all the saved NYEP files and had become intrigued with all the good questions that could be put to this distinguished group of youthworkers seven to ten years after their training at the center. She also had a particular institutional interest in pursuing that idea. Gisela Konopka had retired, leadership at the University of Minnesota had changed, and the future of the Center for Youth

Development and Research was in question. Erickson hoped that a study among a group of the center's alumnae would suggest future roles for the center and help it survive. Upon approval of a $41,000 grant from the Lilly Endowment, she dusted off lists of names and addresses, the fact sheets of information on each participant, action plans, and other materials, and with the help of others on the staff, began to track people down for telephone interview appointments.

Follow-Up Study Design

There were 545 alumni names available. Erickson decided to select at random 25 percent of the youthworkers from each of the eight agencies, and then add more where necessary to get at least 15 alumni from each agency. Thirty-one of the juvenile justice system personnel were also randomly selected, representing 20 percent of the total of that group. This process yielded an initial sample of 157.

The search for the 157 alumni began with calls to the local offices of the agencies where they had been working when they came to NYEP. The subsequent process shows the typical difficulties follow-up studies often face. If an agency was no longer in the local phone book, calls were made to the national office and to the local United Way, to ask about a possible agency name change, merger, or new job for the youthworker. If the agency could be contacted but the youthworker was no longer there, the researcher explained the purpose of the inquiry and asked for help. Erickson's report on the study says that "most agencies were very helpful, and provided some clues for continuing the search" (Erickson, 1986).

If that route did not work, the staff checked area telephone directories within a forty-mile radius, and called anyone with the same full name as the youthworker. If there were no such listing or if it was the wrong person, they looked for individuals with the same last name. Unless there were entirely too many of these people, they called their numbers, hoping to find relatives. "In this way," comments Erickson's report, "we ended up talking to siblings, children, ex-husbands, parents, and distant relatives" who often provided the information needed.

Erickson and her crew were able to get in touch by phone with 118 of the 157 alumni (80 percent). Each of these 118 was then mailed a letter with a further explanation of the study, a copy of the interview questionnaire, and a request that the youth-worker call and schedule a time for a telephone interview. Those who did not respond within three weeks were called again and asked for an interview time. The final sample was 81. When the characteristics of this group were compared to NYEP participants as a whole, as well as to those who had been located but could not be interviewed, the sample was reasonably representative of the program's enrollment over the four years of its life. This whole process of building the interview group is carefully documented in the evaluation report.

When letters were sent confirming interview appointment times, copies of the participants' action plans from the files were enclosed—in all but a few cases where they couldn't be found—to refresh participants' memories.

The interviews, conducted in early 1986, lasted anywhere from fifteen minutes to nearly two hours, depending mainly on whether the interviewee was still involved in youthwork. With the participants' permission, the interviews were recorded and later transcribed for analysis. The researchers' interests took them well beyond the scope of the NYEP experience specifically, but some of their interview questions were very pertinent to NYEP and their findings added substantially to the original evaluation of this program.

Follow-Up Study Findings

- Fifty-seven percent were still in youthwork, seven to ten years after participating in NYEP:

Same agency, same position	13.6%
Same agency, different position	14.8%
Same organization, different location	7.4%
Still in youthwork, different agency	21.0%
Has left youthwork	28.4%
Retired	7.4%
Not in labor force	7.4%

- Forty-five percent now said that their action plans had been fully implemented as planned, and 32 percent said that their plans had been implemented with modifications. The study report gave a few good examples of these plans and the initiatives that had come from them.

- Eighty-nine percent of the respondents were presently using the action planning process in their work, although a little less than half were not able to say for sure that it was because of their NYEP experience.

- Eighty-eight percent of the thirty-five alumni who were still working for the eight original participating agencies or the juvenile justice system were still using NYEP materials in their work.

- Twenty-four percent said among the most frustrating aspects of their jobs in youthwork agencies were "problems with the board representing the agency power structure." In the 1979 survey, only 1 percent had mentioned such constraints against the implementation of action plans, and the increased frustration may reflect increased experience.

- The follow-up study also produced a useful reminder that findings from early feedback are not always dependable predictors of future attitudes and behavior. Exit evaluations after the NYEP sessions, comments on some of the 1979 questionnaire forms from alumni, and remarks from national agency staff had led those who were running NYEP to conclude that there was a distinctly antiacademic, pragmatic bias among the youthworkers. As the follow-up study report points out, the original evaluation reports had quoted a youthworker as saying, "We're doers, not thinkers." This impression that the youthworkers were nontraditional, hands-on learners had caused the Center for Youth Development and Research to make significant changes in the curriculum after the first year or so, moving away from anything that smacked too much of university scholarship.

Now, however, seven years later, 31 percent of the alumni reported that since NYEP they had earned one or more academic degrees — mostly master's but a few bachelor's and Ph.D.'s. Another 13 percent were in a degree program at the moment, and several others were planning further academic work in the next two years.

Furthermore, 72 percent of those who had stayed in youth-work now reported that there were training programs offered outside their own agencies that they wanted to take but couldn't, usually because they could not afford the programs and their agencies would not pay for them. This was one of several findings in the follow-up study that would be useful in planning for any new programs at the center that might carry on from NYEP. All of the NYEP participants' costs had been paid by the Lilly Endowment. Any new similar program at the center would have to cope creatively with the need for financial aid.

Unlike the original reports, the follow-up report is explicit about the ultimate goal of the temporary systems model. It states that those responsible for NYEP had "hopes that participants in the NYEP would form a nationwide network of youthwork professionals who would continue to share ideas . . . and be in the vanguard of inter- and intra-agency collaboration efforts." Although 29 percent of those who were still working for one of the eight national agencies or the juvenile justice system said they were regularly in touch with other NYEP alumni, no organized network had developed. On the other hand, the values of collaboration had been well taught; 71 percent reported that they had collaborative activities that were "functioning well" with other youth-serving agencies, and half said they were involved in joint training or advocacy efforts with other agencies.

Finally, the alumni were asked what they now felt were the most important benefits of their NYEP experience, and the follow-up study report compared these answers to those from the 1979 evaluation. The importance of contacts with other youthworkers and the acquisition of specific skills and helpful materials, two benefits cited frequently in 1979, were no longer mentioned as often. Instead, there was now considerably more emphasis on personal growth and the new understanding gained about youth problems and coalition building. The "sense of professionalism" that had been generated by NYEP came up frequently in the 1986 interviews; this kind of comment had apparently not been common enough in 1979 to be reported in that study. Perhaps this change in attitude about oneself and one's work was just a matter of maturity, but it may also reflect the impact of NYEP over the years. NYEP may have helped a lot of youthworkers see new importance and respect for what they were trying to do with their lives. Among other things, it may have led many of them eventually to decide to go back to school, as reported above.

It is tempting to wish there had been a control group moving along through the years, with whom the lives of these alumni could be compared. But checking for changes directly attributable only to NYEP is probably asking too much of a program as brief as it was. Because there is so much else going on in everybody's lives, it is often unrealistic to try to isolate the influence of a single experience.

Just looking at the responses from the alumni, however, adds a great deal of depth and veracity to what had been known about the participants' NYEP experiences and what they give the program credit for. The high quality of the information produced by looking at findings over time usually makes the data contemporary with a program look shallow by comparison. The problem that frequently limits the usefulness of longer-term information, however, is the often fleeting life of a program such as NYEP. Interests and activities keep changing at agencies, university centers, and foundations, and old programs just fade away. Even by 1979, NYEP was out of business and not likely to be followed by anything similar. By the time of the 1986 follow-up study, NYEP was even more remote from the activities and personnel of the eight national agencies. Judith Erickson and Susan Wisely called the agencies together again for a report on this follow-up, but the representatives who came were not the same people, and they were all in the middle of the 1980s' cuts and crunches. It is difficult to find tangible consequences of that meeting.

The 142-page report on the follow-up was released jointly by the Lilly Endowment and the Center for Youth Development and Research at Minnesota. Erickson feels that the follow-up study has found its greatest use among newer arrangements of organizations and individuals addressing problems of adolescents. She particularly cites the Carnegie Council on Adolescent Development, an operating program of the Carnegie Corporation. Jane Quinn, director of the council's Project on Youth Development and Community Programs, said in a 1991 conversation that she happened to be using the report "at the moment," as a "jumping off point" in planning a national meeting about professional development through pre- and in-service training in the field. She added, "We don't want to reinvent the wheel, we want to build on lessons learned."

Evaluation Cost

The evaluation work began in December 1978 and was completed in early 1980. The cost of the evaluation to the Lilly Endowment was $45,000. Lilly's grants to NYEP itself had totaled $1,661,000 over the four years. It was the first time an evaluation had been initiated and organized within the foundation and charged as an administrative expense, rather than being part of a program grant.

Evaluation Strengths and Weaknesses

This was a strong evaluation design. The combination of an extensive survey among the program participants, personal interviews among the executives of the institutions targeted to be affected, a few case studies in depth in the field, and follow-up telephone interviews with participants a few years later (even though this was not part of the original plan) can be a model for others who wish to evaluate efforts to stimulate change in service institutions. It is just as appropriate locally as nationally.

The evaluation's questions were directly related to the purposes of the underlying program, and the way they were framed reflected good practice. To the extent possible, they looked for answers about specific behavior — asking, What have you done? instead of only, What do you think? — and they asked for specific examples.

The only disappointment in the design is that close contact with girls and young women themselves — so important to the Project Girl research — was not a feature of the evaluation as well. Instead, the evaluation investigated the program's effects on the professionals involved, albeit professionals largely at the level where the agencies encountered the consumers of their services. Because there was no part of the design that brought consumers into the assessment of NYEP in the way in which they had been involved in Project Girl's assessment of the needs NYEP should meet, the evaluation was less informative than the research had been. The case studies might have served this purpose to some extent, but they too were written from another point of view.

With such a good design, however, findings and interpretations could have dug deeper than they did. The 1979 survey of youthworkers, with its excellent return from identified respondents, potentially included a host of variables. These answers could have been analyzed in terms of the youthworkers' jobs, age, experience, gender (12 percent of the participants were men), types of communities they worked in, types of action plans they wrote, and so forth. The first NYEP classes had been back out in the field for three years. How many were still with the agency that had recommended that they attend the training? How many had been promoted? To what extent were they still in touch with one another, and for what reasons? Such information was analyzed to some extent in the follow-up study, but not in the original evaluation. Even within the framework of the data that were reported, interpretation was at a minimum. The principal summary report has a brief section of conclusions, but they seem fairly independent of the evaluation itself; they seldom tie back to reported findings.

In fairness, however, it needs to be remembered that this was not intended to be a formative evaluation providing feedback to NYEP for program adjustments and improvements. Nor did the Lilly Endowment regard it as a test of whether or not funding should be continued. The program, at least as it stood at the time, was virtually over at the time of the evaluation. Nor was the evaluation an initiative taken primarily by the eight national agencies, with crucial questions that they wanted answered. The major stakeholder in the evaluation was the endowment, and it got the answers it wanted for itself through its own involvement in the whole process of program and evaluation, not through formal detailed analysis and reports. Its NYEP experience helped Lilly understand a new grantmaking model that revolved around a cluster of grants in a particular field, an institutional change strategy, and an evaluation practice that was much more ambitious than anything it had done before. "This evaluation was helpful to us in several ways," says Susan Wisely. "It informed our future efforts to serve youth. It shed light on an effective grantmaking strategy with broad application throughout the foundation's work. And it demonstrated the benefits of evaluation at a time when our evaluation program was in its infancy."

But a foundation never knows how useful evaluation findings might become in the future, either among the original grantees and institutions or among others not yet predictable. It may therefore be good to get everything out of the data that seems *potentially* worth knowing and to record the findings in a manner that will let others use these findings with confidence. Working over the numbers in that way is a bargain among evaluation costs, especially with today's computers.

The National Youthworker Education Project evaluation has found some extended usefulness. Carnegie's Jane Quinn is paying attention to the follow-up study because she is familiar with NYEP historically, largely through the evaluation. She remembers that she heard about NYEP in the early 1980s through "a lot of grassroots testimonials from youthworkers who said it had made a difference in their lives," and she obtained a copy of the evaluation summary at that time. Today she says, "It verified, in a systematic way, what I had been hearing anecdotally. Youthwork is a field in which practitioner's beliefs and experiences are not documented very well. It's great to have an evaluation that gives us facts about what a program actually did for front-line workers."

9

Annual Check-ups for Program Progress: Evaluating the Philadelphia Summer Youth Employment Career/Vocational Exploration Program

Site:	The Philadelphia metropolitan area.
Date:	Annually, 1982-.
Underlying program:	An annual summer program for disadvantaged youth, offering jobs and counseling that help them test future career inclinations.
Evaluation purpose:	To get feedback every year that can be used to improve the program the following year and to raise money for it.
Evaluation initiator:	The lead foundation: William Penn Foundation, Philadelphia, Pennsylvania.
Stakeholders:	The lead foundation and other funders, the service agencies involved, and to a lesser extent, the youth employers.
Evaluator:	C. Richard Cox, senior program

Evaluator, Cont'd.:	officer at the William Penn Foundation, with the help of an intern and the other funders who, with the William Penn Foundation, make up the Foundation Collaborative for this project.
Information sources:	Youth in the program (directly and through program data), agency executives, college student monitors, and employers. Participating agencies provide much of the data.
Evaluation methods:	Collection and analysis of program data, questionnaires, and personal interviews. (Exemplifies descriptive, formative, process, and summative evaluation.)
Evaluation cost:	$6,050 plus in-kind contributions.
Paid by:	The lead foundation, with in-kind contributions from other funders.
Program cost:	$1,437,000 among eleven grantees in 1990.
Sources of program funds:	William Penn Foundation and twenty-five other area foundations and corporate giving programs.
Reports:	Annual reports of findings and recommendations, produced by the evaluators, and a five-year summary published by the lead foundation, distributed on request to those interested in the field. A separate report is given to each agency with the agency's own performance data.

The Program to Be Evaluated

All cities have summer jobs programs for youth, but Philadelphia's summer youth employment Career/Vocational Exploration Program is several cuts above the routine. Youngsters who wish to explore careers get counseling, interviews, a choice of over 1,100 employers, and a trained college student "monitor" for every twelve high school students in the program. The program also helps the youth persuade employers to hire 84 percent of them to work more than the program's basic twenty hours a week, and to keep 42 percent of them working a while after the six-week program is over—with many of those who do not go on working at a job choosing not to continue in that particular job anyway.

The work is virtually all in private, profit sector jobs, and 71 percent of the students find jobs that are related to their current career interests. (Half of the remaining 29 percent say they don't have a specific career interest yet.) The program is open only to youth in the summers following their tenth- or eleventh-grade years, or immediately following their graduations. The youth are mostly from the less-advantaged comprehensive high schools; dropouts are excluded. Family income must be below the poverty level—$19,013 for a family of four in 1991. Ninety-two percent of the youth are African American, Hispanic, or Asian.

C. Richard Cox, senior program officer of the William Penn Foundation, says, "We hope we've come a long way from the days when for many funders the idea in the summer was just to keep youth off the streets." Gerson Green, executive director of the Greater Philadelphia Federation of Settlements, feels this is the best youth work program he has ever seen: "It's the elite, 'prep school' program of its kind." William Parshall, director of community affairs for Hunt Manufacturing Co. and secretary of the Hunt Foundation, adds: "The image of many of these programs around the country has been that summer work for youth has to be simple pretend jobs working for the city, because these youngsters are losers who can't hack it in private sector employment. This program in Philadelphia shows that's not true."

Close monitoring and evaluation every year for the past nine years has played an important part in showing "that's not true," and in making the program work better every year for the youth of Philadelphia.

The design of the Career/Vocational Exploration Program is influenced by impressive data from efforts funded nationally in the 1970s and early 1980s under the federal Youth Employment and Demonstration Projects Act. Cox, with some good Philadelphia experience in youth employment, found out about the federal model in 1982, from a report written by Andrew Hahn of Brandeis University. Hahn had distilled the literature and experience on career exploration for adolescents into a useful overview, which included the federal model. After a year of organizing and funding the program on their own, Cox and the William Penn Foundation responded to overtures from other funders and established the Foundation Collaborative to develop and support it. At the outset, in June 1983, there were fifteen foundations and corporate giving programs engaged. There are now twenty-five.

Each November, the collaborative sends a request-for-proposals to a variety of community-based agencies in Philadelphia and selected areas outside the city, in anticipation of the following summer's program. Each agency proposes to find the employers; recruit, counsel and place the students; recruit and train the college student monitors; keep in touch with all participants; and maintain records and help evaluate the program. The students' basic experience in the program is six weeks on the job at twenty hours a week. The funders in the collaborative pay for the students' stipends ($4.25 per hour minimum wage in 1991), the monitors' stipends (up to $6.50 per hour for first-time monitors, $7.50 per hour for returning monitors), and part of the program operating costs for the agencies, calculated as 17 percent of total stipends.

There are specifications established for the participating agencies that spell out the type of jobs to be developed and other standards: all employers should be for-profit enterprises, no fast-food places as employers, only one contracting agency deals with each employer, only two placements per employer in most cases, and no other summer job placements at participating sites. Written work-site agreements have to be negotiated with the employers about their role. Each youth is to get career/vocational exploration counseling from the agency, training in job-readiness skills, and on-the-job support. Youth are not to be placed arbitrarily at job sites but are to be interviewed and accepted or rejected by potential employers; there is a consistent effort to make this program part of the real working world. The agencies are to give monitors training and supervision under a plan spelled out in a monitors' manual. ("Monitors" is not descriptive of their true roles; they are to be "effective role models, counselors and administrators.") There are also minimum standards for agency success rates in helping youth to gain extra hours over and above the basic twenty hours a week and to get continued employment after the six weeks.

In spite of such specificity, variations in the way agencies propose to work are common and encouraged. Exceptions are made, "waivers" are approved, and the program prides itself on its diversity.

A committee of the collaborative reviews the proposals, but the funding is not pooled. Early on, the foundations and companies decided they wanted to maintain their individual autonomy and make grants to the agencies separately. Each year, they get together and hold "the auction," at which each member of the collaborative chooses the proposal, or shares of proposals, that seems most appropriate and within the members' desired grant level. Companies with some or all of their operations outside the city, for instance, choose program sites wherever their corporate interests are. Grants are then considered in the regular grantmaking process of each member of the collaborative.

The total amount granted by the collaborative determines the size of the program for the year. In 1990, grants totalled $1,437,242, enabling 1,890 high school students to be in the program and 163 college students to be hired as monitors. Eleven agencies received grants to participate. Several agencies have more than one neighborhood center—the Federation of Settlements had fourteen of its member agencies participating in 1990—so a total of thirty agency sites were involved.

Dick Cox is given great credit for making everything work. As Gerson Green of the settlement federation says, "He's tremendously capable, and although he has plenty else to do he somehow keeps all four hands and feet in this program." The William Penn Foundation hires an intern every summer—usually a graduate student—who helps Cox with the evaluation and whatever else comes up. As Cox says, "The lead organization in a collaborative like this has to be ready to bear additional costs and expenses."

The Evaluation

The government program on which this program is modeled was carefully evaluated; that is how Hahn, Cox, and others knew it worked well. It was natural, then, that this Philadelphia program should have a strong monitoring and evaluation component. When asked if the government program evaluation influenced this one, Cox replies, "Absolutely. From the beginning, we felt we had to follow their lead and know what we were doing."

The evaluation process is an internally generated one, yielding a great deal of quantitative and qualitative information every year. The participating agencies are responsible for submitting three statistical reports during the six-week program. Inputs from these reports about the characteristics and status of participants are promptly computerized, so that problems with either the program or the evaluation can be anticipated. At the end of the summer, with the help of the program intern, each agency compiles a final report, with both statistics and comments about the youth in the program and, more specifically, about applications, characteristics of the accepted candidates, job development, counseling, placements, work records, career exploration, extra employment beyond the minimum, attrition, terminations, and the hiring, training, and performance of the monitors.

The agencies are also responsible for having their students and monitors answer questionnaires prepared by the collaborative. These are distributed during the fifth and sixth weeks of the program. In addition to demographic and school information, the students' questionnaire asks about the orientation they received from their respective agencies, their experience with the jobs, and their supervision, career exposure, problems, help with problems, contacts with their monitors, extra work for extra pay, and future plans. Monitors are asked about the usefulness of the monitors' manual and training, the reasonableness of their case loads, their experiences with the youth, and their estimation of the success of the placements and the program as a whole. Both questionnaires call for all the vital profile data necessary to make comparisons among various subsets of the youth without having to use names, so the questionnaire responses can be anonymous; the forms say: "Please do not give your name."

According to the evaluation report for the year, ninety percent of the 1,644 students who went on to complete the program in 1990 and 91 percent of the monitors responded to the questionnaires (Foundation Collaborative, 1990). Cox attributes the high response rates to good organizing: "The agencies understand that the evaluation is a critical component of the project. They get the questionnaires out to field staff on time, and field staff give them to monitors who do their own questionnaires right away and hand the participant questionnaires to the youth they are responsible for. I think most of them usually wait right there to get the questionnaires back."

Representatives from the collaborating foundations and companies, accompanied by the program intern, conduct interviews with employers and students towards the end of the six weeks. In 1990, they visited 165 work sites and talked with roughly that number of employers and youth. A form is used so the results can be compiled. It calls for information from the employer about the job, student performance, interaction with supervisors and other employees, whether the student will be hired after the six weeks, and so forth. Information from the youngsters in these interviews includes their perceptions about the quality of the experience and its relevance to their career ideas, their attitudes about work, and what their friends are doing during the summer.

The different parts of the evaluation reinforce each other on some important points. For instance, as noted earlier, the agency statistics indicated that 84 percent of the students in 1990 got extra pay for extra hours. A 77 percent finding on the same point in the student questionnaire confirmed the figure accurately enough, considering differences in interpretation. The answers to the questionnaire also revealed that half of the remaining students chose not to work extra hours.

Other valuable combinations of findings link quantitative and qualitative information. The statistics generated from the reports and questionnaires tell a great deal about how the participants are doing, but as Cox says, "It's the interviews with the youth themselves that show us how well they can articulate the applicability of what they have been doing. That's when we find out they are mature enough to grasp the idea that what they learn about working and about the people they meet is going to be useful later on."

Evaluation Findings as a Management Tool

Cox and other members of the collaborative work with the program intern on the yearly preparation of the evaluation report and its recommendations. A draft is circulated in early fall among all the members, and it is discussed at a meeting before the final version is released. Then the final version is used as the basis for discussing the program at an annual meeting with the agencies in December, and it is also the central reference for a spring meeting organizing the coming summer's program. Funders and agencies, both, are truly stakeholders in the evaluation, as well as in the program itself; there is a real feeling of ownership, and the evaluation findings are taken seriously.

Disseminating Information

Copies of the report are sent to key people in the area who are involved with youth employment and to a few others out of town. In 1987, the William Penn Foundation published a booklet (Foundation Collaborative, 1990) on the program's first five years. That booklet's wide distribution among foundations and others, plus an article or two and word of mouth, continue to bring in a few requests every year for the annual evaluation report. Recognizing that these requests often are from people considering similar programs and evaluations, Cox does something few of the other foundations and agencies in this set of case studies have done when responding. He includes copies of the questionnaires and report forms, as well as a copy of the RFP, in the appendix to the report. These show the contexts in which people have given their answers to questions. The 1990 report also included a three-page summary of the "theoretical and research background," which was based on the evaluation of the government program that provided the "philosophical and operational framework" for the Philadelphia plan.

The Program-Evaluation Improvement Cycle

There are many examples of evaluation feedback leading to important program improvements. For example, attrition rates — percentages of participants not completing the six weeks — were increasing in the mid 1980s. The annual evaluation reports showed a good deal about when and why this was happening. They also showed that youth paid attention to good monitors. Up until 1988, there had been no formal manual for monitors; with this indication of the importance of quality monitor work, a committee of collaborative members and agency people designed the current manual and a suggested monitor training program for agencies to use. In preparation for the 1989 program, virtually all of the participating agencies established formal monitor training based on the manual. The attrition rate went down, from 18.5 percent in 1988 to 13.9 percent in 1989 and to 13 percent in 1990. When asked in the questionnaires after the 1989 program who had been most effective in helping them stay on the job, students gave their "parents and other relatives" the highest ranking, with the monitors a close second. In 1990, parents and relatives were still a very useful source of help, but monitors had increased their ranking past them, as well as past the four other possible sources of assistance listed in the questionnaire.

Such is the cycle of program activity, evaluation findings, program improvement, and measurement through the next year's evaluation of whether the improvement worked. This process continued in 1990. To get further specific standards for the monitors' activities, the collaborative added some appropriate questions to the students' questionnaire. They were asked how often their monitors had met with them, and how much time they had spent talking to the monitors about the jobs they were experiencing. Answers were cross-tabulated with other answers about how the students were doing, including their problems on the job, whether they had considered quitting, and how helpful their monitors had been. The comparisons showed that those youth who had been able to talk about their jobs with their monitors for at least fifteen minutes twice a week were more likely than others to be doing well and crediting their monitors with being helpful. From these findings came recommendations for 1991 that have led to specific norms for how much time monitors should spend with youth assigned to them.

Another example of program improvement involves the discovery in one of the early years' evaluations that some employers were paying the students to work extra hours. Employers were doing this on their own; it was not part of the program plan. The collaborative and the agencies were impressed with this development as an unexpectedly strong feature of the experience the program could offer to youth. Since then, objectives of extra time and continued employment beyond six weeks have been built into the program design as essential components, tested every year in the annual evaluation.

A current example of important evaluation feedback concerns a gender gap. In the early years, evaluation reports showed slightly more young men in the program than young women. That proportion has changed, and the change has accelerated in the past two years. In 1990, 63.4 percent of the participants were young women. New strategies have been discussed, and shared among the agencies, to try to keep this gender gap from increasing further. For the future a watchful eye is also being kept on the age mix of the youth. The collaborative wants the program to take more tenth graders and fewer juniors and se-

niors especially when they already have had job experience. "This
program should be particularly for the students who haven't had
real jobs before," explains Bill Parshall of the Hunt Foundation, "the ones who are up against the old catch-twenty-two that
says you have to have experience to get a job but you need a
job to get experience." The evaluation reports help him and the
rest of the collaborative work on this issue. Participants' ages
and grades in school can be related to information on job interests and job experiences.

Just as gender and age analyses now inform the planning
processes, there are new categories of information that may be
necessary to aid future attention to particular groups. Gerson
Green of the Settlement Federation gives the example of youth
with criminal or juvenile court records. It is not known which
or how many participants in the program have been in trouble
with the law in various ways. If this information could be added to the evaluation and compared with data about performance
in the program, Green suspects it might lead to some useful new
arrangements for youth with records, who normally have special difficulties in getting job experience.

The recommendations in each annual evaluation report
tend to be implemented before the next summer's program. The
principal recommendation in 1989 was that there should be a
mandatory one-day workshop for "the individual from each operations site who is directly responsible for the program." It had
become evident from personal contacts that top agency management were increasingly delegating oversight responsibilities
to new people who didn't necessarily have an appreciation for
the features that had established this program's high quality and
who were placing too much emphasis on the gross numbers of
people served. The first such workshop was held in May 1990
at a corporate retreat center, and a whole new generation of
project directors were brought into the high standards and career
development culture of the program.

The annual evaluation yields many different insights that
are of varying interest to different people. To Dick Cox, "the
most exciting thing" about recent years' evaluations has been
youth's change in attitude about the meaning of the program.

When they are asked before the program begins why the opportunity is important to them, the most frequent reply is "earning money." After the experience, the incidence of that acceptable but limited answer is cut in half and other responses about new skills, career ideas, and personal success move up proportionately. The program itself works well because of attention to detail, and the evaluation findings tell the collaborative and the agencies how those details work out every summer.

All the findings are available in agency-by-agency breakdowns. Each year, the collaborative gives each agency the major findings about its own performance alongside the data for the whole program. Agency performance that does not measure up to the standards set forth in the RFP is called to the agency's attention. On the whole, however, the collaborative and the agencies try to establish some distance between the evaluation and the consideration of proposals. The annual evaluation is of so much value in other ways, it would be unfortunate to undermine its usefulness by letting it become primarily a tool for "fund or don't fund" decisions. The funders are close enough to the agencies to be able to consider proposals on a broader basis, using the evaluation results as only one component.

Evaluation Consequences

The annual evaluations have had a considerable impact on the youthwork field in Philadelphia. The Philadelphia Urban Coalition is one of the grantee agencies for this program. It also runs other youthwork activities, especially a major summer employment program sponsored by the Private Industry Council and strongly supported by city hall. Ernest Jones, executive director of the coalition, readily acknowledges that this and other programs have been modeled after the Career/Vocational Exploration Program — not necessarily doing everything the same way but certainly showing signs of constructive influence. He says: "It was the evaluation reports that gave us the set of ideas we could pick up and use."

In a program organized and funded by a collaborative, evaluation has a special importance. Cox is particularly sensitive to this fact. He says that the evaluation gives a high degree of reassurance to the foundations and corporations putting up the money: "It is no good to have people coming into the collaborative assuming that the program must be okay because the William Penn Foundation gives it a million dollars a year. Any hint of that is an insult to everyone and too much trust. Instead, this evaluation component gives each of us the facts, and each of us can come to our own conclusions. That builds confidence and ownership among the funders."

The Hunt Foundation's Bill Parshall observes that "the collaborative is a process that people have come to accept, which is remarkable in Philadelphia where no other cooperative arrangement like this has worked so well or so long. With corporate contribution programs, despite the way we all make separate grants in this program, you are asking donors to give up some individual advantages, including public relations, when you propose a collaborative model instead of everybody being entirely on their own. So you have to prove that the companies are getting something else for their money — more program effectiveness — and that's what this evaluation helps accomplish."

The collaborative uses the offices of the Delaware Valley Grantmakers Association as the address for the RFP responses and for meetings to review the proposals. Alexandra Fogel, executive director of the association, reports that "the program and its evaluation have helped stimulate other collaborative projects. When people see impressive factual information about a program being run like this, and realize that these funders actually get this done without biting each other's heads off, they begin to decide that there can really be a productive level of trust in working together."

Evaluation Cost

Dick Cox says he can't even estimate a total cost for the evaluation because so much of the work comes from in-kind contributions from William Penn, the other members of the collaborative, and the agencies. Direct costs of the intern's time spent on the evaluation, the intern's expenses, and the expense of having the questionnaires tabulated came to $6,050 in 1990.

Evaluation Strengths and Weaknesses

The evaluation monitors the program well, feeds back performance information promptly, and stimulates creative thinking about improvements among grantors and grantees, year after year. There is a richness that comes to an evaluation when it looks at change over time. It can contribute significantly to both stability and progress. The whole culture of a program, its values and details, are not locked up in somebody's head but are laid out annually in a process in which everyone participates. This is a fine example of continuous formative evaluation having a compounding influence on the quality of a program.

Yet each year it is also a summative evaluation, giving each of the members of the collaborative, the agencies, prospective new funders and agencies, and others in the community the information they need in order to judge the program's merits.

The evaluation looks at the program from several perspectives and with different methods. Quantitative and qualitative data complement one another and give each other depth and breadth. The results provide what Cox calls "a multifaceted review," yielding "cross checks." Such multiple views build credibility.

The evaluation goes to the level of the youth themselves; it provides firsthand information about their experience in the program and what it has or has not done for them. The student questionnaire and on-site interviews are key components of the evaluation design. Evaluations in which the consumers of the program being evaluated are primary sources of judgmental information about the quality of the program are refreshing to grantmakers.

The program is a demanding one, and the people who make it work have hard jobs. However, they are generally successful, and the evaluation shows them so, every year. "We need all the positive reinforcement we can get around here," says Gerson Green, "and the evaluation findings give us some."

In a field he knew was full of experiences to learn from, Dick Cox looked for helpful models and found them. He made good use of previous evaluation research about employment opportunities for youth, and he is adding to that body of knowledge.

When compared with most summer job programs, this one has an exceptional evaluation component. But leadership imposes new standards, and there is always good reason to consider improvements, even in exceptional evaluation projects. In this case, funding support from the most immediate sources is leveling off — there are limits in funding even for programs as impressive as this one. On the demand side, there are thousands more youth each year who could qualify for the program. Yet as stipend costs keep rising to match minimum-wage levels, the same total dollar investment helps fewer youngsters. To let this program realize its own potential by helping Philadelphia youth realize theirs, present funders and agencies realize that new private, and perhaps public, sources of support have to be cultivated. New arrangements — such as employers paying for part of the basic twenty hours as well as the extra hours — have to be considered.

The evaluation becomes essential to the processes of planning and persuasion that are involved in working on these possibilities, and it needs to be increasingly effective and fine-tuned, just like the program itself. For instance, the present evaluation makes no effort to measure any benefits or influences that affect the students beyond the short summer job period. The collaborative has been told by research experts that a six-week summer program for teenagers just isn't a momentous enough event in their lives to show up convincingly as a determinant in a multiyear longitudinal study, but that shouldn't dissuade the collaborative from at least following the students through high school graduation.

Some questions the evaluation could tackle are: Among tenth graders, what happens the next summer? How many of what kind of participants go back to work for their program employers after school or after graduation? How many go to work at some other place where there is a discernable link to the program experience? How many get completely different jobs because the program experience with one type of employment convinced them it was not right for them? How many go on to college or other post–high school training with goals in mind that were clarified by this work experience? What is the high-school drop-out rate for youth who have participated in this program? Such information, sometimes set against findings about a comparison group, would seem to be a good next step in assessing the value of the program.

At the moment, the evaluation has no systematic way to collect data for articulate narratives and anecdotes about the specific experiences of individual youth or small groups of them at particular job sites or agencies, either as case studies or as more modest accounts of their experiences. Several of those active in the program's administration—probably everybody if you had a chance to ask them—have impressive descriptions of times when this program has shown not only a beneficial impact for a specific youngster but also the start of a significant relationship between employer and employee that may have positive repercussions in a community. Ernie Jones of the Urban Coalition talks about the placement of African-American youth in Korean-run shops in black neighborhoods. Good relationships develop where there had been prohibitive interracial distance before, and these experiences have led to new patterns in employment generally. Among other things, says Jones, "That whole process helps respond to the African-American community attitude that says, Why don't we ever see any of our kind working in those places?"

There are many reports of employers becoming mentors, taking youth on trips, giving them unusual responsibility, helping them with longer-term job or education plans, and helping them with personal problems, as well as, of course, offering them permanent jobs. Close relationships have developed, often in spite of negative racial stereotypes on both sides. Cox values several on-the-job experiences in this program where traditional gender roles have been reversed. Young women have done well in jobs usually held by men, young men have done well in jobs usually held by women, and old workplace habits have been affected.

People also tell anecdotes about just plain employment successes. Many of these show the benefits of placements in small companies and small professional offices—dentists, doctors, lawyers, architects—which have become the vast majority of job sites. Youth are exposed to all the different parts and issues of a business, they often get a chance to work at a higher level than anyone would have predicted beforehand, and they gain recognition when they do it well.

Though the informal reports concentrate more on the positive experiences, there are failures and disappointments to learn from too. In 1991, Green distributed to his fourteen member agencies that participate in the program a form on which he is asking for at least clues to notable experiences, good or bad. The resulting narratives, if written or filmed with sensitivity and telling detail, could become just as important a part of this evaluation activity as the performance numbers. Some say more so.

Finally, the importance of the data deserves some refinements in the collection. For instance, the participating agencies normally select the work sites where employers and students are interviewed, and the agencies are likely to choose successful sites and successful youth at those sites. Cox and Parshall say they get around this partly by insisting that they be taken to visit different employers each year, but something closer to a true sample would make the visits more productive.

10

A Collaboration of Program and Research
on a Crucial Social Issue:
Evaluating the Gautreaux Program

Site:	Chicago metropolitan area.
Date:	1981–.
Underlying program:	Demonstration and advocacy program to enable minority inner-city public housing families to find better housing and living conditions, in nonracially impacted communities.
Evaluation purpose:	To determine what happens to the families, and make that information available for public policy consideration locally and nationally.
Evaluation initiators:	Leadership Council for Metropolitan Open Communities; Business and Professional People for the Public Interest (both of Chicago), and the researchers.
Stakeholders:	Same.
Evaluators:	Outside evaluators Leonard S. Rubinowitz and James E. Rosenbaum,

Evaluators, Cont'd.:   faculty connected with the Center for Urban Affairs and Policy Research at Northwestern University, with graduate, undergraduate, and former students.

Information sources: Families in the program.

Evaluation methods: Personal and telephone interviews, mail questionnaires, comparisons with control groups, and a longitudinal study with comparisons among three panels. (Exemplifies impact or outcome evaluation.)

Evaluation cost: $561,000 for a series of five studies.

Paid by: Spencer, Mott, and Ford Foundations, after initial planning grants from the Taconic and Wieboldt foundations.

Program cost: $470,000 in 1990, exclusive of rent subsidies.

Sources of program funds: U.S. Department of Housing and Urban Development and the Illinois Housing Development Authority, for specific Gautreaux program costs. General operating support for the agencies and the university center comes from a wide variety of foundations, corporate giving programs, and other institutional and individual donors.

Reports: Published reports and news releases from the university center.

The Program to Be Evaluated

Low-income single-parent African-American families from seg-
regated inner-city housing can succeed in largely white suburbs
when they are given counseling and housing assistance. Children can cope with suburban schools, and more of their mothers
can and do find jobs — better jobs — than they would have back
in the city. It isn't easy; there are obstacles and hard times, but
families are making it and glad they moved.

These are the findings of a series of studies of a program
initiated by private nonprofit organizations in the Chicago metropolitan area. The studies have enabled the program to become
an influential laboratory for researching at least one aspect of
a basic social issue of our time. Funding for the ongoing work
of the organizations and for the evaluations has come from foundations and corporate giving programs. Funding for the rent
assistance to the families and the administration of this program
comes from the U.S. Department of Housing and Urban Development (HUD). HUD is carrying out the requirements of
court decisions that would not have happened without the legal
activity of a nonprofit agency funded by the private sector. The
program is a remarkable example of sound, constructive, collaborative work by nonprofits addressing fundamental public
problems. Evaluative research is playing an important role in
testing the program's impact.

Three very different nonprofit organizations have worked
closely together: the Leadership Council for Metropolitan Open
Communities, a Chicago fair housing agency determined to break
down racial barriers; Business and Professional People for the
Public Interest (BPI), a Chicago public interest law firm; and
the Center for Urban Affairs and Policy Research at Northwestern University. In 1966, Alexander Polikoff, who was soon
to become executive director of BPI, began serving as general
counsel to a group of Chicago public housing residents and applicants. Their class action suit in federal court charged that
HUD, as well as the Chicago Housing Authority, was responsible for the racial discrimination in site selection and tenant

placement that restricted housing opportunities for eligible African-American families. As the litigation moved to the U.S. Supreme Court, it became well-known as the *Gautreaux* case, named for Dorothy Gautreaux, the first-named plaintiff. The plaintiffs prevailed against the housing authority in 1969 and against HUD in 1971. In 1976, after several years of further litigation concerning the relief to be given, the Supreme Court ruled that the remedies need not be confined to Chicago but could embrace the entire metropolitan area in which HUD operates its housing programs.

As part of the settlement, HUD and Polikoff agreed to adopt the remedial strategies of a demonstration program just getting underway under the auspices of the Illinois Housing Development Authority (IHDA). Under a much-expanded program based on IHDA's approach, *Gautreaux* plaintiff families would be enabled to secure housing in the private market throughout the metropolitan area. The Leadership Council for Metropolitan Open Communities — founded in 1966 in response to Martin Luther King's campaign for open housing in Chicago — was asked by BPI, IHDA, and HUD to administer the Gautreaux program. It began doing so in 1976 and recently served its four thousandth family in that program.

Program participants pay 30 percent of their income for rent. The balance comes from HUD Section 8 subsidies. The program cost of developing housing opportunities and placing the participants is largely a one-time expense of approximately $1,000 per family. Ninety-nine percent of the families are African-American, virtually all are from Chicago neighborhoods that are over 90 percent black; many are public housing families — tenants or former tenants, or from the public housing waiting list.

Slightly more than half of the Gautreaux family moves have been to qualifying suburban communities that are less than 30 percent black. (That was the criterion set by the court, but in actuality, almost all the families moving to the suburbs have gone to communities that are less than 10 percent black, and the average is less than 5 percent.) Well over 100 communities in the six-county area have been included in the suburban part of the program. The remaining families have moved to largely African-American neighborhoods in Chicago itself. The Section 8 support for both groups is the same, and there is little difference between the families. The mechanics of the process through which families are offered Section 8 rental opportunities make selection between city and suburbs effectively random.

Program Evaluators

In the early 1970s, when the *Gautreaux* litigation was still in its formative stages, Alexander Polikoff of BPI felt strongly that housing mobility made possible by *Gautreaux* was an experience that needed and deserved research, and that findings from such research would strengthen his case for a metropolitanwide remedy for the problem. He helped arrange a position at Northwestern University's Center for Urban Affairs and Policy Research for Leonard S. Rubinowitz, then at the midwest regional office of HUD, now professor of law at Northwestern and member of the research faculty at the center. In 1977, Rubinowitz and the center conducted a modest study (funded by the Ford Foundation) of the first year of the Gautreaux program for the Leadership Council, and then helped the council do some in-house evaluating of the program. By this time, the program had grown in size and had important potential as a national model. A more ambitious analysis seemed a wise investment. The center, with Polikoff's help, approached the Spencer Foundation and received the first of a series of grants it would get from different sources for evaluative research about the effects of the Gautreaux program on the families it serves.

Rubinowitz has been codirector of the studies about the Gautreaux children. James E. Rosenbaum, professor of sociology, education, and social policy at Northwestern, and also a member of the research faculty at the center, has been the other codirector of these studies and director of the studies about the mothers in the Gautreaux program.

Program and Evaluation Funders

It would take many pages to give credit to all the private sector contributors who have made the Gautreaux program possible. Although HUD pays the rent assistance and the costs of finding housing and placing families, and IHDA pays for a supportive services component of the program, the Leadership Council relies on foundation and corporate funds for its basic operations and several parts of its overall program that support Gautreaux activity. The Chicago Community Trust has made a rare exception to its practice of limiting year-after-year support; it has made grants totaling $2,334,000 in general operating support since the council's inception. Other prime contributors to the council have been the Joyce Foundation, Continental Illinois Foundation, First National Bank of Chicago, Commonwealth Edison Company, and Inland Steel-Ryerson Foundation. BPI is supported by foundations, law firms, individuals, and corporate giving programs. It has received support earmarked for its Gautreaux work from the Taconic Foundation, Amoco Foundation, Continental Illinois Foundation, and Borg Warner Foundation. The Center for Urban Affairs and Policy Research plays an important interdisciplinary academic role at Northwestern, supported by that university's many institutional and individual donors. Specific funding for Rubinowitz's early work at the center came from the Taconic and Wieboldt foundations. Grants for the specific studies of the Gautreaux program described here have come from the Spencer, Mott, and Ford foundations.

The First Evaluation: The Children and Their Schools and Neighborhoods

The first evaluation study was conducted in 1981 and 1982. Called Low-Income Black Children in White Suburban Schools, it focused on how the children in the Gautreaux families were doing academically, socially, and emotionally in their new schools. Parents coming into the Gautreaux program had always emphasized their hopes for better schools as a prime reason for leaving their old homes and taking advantage of the program. It was important to find out if their hopes were being fulfilled.

Furthermore, it was a grand research opportunity. The report on the study cited three reasons why: the children and their families in the two groups — those moving to the suburbs and those staying in the city — were very much alike and lent themselves well to comparisons; few other studies have been able to look at how low-income minority children fare in suburban integration situations, because it has happened so rarely; and school integration in this case is a result of residential integration, rather than busing or other school-specific efforts. There was less of the highly charged emotional atmosphere that has made it so difficult to evaluate how children of different races would do if integrated settings were the norm. Furthermore, racial integration has not been a mandated requirement or goal of Section 8 assistance, and the administration of funds has not encouraged or effected changes in that direction. Therefore, Gautreaux was unusual as a federally funded housing program that encouraged racial integration, and this feature made it all the more attractive for research.

The fact that the program centered around housing suggested to the evaluators that the evaluation about schooling should encompass more than school experiences alone. Because the program was bringing the children out to live in communities that were very new and different for them, the total effects of that change needed to be the central focus of the study.

Evaluation Design

The evaluation was to use three complementary designs: a retrospective comparison based on the families' knowledge about their lives now versus their lives before; an experimental/control group comparison looking at the experiences of the suburban experimental group versus those of the city control group; and comparisons across different suburbs to identify characteristics that helped or hindered the move to the suburbs. In describing the value of the multiple designs, particularly the first two, the evaluation report says, "While each of these designs has inherent weaknesses, using both designs to study the same issues helped to overcome the weaknesses of each. The use of both designs permits our study to test most variables of interest in two different ways. Where both sets of analyses lead to the same finding, we may be more confident of our conclusion" (Rosenbaum, Rubinowitz, and Kulieke, 1986).

Data sources other than the family interviews were also used. For instance, school records, where available, were used to validate mothers' reports on their children's grades. Nineteen eighty U.S. Census reports were relied on to characterize the neighborhoods families were coming from and moving to.

Conceptual Model

Before the questions for the interviews could be framed, a conceptual model was established to identify the important considerations in each child's experience. Taking school outcomes as the bottom line of these considerations, the Northwestern team devised the model illustrated in Table 10.1. The cause-and-effect sequence of the model moves from left to right, from givens to consequences. The first column concerns the basic characteristics of each child and of the community he or she came from. The second column identifies at least some of the influential institutional factors in the new school and neighborhood. The third column brings the family into consideration, both as it is influenced by the factors in the first two columns and as it, in turn, has a bearing on the factors to follow. The fourth column lists some of the ways in which the child's social interactions outside the family will be influenced by the environment described in the previous columns, and will then influence further consequences. And the fifth column identifies the outcomes for each child's performance, attitudes, and behavior at school. Rosenbaum says: "This conceptual model helped us organize our thinking about the many factors affecting these children. Once we did this, we could invent the interview questions in a fairly systematic way. Without this preparation, you're just coming up with questions at random, in a way that is likely to miss a great deal."

Establishing the Set of Families to Interview

A search had to be made among the 700 Gautreaux families that had moved to the suburbs up to the time of the study to find those who were still in the suburbs and still in the program and also met other criteria. For example, a family had to have at least one child old enough to have been at school in the city before the move to the suburbs. Although the researchers had intended to develop a random sample of participants in the program, these limitations, plus considerable difficulties finding the families, caused the evaluation to end up being what the research report called "a nearly universal survey" of the families available. One hundred and thirteen suburban mothers were interviewed. The group as a whole matched as closely as possible the known characteristics of all Gautreaux families at the time. One child in each of the families was randomly selected from among his or her siblings for interviewing. For a variety of reasons, however, including resistance among the parents, only 61 children were interviewed.

There were 48 families in the control group of those who had also moved to Section 8 housing but within the city. To make the comparison more rigorous, the families selected for the control group were those who had moved to neighborhoods most like the premove neighborhoods of both the city and suburban groups.

Many characteristics of the two groups were compared to ensure their similarity. For example, 86 percent of the suburban group and 88 percent of the control group, were one-parent families (mothers). Seventy-five percent of the heads of families in the suburbs and 80 percent of them in the city were at least high school graduates. The children's mean ages and whether the children had attended Chicago public schools were also examined. In their report, Rosenbaum and Rubinowitz acknowledged that Gautreaux participants, whether in the city or the suburbs, were not entirely representative of all low-income inner-city families, especially in these early years of the program. The families were somewhat smaller, the women better educated and more frequently employed. However, the researchers asked that

Table 10.1. A Model of Social Processes Influencing School Outcomes.

Former Community Characteristics	Environmental Influences	Family	Social Interactions	Outcomes for Children
Racial composition	School	Mother's personal	Child's social interaction	Child's attitudes toward
Socioeconomic	Class size	characteristics	Number of friends	school
	Curriculum and extra-	Mother's fate control	Time alone	School attendance
Individual Characteristics	curricular activities	Mother's education	Time outside	Child absent from school
Age (present and at	Curriculum appropriate	Mother's expectations for	Social status	Stay away from school
time of move)	Academic standards	child	Interracial friendships	when not sick
Time since move	Extracurricular activities	Educational expectations	Peer influences	Child away from school
Sex	Teacher-related behaviors	for child	Types of peers	because afraid
	Teacher help	Occupational expectations	Influence of peers	School behavior
	Teacher treatment of child	for child		Amount of school trouble
	Special Education		*Socialization*	Achievement
	Amount		Child's self-esteem	Grades
	Perceived appropriateness		Child's fate control	Relative performance in
	School-parent			school work
	communications			Child's aspirations
	School provided informa-			Educational aspirations
	tion on subjects, progress,			Occupational aspirations
	and programs			
	School provides open house			

School environment
  School provides right
    type of environment
  School dangerous, day
  School dangerous, late

Neighborhood
  Neighbor interaction
    Contact and friendliness
      of neighbors
    Amount and kind of
      interaction
    Racial composition and
      number of friendly
      neighbors
  Safety
    Child/mother feeling of
      safety
    Perceived dangerous places
    Incidence of break-ins,
      robberies, attacks, or
      threats

Source: Rosenbaum, Rubinowitz, and Kulieke, 1986. Reprinted with permission.

such differences not be exaggerated, because there were still great
contrasts between the Gautreaux suburban families and their
new neighbors. "All the children" in the study, says the report,
"came from very low-income families, and most had lived all
their lives in predominately black, low-income city neighborhoods. . . . The move to a predominately white, middle-income
suburb represented a great many changes for these children."

The interviewers, present and former Northwestern graduate students, were African-American women, "to increase rapport with the respondents." Interviews averaged over two hours.
The suburban families were asked both the retrospective questions and those necessary for the suburban-city comparisons.
The city families were asked only about suburban-city comparisons. Nearly all the parents (well over 90% of whom were
mothers) permitted the interviews to be tape-recorded, and the
tapes were studied for both quantitative responses that could
easily be counted, totaled, and compared with others and responses that could be treated more qualitatively. "The senior
staff," says the report, "listened to all the tapes to find descriptive examples and counter-examples" relevant to the conceptual
model, and many examples were quoted in the report.

Evaluation Findings

The study report was organized to match the conceptual model
on which the interviews were based. As one might predict, there
were influences up and down as well as across the model's format. For instance, the environmental influences of class size and
special education turned out to be related. Both the retrospective survey among the suburban Gautreaux families and the
comparison between the suburban and city groups showed that
the children were in smaller classes in the suburban schools,
but they also showed that one reason for this was that Gautreaux
children in the suburbs were more likely to have been placed
in special education classes, including many children who had
not been in special classes before they moved. These classes tend
to be smaller than regular classes. The study examined how
much of the difference in class size was due to this reason and

also reported suburban parents' varying reactions to these special education placements. Some were accepting, others critical.

There were times when quantitative and qualitative findings didn't match. For instance, when the parents were asked specific questions about academic standards and how hard it was for their children to get passing grades, the quantitative data from their answers, in both the retrospective analysis and the suburb-city comparison, showed no significant difference between city and suburbs. Parents felt there was actually more homework assigned in the city schools.

On the other hand, the spontaneous comments of suburban Gautreaux parents often paid explicit tribute to the higher academic standards at the suburban schools. The report quotes such remarks as: "The level of everything is so much higher." "The school work is much harder." "There's always an assignment." "They don't accept any excuses like they do in the city." "I went up there and actually saw what the first-year kids were doing and I knew in my heart he couldn't do that." "They just have different standards."

In their first report, Rosenbaum and Rubinowitz attempted to reconcile these different findings, saying: "It is possible that the suburban schools demand higher levels of achievement in a way that is not significantly more difficult for the children and requires no more homework time than the city schools." They suggested several likely contributing factors, such as teachers working with students individually, less make-work, and ability groupings of various kinds. They also discussed the possibility that at least some of the Gautreaux children were experiencing a "subenvironment," which may have been less demanding than the regular (white) school environment their parents assumed they belonged to.

Such efforts to make sense of different indications from quantitative and qualitative data show clearly the value of having both kinds available. They play against one another and stimulate new insights.

There were several topics in this section of the conceptual model that dealt with environmental influences and allowed the interviews to examine race relations. Ninety-two percent of the suburban parents (again, almost all are mothers) said school teachers were generally treating their children the way the parents wanted them to. There were, however, even among this majority, reports of difficulties more often than not related to race. Some parents complained of willful discrimination. Others reflected on the role of familiarity, saying, for example, "The teachers [in the city] were more open with him and me, because there are more blacks there and I guess they understand each other."

Parents also had suspicions that school personnel had low expectations for their children. One parent reported, "When [my son] first got into school they had him in the lowest reading and math classes because they took for granted that he was a black child from the city and his reading scores had to be lower and his math scores had to be lower."

Several parts of the study dealt with the social relationships experienced by the Gautreaux families. Just a few findings can serve as examples.

- After the move to the suburbs, 44 percent of the children's friends were black, compared to 95 percent before the move.
- Among the group that had moved to the suburbs, however, there was no correlation between the *number* of friends they now had and the number they had had in the city. Children with the most friends before the move often had average or less than average numbers of friends after the move, and vice versa. The report examined some of the variables and possible implications of this finding.
- The types of peers children chose as friends in the suburbs were much the same as they chose in the city, according to the children's own answers in both the retrospective analysis and the suburban/city comparison.
- Parents indicated that suburban neighbors were less friendly overall than city neighbors. Furthermore, 36 percent of the suburban parents reported experiencing negative incidents ("where people treated you or a member of your family badly") during the first six months, compared with only 15 percent of those who stayed in the city.

- Yet in terms of interactions with neighbors for specific activities, there was more contact in the suburbs than in the city. Parents visited neighbors, talked on the phone with them, shared baby-sitting, ate at neighbors' homes and had neighbors over for lunch or dinner more often than in the city. By looking at these responses in relation to others, it was found that these interactions were largely with white neighbors, and that "several" neighbors were involved more often than not.

Such findings as these suggest the wealth of interrelated information available in these studies for painting an accurate overall picture of what happens to people in the program. As Rubinowitz says, "it's a patchwork quilt. You are never going to fit in all the patches where they belong, but there are enough of them to suggest what the whole thing looks like."

Following the conceptual model, the report also examined a variety of outcomes at school. On average, suburban Gautreaux children "liked school a lot," in contrast to their recollections of having "liked school a little" when they lived in the city. Attendance and absenteeism seemed about the same in city and suburbs, but the reasons for not going to school were very different. For instance, when correlation coefficients were computed between absenteeism and children's reports about whether they felt safe in their neighborhood, it was clear that perceived danger was a significant factor in deterring children from attending school in the city but not in the suburbs. In the suburbs, distance from school, lack of transportation, weather, academic and social difficulties at school, and other reasons were more important.

Grades in city and suburbs were surprisingly similar and to the extent grades are a convenient, if incomplete, ultimate indicator of how the Gautreaux children are coping with their radical move, this study indicated they were at the very least surviving the change.

The final chapter of the report looked at the third of the three designs in this study — the comparison of variations in outcomes among different suburbs. This was important to the evaluation because of the choices the Leadership Council makes in finding housing opportunities and recommending that Gautreaux participants take advantage of them. Once they were sure that the determination of which families would go to which communities was indeed carried out in a way that was close to random, Rosenbaum, Rubinowitz, and their team used regression analysis to test if differences among the suburbs might be responsible for the outcomes reported in the study.

Community socioeconomic status (SES) was seen as the principal community characteristic that might affect the lives of the Gautreaux families. The regression analysis determined that students' grades were best in the low and high SES communities and worst in the middle SES communities. Parents' expectations for their children, which were evidently influential on grades, tended to follow the same pattern. These findings coincided with the original premise of the analysis, which was that "low SES communities are supportive because of their closer social similarity to the program participants, and high SES communities have positive impact because of their greater resources, low teacher/student ratios, and racially tolerant attitudes." Middle SES communities may present none of these advantages. Although the report was clear that this premise needed to be empirically investigated, the report did draw the conclusion that the "program participants may receive the most educational benefits . . . by moving to either low or high SES suburbs," whereas middle SES suburbs are "places where these children's social integration and grades may be particularly problematic."

The Second Evaluation: Women in the Program — Their Satisfaction, Social Life, and Jobs

In the fall of 1988, James Rosenbaum directed a second study, this time concentrating on the experiences of the Gautreaux program women. This study was funded by the Mott Foundation. Rosenbaum and his researchers felt the important reasons for the study were to see how the program was working and whether it was producing useful new answers to old problems. Their report (Rosenbaum and Popkin, 1990) said:

Relations among people of different races and different classes remain a fundamental problem in American society. . . . The problems seem more intractable than they did decades ago. We have less sense of the definition of the problem than in that apparently simpler era — and consequently less agreement about the appropriate solutions, even in theory. We have an acute need for new workable alternatives . . . , and we especially need detailed analyses of the mechanics and consequences of programs embodying new alternatives.

Rarely do people of different races and classes live and work together in this country. As a result, there are few opportunities to discover what these experiences are like for the people involved. . . . The Gautreaux program has the distinctive feature of placing low-income blacks in middle-income white suburbs. No other housing assistance program of which we are aware has accomplished — or attempted — this sort of integration on so large a scale. . . .

While racial integration is a societal ideal, it may be costly to the individuals involved. Some research suggests that blacks do not desire to move to mostly white areas. . . . Some critics have argued that Gautreaux participants will be highly dissatisfied with their moves because of race and class discrimination. . . . These fears are plausible, but until now no information has existed to test them.

In 1988, Rosenbaum and his team had available to them over 2,000 dependable names and addresses of women currently participating in the program in both the suburbs and the city. They randomly selected 515 and mailed them questionnaires. A follow-up reminder was sent two weeks later to those who had not responded. There was a 67 percent response rate — 230 participants in the suburbs and 112 in the city.

To add a qualitative element, which could investigate questions in greater depth and test the accuracy of the questionnaire responses, in-person interviews were conducted with 95 other program participants, 52 in the suburbs and 43 in the city. These women were selected at random from those who had moved into Gautreaux housing in one of three years of the program — 1980, 1983, or 1986 — and who were still in the program. The refusal rate on interviews was less than 7 percent.

The Sample

Characteristics of both the questionnaire and interview respondents were analyzed and found to be reasonably representative of the women in the program. There was, as had been shown in the previous study, little difference between city and suburban participants. The report for this evaluation added a few more demographics: the women's average age was thirty-six, they had been in the program an average of almost six years, they had an average of two-and-a-half children, about 9 percent were married now, 43 percent had never married, about half were currently receiving Aid to Families with Dependent Children (AFDC), half of these were second-generation AFDC, and 22 percent had at least one disabled person in the household.

This report also calculated the possible impact of the Leadership Council's screening and placement processes on the representativeness of the Gautreaux families compared to public housing residents as a whole. This is an important exercise in evaluation work, although frequently not conducted. It is especially valuable in a case such as this, where the issue of the program's potential to be used elsewhere is so critical. Too often it is just assumed that the participants in the program — and in the evaluation — are representative of whatever group they supposedly come from, and that the report's readers can take that for granted. Specific attention to the degree to which those served and those evaluated represent the target population adds considerably to the credibility of the findings.

Rosenbaum and his team proposed that there were three

significant criteria in the Gautreaux selection process that could make all its participants less representative: the scarcity of large apartments, so that families with more than four children had a hard time being placed; the check on applicants' credit or rent records to see if they could and would engage responsibly in the shared-payment program; and the visits to applicants' homes (by appointment) to evaluate housekeeping habits. These criteria appeared to eliminate sequentially 5 percent, 13 percent, and 12 percent; this means that together they reduced the eligible pool by less than 30 percent. The researchers also discussed the self-selection process whereby public housing residents choose to apply or not to apply and determined that this self-selection would not add much more impact. They pointed out the diversity of the program participants and concluded: "Although the participants are not totally representative of the average housing project family, they probably represent a majority of project residents." Lastly, a separate comparison was made between Gautreaux families and a random sample of AFDC recipients in Chicago.

In all, the report gave anyone interested in replication a lot of data with which to characterize the program's constituency and come to some conclusions about whether or not it matched the relevant universe in Chicago, or anywhere else.

Evaluation Approaches

Like the study of the children, this one had two main evaluation approaches with which the researchers organized and interpreted the questionnaire and interview data: a retrospective comparison and an experimental/control group comparison in which the suburban women were the experimental group and the city women the control group. As the report said, those in the two groups were similar and both groups had improved their housing. The only major differentiation was that one group had moved to the suburbs while the other was still in the city in predominately African-American neighborhoods. Therefore, the city women could be considered a "no-change" control group, and comparisons between them and the experimental suburban group would help determine the effects of living in integrated settings in the suburbs.

Evaluation Findings

Three aspects of the Gautreaux participants' experiences were examined: satisfaction with their new communities, the extent to which they were becoming socially integrated into the communities, and their experience with employment.

Community Satisfaction

The evaluation identified comparative satisfactions among the suburban women — for example, more satisfaction than their city peers as far as schools and police services were concerned, less satisfaction with transportation and medical care because they no longer had a convenient public transportation system to depend on, and suburban medical resources were not serving Medicaid patients well. The evaluation's documentation of these program impact problems became valuable feedback for the Leadership Council in adjusting the program.

The questionnaire had asked women to rate community services on a scale from 1 to 5, where 1 was "very dissatisfied," and 5, "very satisfied." Transportation facilities, for instance, were rated 3.03 by the suburban women and 4.25 by the city women, a statistically significant difference.

In contrast, the interviews had open-ended questions about program satisfactions and dissatisfactions, which provided a chance for qualitative documentation. By and large, the women in both suburban and city groups believed their moves "had a generally positive effect on themselves and their families." Suburban women were more likely to speak of the benefits for their children — the schools and the general environment. They also talked a lot about the safety they felt now, compared to their lives in the city. On the other hand, over half of them mentioned incidents of racial harassment. Observations about the dangers faced in the city and the suburbs, often equal in stress but different in kind, were especially enlightening in this qualitative aspect of the research.

Social Integration

Both the quantitative and qualitative data of the study showed that, despite risks of racial harassment, the suburban women became part of their new communities as successfully as the city women. The evaluators concluded, "These findings suggest that Gautreaux participants receive enough acceptance from their new communities to prevent them from becoming socially isolated."

Employment

The most dramatic finding was about jobs. The Gautreaux program has had no employment component or any suggestion of a requirement that participants try to find jobs. It is a housing program. Yet by examining employment, this evaluation showed that the move to the suburbs was advantageous. The city and suburban groups began with very similar employment circumstances — just under two-thirds had been employed at some time before moving — though not necessarily immediately before. By the time of the survey, however, even including those who had moved in recent weeks and months, 63.8 percent of the suburban women were employed, versus only 50.9 percent of the city women. The difference is all the more impressive when one considers that for virtually all the suburban women the jobs had to be new ones, whereas for about a third of the city women who had been employed before, their jobs now were the same as those they had held before moving. Furthermore, when only those women who had not been previously employed are considered, those in the suburbs were 53 percent more likely than those in the city to become employed after their move.

The suburban women were also more enthusiastic about their jobs. Although their pay levels were not higher than the city women's, they were more likely to agree with statements saying that they now had a better job that gave them more advantageous job experience. "The results," said the report, "clearly show that suburban movers believe that the move has improved their labor market experiences while the city movers do not."

The report discussed the implications of this finding by noting that there are two conflicting ways of looking at the employment problems of the poor. First, the Culture of Poverty hypothesis says that there are "deeply ingrained habits" which prevent poor people from benefiting from any improved circumstances such as a new community with better job opportunities. Second, the Spatial Mismatch hypothesis proposes a structural explanation of poverty: people suffer because there is no geographic match between where they live and where the available jobs are. For this discussion, Rosenbaum and his researchers called upon a variety of scholarly references, quoting several and noting that Chicago was losing appropriate jobs, while the suburbs represented "a growing labor market with a strong demand for low-skilled workers." The women in the Gautreaux program were shown by this study to be willing and able to take advantage of those opportunities. Therefore these findings, by and large, supported the Spatial Mismatch hypothesis. As Rosenbaum wrote in the newsletter of the Center for Urban Affairs and Policy Research, "These findings imply that intensive relocation assistance should be an option that policy makers consider to help reduce the problem of long-term poverty."

The report also used the evaluation's interviews to document what the women had found out about employment in the suburbs: availability of jobs, safety both for themselves and for their children (who no longer needed to be watched and worried about so much), an environment that gave them stronger motivations to move ahead to better jobs, and the barriers they were finding as they tried to do so.

The report ended by noting again that the Gautreaux program had, up to that point, "provided no assistance or encouragement" about employment, and the report suggested that, based on the findings of this evaluation, Gautreaux or any similar program "that provided such support might produce even more encouraging results."

Additional Studies

The Center for Urban Affairs and Policy Research at Northwestern has three more Gautreaux studies underway. The first is engaged in reinterviewing the parents and children interviewed in the first study. As James Rosenbaum says, most of the children are now about twenty, "which means that we can examine whether the benefits of living in the suburbs held up over time. Further, we can learn about the kinds of choices these participants are making about higher education and careers." The Ford Foundation is funding this follow-up.

The second new investigation is a longitudinal study, also funded by the Ford Foundation. Three panels are being selected: 150 Gautreaux families in the suburbs and, as comparison groups, 150 families in Section 8 housing in Chicago and 150 families in Chicago public housing projects. Plans are to track these families over the next five to ten years, with major emphasis on school experiences and their consequences. The original study about Gautreaux children was limited in that it was a snapshot or a slice of life at a particular time. It could do little more than speculate, for instance, about the impact of suburban schools and the way they were handling Gautreaux students. These two new studies will provide information over time, which is of an entirely different nature than "snapshot" information.

The third new evaluation is a sequel to the women's study, to gain more information about employment. As mentioned, jobs were not initially a priority consideration in either the program or its evaluation, and the findings so far have stimulated as many questions as they answered. In the new study, telephone interviews will examine such issues as the nature of the suburban jobs the women are getting through the years, how they get them, how much they are paid, what the benefit programs are, and what the experiences have been with respect to promotions, job switches, and other aspects of employment. This study, like the original women's study, is funded by the Mott Foundation.

Consequences and Use as a Management Tool

When Kale Williams, executive director of the Leadership Council for Metropolitan Open Communities, is asked about the usefulness of the Northwestern urban center's evaluation studies, the first thing he talks about is "the management of the program."

From the beginning, the council has looked at findings and raw data from these evaluations to learn what needs to be done differently and what new issues or opportunities need to be attended to.

Examples of Evaluation Feedback

Early responses from participants, for example, showed many families were having problems using food stamps in suburban supermarkets not accustomed to serving food stamp customers. The chairman of the largest chain in the area, who was on the council's board of directors at the time, saw to it that company-wide practices of acceptance and courtesy were established immediately and were monitored. Findings such as this emphasized how frequently suburban ways were out of sync with the needs of Gautreaux families, and vice versa. Additional follow-up and supportive services were needed, and feedback from the evaluations documented these needs well enough to convince the Illinois Housing Development Authority and HUD to fund such services. "The studies," says Williams, "were instrumental in getting supportive services incorporated into the program." He adds, "Since then, we have used the experiences and attitudes reflected in the evaluation responses to help us refine these services. Along the way, we have shifted the emphasis from being a service provider to helping participants organize themselves to get what they need. As the program moves along, we want to help them get engaged in the life of their new communities rather than just try to pull strings for them."

Although the council had never perceived the Gautreaux program as having to do with employment, the dramatic findings about jobs in the second evaluation changed that. They showed how realistic the potential for employment is for the women in the program and how many of them place a high value on the prospects of getting a good job. Following the evaluation report's recommendations, referrals to job counselors have become a routine part of council services, and a new program integrating the development of job and housing opportunities is being established in conjunction with the Minority Information Referral Council. Williams reports that the research findings themselves are now used in meetings with women in the program, to show them how others have successfully taken advantage of job opportunities.

The evaluations underscored the troubles Gautreaux families have using Medicaid to get health care in the suburbs. In response, the council has worked with families in meetings with hospitals, clinics, and county health departments. Council staff have also published regional directories that list health-care resources and talked in group meetings about how to get satisfactory care, and Williams reports that the problem is "much resolved since the early days."

Council staff know a lot about Gautreaux families from personal contacts, but those are on a one-on-one basis, with different participants at different times and mostly about housing issues. The evaluation findings are broader in scope and more systematic in showing trends and tendencies across the whole group of participants. According to Williams, "Having this detailed and broad-reaching information helps us [on the council] confirm or dispute our own anecdotal observations, and it lets us put our work in a larger perspective."

Another useful consequence is that the evaluation process imposes the discipline of keeping track of participants' whereabouts.

Program Strategies and Dissemination

"The other set of uses for the evaluation studies," says Williams, "is in our strategies to convince policy makers that housing choice for poor people is a good and desirable thing, and that there is a way to make it happen." Some of this advocacy involves local activity. Williams describes how council staff use the findings in "the constant education job we have to do in communities." Evaluation reports are shared with landlords and prospective landlords, school and police officials, and mayors and others on local government and real estate. Says Williams, "We try to build a favorable view of affordable housing. The research shows we have a program that works."

Williams and others also use the findings when they speak at meetings of such organizations as the local chapter of the Institute of Real Estate Management and when they hold meetings with developers. Evaluation results are always reviewed in the council's newsletter, and summaries are submitted to other newsletters and local media.

Outside the Chicago area, the crucial impact of the evaluation studies has to be on HUD itself, in the effort to persuade that federal agency to support programs like Gautreaux nationally. After several years in which HUD had shown no interest in encouraging housing mobility and integration, the current administration has listened carefully to the Gautreaux story. A recent request took BPI's Alexander Polikoff, the council's Kale Williams and Northwestern's James Rosenbaum to Washington where, at the insistence of HUD policy analysts, the first half of a daylong meeting at HUD was devoted to the evaluation studies and their findings. "You never know when the time is going to be right," remarks Rosenbaum. "It just happens that now is a time when the Gautreaux type of program fits into the HUD agenda—especially with the consideration of employment as well as housing." Authoritative information such as he and the others were presenting is obviously not only persuasive among the policy analysts themselves. These analysts recognize it as the documentation they need to bring about the administrative and legislative action required to mount similar programs elsewhere. In 1992, President Bush signed legislation establishing Moving to Opportunity, a HUD national demonstration program based explicitly on Gautreaux.

The evaluations have also become important to the help Williams and Polikoff give to people in other cities working on housing reform through litigation or legislative or administrative channels. In Dallas, Cincinnati, Memphis, and other cities, reports about the program are proving to be of special interest to those involved in remedial stages of similar litigation. Gautreaux generates enthusiasm because, as Polikoff says, "The studies show it is a remedy that obviously works." Rosenbaum adds that public housing authorities across the country have asked about Gautreaux. Their housing is deteriorating; rehabilitation or replacement is tremendously expensive if desirable at all, and they are looking for alternative solutions. The evaluation studies show them that the Gautreaux program is a successful, credible model. Williams also reports interest from those in other cities who are examining school desegregation. He feels that the new longitudinal evaluation will be especially useful for those looking at such cross-jurisdictional metropolitan remedies as the Gautreaux program represents.

Extensive newspaper and television coverage of the program's evaluation studies has sometimes been the initial stimulus for calls from other cities. News releases about the findings from the first two major studies "have been events in themselves," according to Rosenbaum. The center's clipping file shows major articles and editorials in the *New York Times, Washington Post, Los Angeles Times, Miami Herald,* and several other newspapers, plus *Fortune, U.S. News and World Report,* and other magazines, and interviews on the "Today" show and the "MacNeil-Lehrer News Hour."

Student and Professional Education

This is another example of an evaluation project that benefits from being valuable to the evaluators. Rosenbaum brings graduate and undergraduate students into the research, increasingly involving them in analysis as well as interviewing. He says: "It is an especially unique and useful project for minority students, because it is research in a field with major social issues relevant to them. And, contrary to what a lot of urban research has to conclude today, Gautreaux is by and large a success story that excites people and leads to good ideas for them personally."

The studies are becoming significant references in professional and academic fields. The Gautreaux program and its evaluations have been the subject of several presentations to professional and academic groups, journal articles, and a chapter in the book *The Urban Underclass* (Petersen and Jencks, 1991). One book just about Gautreaux has been published—Alexander Polikoff's *Housing the Poor: The Case for Heroism* (1978), which was written with the help of a grant from the Twentieth Century Fund. Another, by Leonard Rubinowitz, James Rosenbaum, and their colleagues, is underway. Notes Rosenbaum: "Not too many years ago, it was unthinkable to consider low-income blacks moving to affluent white suburbs. Then metropolitan school integration projects came along, but they were all about busing and politics and racism at its worst. Gautreaux has given us the chance to look at what happens to people under more ordinary circumstances. It means we have been able to build on theories such as the Spacial Mismatch idea. . . . That's important not just from a scholarship point of view but to people who have to make policy decisions about the connections between people and housing and jobs."

Evaluation Costs

The costs of the two original evaluations were met with grants of $163,000 from the Spencer Foundation and $99,000 from the Mott Foundation. A repeat of the grant from Mott will pay for the follow-up to the women's study, and a $200,000 grant from the Ford Foundation is paying for the follow-up to the initial research about the children and the new longitudinal study. Grants specifically for evaluative research, therefore, total $561,000. There have also been some additional costs, primarily incurred by the Leadership Council in record keeping and helping the researchers gain access to the families.

The Leadership Council estimates that the cost of its Gautreaux program for 1991 will be $400,000 for assisting 400 new families to find housing, plus $70,000 to provide supportive services to a predicted 700 families. Overall considerations of the investment in these families need to include the HUD certificates given to them for rent assistance. Most of the 400 families in 1991 received five-year Section 8 existing-housing certificates worth $30,000 ($500 per month).

Evaluation Strengths and Weaknesses

This series of evaluations of the Gautreaux program's impact is a good example of research producing intelligence that becomes part of an active advocacy program, as well as a contribution to scholarship. The work at Northwestern

University's Center for Urban Affairs and Policy Research is independent research with a life of its own. The Leadership Council was certainly not the center's client, yet the connections between the research and the program are strong. The research gives good service in the two ways that demonstration programs require of evaluation: first, it feeds back information internally that shows whether the program is worth pursuing, and it suggests improvements, and second, it provides the core material for convincing outsiders of the program's merits and worth. It is difficult to think of the program's impact without considering the evaluations; without them, the work would certainly not have the strength internally or externally that it does have.

All that is easy to say, but there are traps and snares in this kind of situation that need to be recognized and dealt with. Leonard Rubinowitz speaks from the perspective of having been involved in building the relationships between BPI, the council, and the center, being active in the research, and now taking the lead in writing a book on Gautreaux. He recognizes the potential value of arrangements between nonprofit organizations and university research centers. As typified here, such arrangements can make it possible for university researchers to gain access to and investigate real-life events where something specific is happening to a given set of people. University teachers and students can become connected with efforts to improve the human condition. The nonprofit organizations, in turn, can get a great deal of accurate, independent feedback information and gain whatever validation of the program the research provides. Both types of institutions, very different from one another, are likely to benefit from the process.

All of this has ultimately worked out well in the case of the Gautreaux program. However, Rubinowitz has lived through some tensions and surprises along the way, and he has advice for nonprofit organizations and their funding sources. He especially suggests that they "read the warning labels" when looking at possible arrangements with university sources. One of the most important labels should emphasize that it is in the best interests of the nonprofits to see that the research effort "follows the rule of letting the chips fall where they may." Going contrary to conventional wisdom that might say researchers are eager to expose and be critical, Rubinowitz counts the ways he and his peers may be apt to emphasize successes and minimize failures: they are the desire to be with a winner — to be researching a success, the need to have something promising with which to raise money, the convenience of a successful program when trying to involve students, and the advantages of submitting positive rather than negative manuscripts for publication.

The leaders of an organization working in good faith want to learn as much of the truth about their programs as the research can provide. Findings that only count the hours that shine are worse than none at all. Rubinowitz says it behooves the organization to keep insisting on evaluation work that counts all the hours, rain or shine, in its dealings with research sources.

Much of the strength of the research work here is that it is by no means a one-time shot. Its ongoing nature, including a follow-up and a longitudinal study, assures that there will be an increasingly long view of what happens to Gautreaux families. Evaluative research can be a building block process. Everything doesn't have to be discovered all at once; instead, the new insights and uncertainties coming out of one research effort can frame the questions for the next.

Rosenbaum says he wouldn't be interested in the Gautreaux program as a research subject if it weren't obvious that those in charge of the program are in it for the long pull. It takes time to make something of the opportunity in terms of scholarship.

For the Leadership Council and BPI, the ongoing nature of the research means that a steady flow of findings are available, not only for internal use but outside as well. As was mentioned earlier in discussing the Cities in Schools program (Chapter Six), you try for years to get the right people's attention, and when the right moment comes you had better have information that is alive and well.

It is important that the ultimate constituents of Gautreaux — the families — are the major source of information. There are many evaluations where the people interviewed are not the clients or program participants but rather other people — professionals and other intermediaries and observers who may be watching the program. Often the concern is as much or more about what is happening to institutions as it is about what happens to people supposedly served. That is decidedly not true here; the program families are front and center, and that focus does much to establish the credibility of the findings. It is also what makes the program and the research so compatible. The researchers, as Rosenbaum says, "have been interested in what happens to the people in the program, from their points of view." While the program, as Williams says, "is good if it helps people who come through it. If that works, other developments will fall into place — like changing other people's attitudes and policies. If the program doesn't help people on their terms, any other achievements wouldn't be worth the candle. That's why this type of research is so important."

Polikoff and BPI have a similar view. As they all say, there is a natural coincidence of priorities. BPI and the council came from the vantage point of evaluation, with motives about internal and external uses. The research center came from the vantage point of scholarship, with ambitions to add to the body of knowledge about people coping with differences in race and class. There were negotiations about the specifics to be included in the studies and the processes to be used. But the shared focus on what happens to the ultimate constituents of the program gave the three organizations a common denominator of interest.

The program and the evaluative research are concerned with a major social issue of our time, which means they get a certain level of attention and respect that projects about less momentous topics miss. They get more value for their investment of time and money. Better faculty and students come forward and work harder; other people are more willing to cooperate; news releases get picked up and turned into lead stories and editorials; copies of reports reach people in high places.

The early developmental support from the Taconic and Wieboldt Foundations, the Spencer Foundation's grant which got the separate studies underway, and then the grants from the Mott and Ford Foundations, have certainly been an enabling strength of the work overall. They are a fine example of philanthropic support of important evaluative research.

There are impressive design elements. The combination of retrospective analysis and the city/suburban comparisons give a good check, one against the other. The use of multiple regressions to see which of many factors appear to influence different findings produces some of the clearest insights in the reports. The juxtaposition of quantitative and qualitative material presents stimulating comparisons, sometimes complementary, sometimes contrasting. The conceptual model for the children's study, and the calculation of how much the council's screening and placement processes might affect the representativeness of those surveyed are effective commonsense applications of good social science practice.

The way in which the qualitative information is presented does not always do justice to its potential. Particularly in the second study about women in the Gautreaux program, quotations are used to make a point rather than give representative samples of how respondents felt. An introductory comment to the qualitative results says that the material was gathered "to get a richer understanding" of what was going on, but the quotations that follow are all in close agreement with whatever topic they fall under. For instance, the comment, "Suburban movers were more likely to speak of the benefits for their children, particularly the improved schools," is followed by quotations that discuss only benefits. There are no examples of what some of the respondents might have felt about disadvantages.

Everyone writing evaluation reports has to make tough decisions that involve trade-offs. Handling quotations as documentation, fitting carefully selected quotes into the flow of the report wherever they can help make a point, produces a neat, unified presentation. And the quotations do add depth of meaning to the points they support. However, two qualities seem at times to get lost with this method: the realism that comes from communicating a variety of different views from different people, and the impression of the respondents as whole people. When a reader can take in generous chunks of quotations from and observations about people, he or she can begin to see and hear them as they really are. That is the value usually associated with qualitative material. When what the reader gets is mostly brief quotes supporting majority views on one topic at a time, the respondents are not really being allowed to speak.

It was also noticeable that when qualitative material was indeed presented for its own value, the researchers sometimes followed a policy of not quantifying any of their findings from it. The first evaluation report is full of locutions such as, "Some mothers said . . . ," "A few families have . . . ," and "A number of mothers indicated . . ." Especially when the topic is a crucial one, such vagueness about quantities doesn't give the qualitative findings the weight they probably deserve. It is tricky to count items learned in interviews that are substantially open-ended, but the effort needs to be made whenever possible to give the reader some insight into the true prevalence of a viewpoint or reported experience. Is it a fairly common theme, or an interesting exception?

The only ways in which these evaluation results have been reported are as the research reports from the center — which are fairly long, have a good many technical statistical references, and need more careful editing — and as summaries and news releases, which are very brief and simplified. Organizations involved in programs being researched and evaluated, and their funders, need to make some arrangements up front that will assure them of at least one well-written report in a format that meets their needs, and the anticipated cost of this report needs to be in the budget.

Nevertheless, the research center's reports are eloquent about the overriding value of researching the impact of such programs as Gautreaux: "These results should encourage those who hope to promote racial and economic integration in American society. It seems that middle-class communities can incorporate low-income black residents with reasonable success. Thus, implementing the Gautreaux model on a larger scale may help to reduce the problems of racial and economic barriers in housing."

11

A Model for Foundation Programs: The Kellogg Approach to Evaluating Clusters of Grants

Site:	National.
Date:	1988–.
Underlying program:	Various projects funded by the W. K. Kellogg Foundation, especially clusters of related projects.
Evaluation purpose:	To enhance the likelihood of individual project success, to assess the effectiveness of projects, to assist in determining whether a programming focus is having the desired effects, and to assess the extent to which foundation staff activities contribute to project and program success.
Evaluation initiators:	The foundation, in the case of cluster evaluations, and the grantees — encouraged and supported by the foundation — in the case of project evaluations.
Stakeholders:	The foundation and its grantees.

Evaluators:	Independent evaluators chosen by the foundation, in the case of cluster evaluations; grantees and the evaluators they may choose, in the case of project evaluations.
Information sources:	Vary widely.
Evaluation methods:	Vary widely, but predominately formative and qualitative.
Evaluation cost:	Varies widely. In the example described here, the cluster evaluation began with a contract for $270,000 over a four-year period.
Paid by:	The foundation.
Program cost:	The foundation's grants and operated program expenditures in the fiscal year ending August 31, 1991, totalled $151,000,000.
Source of program funds:	The foundation.
Reports:	Annual and other reports from grantees and cluster evaluators.

The Overall Design for Evaluation

There is a grand design for evaluation at the W. K. Kellogg Foundation. It began to take shape in 1988; it is still evolving and growing. The size of the foundation — it is one of the five biggest in the world — gives impressive scale to the work, but the design itself is also applicable to foundations much smaller. This case study will describe the model briefly and then look at it in practice in a specific example.

It needs to be said at the start that the style of Kellogg's evaluation program today is based on a sense of caution. The foundation is familiar with the skepticism its grantees and others in the nonprofit field feel about evaluation. Many of the foundation staff and trustees share such reservations. They have seen evaluation designs that impose severe constraints on programs, and evaluation practices in which little of a project's rich experience is properly appreciated. In commenting on these concerns, the foundation's *Program Evaluation Manual* (Kellogg, 1989) says: "Today this healthy skepticism coexists with an understanding of the considerable benefits of evaluation. The foundation increasingly has acknowledged the complexity of the problems that society faces and, therefore, recognizes that its initiatives should reflect this if they are to have an important impact. The renewed attention to evaluation by the foundation is, at least in part, a statement that evaluation need not interfere with doing important things and that a proactive orientation should be combined with a careful assessment of lessons learned" (Kellogg Foundation, 1989).

Kellogg has always seen itself as a foundation interested in making grants for action and service, rather than research. It prides itself on supportive, non-adversarial relationships with grantees and has resisted evaluation work that might jeopardize those relationships. Ronald Richards, Kellogg's first program director for evaluation, says the key question has always been, "How do we go about strengthening evaluation without changing the nature of the Kellogg Foundation?" The foundation's answers to that question are evident in the characteristics of the evaluation described here: the emphasis on formative evaluation, which primarily helps funded projects succeed; the distrust of comparative quantitative studies; the call for flexibility; the value placed on networking conferences that broadly benefit grantees; the decision for confidentiality within cluster evaluations; and other choices that have been made. All these traits are consistent with the foundation's conviction — based on the work of Daniel Stufflebeam (1984) — that the prime function of evaluation is to "improve rather than prove."

Evaluation Design for Individual Projects

From the beginning, Kellogg applicants and grantees are urged to take charge of whatever needs to be done to evaluate projects, whether they are going to do the work themselves or contract out to independent evaluation sources. Applicants are asked to include evaluation plans in proposals. Seven points of information are requested:

- Purpose of the evaluation
- Intended audiences for the evaluation
- "Important questions" involved in the proposed project that need to be answered by evaluation
- Methods that will be used to address the important questions
- Who is going to do the evaluation work
- How the evaluation will be reported and used
- What the evaluation budget will be

Program staff grantmakers work with applicants on their evaluation plans just as they do on the other parts of proposals. A Kellogg evaluation staff of two is available to help with respect to methodology, costs, the competence of possible outside evaluation sources, and other technical issues.

Important Questions

"Important questions" is a concept that pervades evaluation at Kellogg. Members of the staff work with prospective grantees to see that the questions are articulated so as to be on target and concise. Aiming for a process that stimulates more coherent proposals, Kellogg guidelines point out that the important questions need to be consistent with a project's stated goals and plan and with evaluation objectives. The guidelines add, however, that the evaluation process needs to be alert to the importance of looking for unexpected consequences and new insights. The important questions can change.

Three categories of important questions are called for: *Questions about context* concern the setting for a proposed project, who the constituencies are and their interests and needs, the position of the applicant in the field and the community, and other relevant external conditions. *Questions about implementation* deal with the activities of the project: what it is doing, what it is going to do, and what lessons are learned from these activities. *Questions about outcomes* focus on the nature of the project results and the impact of the project on people, institutions, and policies — short-term, long-term, intended, and unintended.

Evaluation Levels

When the time comes for the program staff to submit an appropriation recommendation to the board of trustees, the memorandum to the board has to include summaries of three of the seven points of information about the intended evaluation of the project: the important questions, the methods to be used, and who is going to do the evaluation work. In addition, the staff rate the evaluation plan's level of ambitiousness. The designations are Level 1, "extensive, complex evaluations employing sophisticated designs"; Level 2, "moderate"; Level 3, "modest"; and Level 4, simple "documentation . . . for purposes of accountability." Staff are asked to justify the level chosen for a project, stating why that level is especially appropriate for the type of activity and grant being considered. James Sanders, who became program director for evaluation in 1991, says that the "choice of level is related to how high the stakes are in the project." The level gets higher, he explains, "if the grant is going to be a major investment, if the project will have high visibility, if there are important policy implications, if it's a pioneering initiative starting from a low knowledge base, or if for some other reason we are looking forward to an extensive dissemination of the results."

When proposals become funded, project evaluation continues to be the responsibility of grantees, just like their responsibility for the projects themselves. The evaluation is theirs to manage and learn from first. Foundation program staff expect that annual progress reports will be based to a large extent on evaluation information, will deal with the important questions, and will talk about the progress of the evaluation as well as of the project itself.

Cluster Evaluations

Like many other foundations, Kellogg makes an increasing number of its grants in clusters, establishing a grantmaking program in a specific field and funding several different approaches. Project evaluation remains an essential ingredient, while cluster evaluation is its new and differently managed companion piece. Evaluation program staff take the lead in organizing a cluster evaluation.

Networking Conferences

The initial grantees involved — often added to later — are called together for a "networking conference," at which the chief task usually is to identify a set of important questions pertaining to the cluster as a whole. Cluster evaluations at Kellogg call for outside evaluators independent of both the foundation and its grantees. Customarily, one or more potential evaluators are invited to the conference with the cluster grantees, so they may observe the process and, it is hoped, submit proposals that will reflect the realities of the cluster, the similarities and dissimilarities among its members, the important questions to be addressed, and the way the foundation wants the cluster evaluation to be conducted.

Cluster Evaluators

Following the conference, a cluster evaluator is selected and a final plan and budget are developed and approved. At Kellogg, there is considerable variety in what a cluster evaluation can look like, depending on the characteristics of the cluster, its members, and their activity. A Kellogg memo that gives background information and guidelines about cluster evaluations for potential evaluators and others states: "One cluster evaluation may be more focused on process questions while another is attuned to documenting change. Still another may look at both intended and unintended outcomes and a fourth will consider ripple effects of project activities that extend beyond the targeted objectives."

No matter what the cluster evaluation's characteristics, the cluster evaluator begins by working with the grantees. As the cluster evaluation memo says, this is a mutually beneficial relationship: "Evaluation is not being done 'to' projects 'by' the evaluators, but rather each is helping the other as projects can call on the evaluators for assistance as well as provide data to them." The foundation's contract with the cluster evaluator usually calls for the evaluator to provide technical assistance to the grantees for their project evaluation. As the evaluator meets with grantees, the list of important questions is refined, and common threads of desired outcomes and strategies among the projects are identified. The cluster evaluator begins to organize material coming in from the projects and to supplement it with whatever is needed from additional sources.

It is at this point that the process can vary, depending on the evaluator and the projects. In one approach, the evaluator proposes to the cluster grantees a set of "working hypotheses" about what they may be learning. Sources for the hypotheses include grantees' project evaluations and progress reports, observations from site visits, interviews with project staff and participants, the cluster evaluator's own surveys, and discussions at subsequent meetings with the cluster grantees. The hypotheses are reviewed and refined by project and foundation staff and the cluster evaluator. Each hypothesis can then be tested over time across each applicable subset of cluster members.

The cluster evaluator feeds a great deal back to the foundation as formative evaluation data. Over the life of the cluster, the foundation also calls for summative information from the evaluator, to inform future decisions about programs. All this information, however, is "reported back to the foundation in aggregate," as the cluster evaluation guidelines say, without singling out the performances of individual grantees or projects. "The relationship between the projects and the external evaluators . . . is confidential. . . . This ensures an environment in which projects can be comfortable in sharing with the cluster evaluators the realities of the work they have undertaken — problems and frustrations as well as triumphs. It greatly increases the usefulness of evaluation findings."

Several other points of policy and procedure among the foundation staff, grantees, and cluster evaluator are made clear by the foundation's guidelines in its manual:

- Cluster evaluators are not representatives of the foundation's program staff. In their relationships with grantees, they are asked to stick to evaluation issues.
- The information gathered through the cluster evaluations is reported to the foundation. Subject to foundation approval, cluster evaluators are then encouraged to disseminate findings in any appropriate fashion.

- The primary emphasis is almost always on formative evaluation work. The first objective is to provide "systematic information that strengthens projects during their life cycle."
- Flexibility is encouraged: "Often evaluation plans will take an emergent approach, adapting and adjusting to the needs of an evolving project."
- The chief purpose of the conferences of cluster grantees is to "establish communication links among projects and with the foundation, [and] aid projects in thinking about their strategies in relationship to other projects [in the cluster]." All of these meetings — from the first one, which determines the important questions, through the periodic follow-ups — are called networking conferences. The foundation finds that the networking process — the exchanges, the broader perspectives, the bridges, the collaborative spirit — yields much that is for the good of the projects, the cluster, and the foundation's grantmaking programs. Formulating the evaluation becomes almost secondary to the larger value of getting the grantees together to share information about their experiences.
- Newly-funded projects are sometimes added to clusters as time goes by. This is a built-in inducement towards flexibility. Cluster evaluators are responsible for integrating new grantees into the cluster, working with them to fit their ambitions, intended outcomes, and important questions into the mix already at hand.
- Kellogg has particular interests in the cross-cluster considerations it calls "supporting strategies," which cut across many of its grants. "Leadership development" and "effective ways to inform policymakers" are current examples. Each cluster evaluator is expected to be aware of these strategies, to see that his or her cluster evaluation contributes whatever relevant information or action it can, and to work with the foundation and other evaluators to put many experiences together in order to develop more understanding about the issues involved in each strategy.
- In both project and cluster evaluations, the evaluation methods used are consistent with Kellogg's convictions about the values and potential dangers of evaluation practice. The

approaches are reflective and qualitative, affirming the work of grantees, nudging projects along. Quantitative studies full of judgmental statistical comparisons are rare. Sanders explains: "We don't see the need for experimental evaluation work, and quasi-experimental approaches are and will be few and far between. We are funding programs to be creative and evolutionary; it would be inappropriate to try to impose comparative field experiments."

Evaluation as a Management Tool

The formative emphasis in both project and cluster evaluations makes the work useful to grantees in the development of their projects. The discipline of systematically and continually asking good questions clarifies program objectives, informs planning, stimulates constructive changes in direction and practice, and works towards a sense of accomplishment. As a project moves ahead, evaluation begins to produce data about outcomes that serve the grantee well, not only in guiding the development of the project but also in whatever efforts it is making to influence others, such as the government, other agencies, institutions, and the public. Formative evaluation also contributes to what Kellogg calls the chances for "sustainment," because it provides the performance information that is essential for building on the best of a project's experience.

It is not just the project that needs to be sustained but also the habit of evaluation. Kellogg's emphasis on encouraging and enabling grantees to take full responsibility for quality evaluation activity is designed to make evaluation a permanent component of its grantees' programs. The *Program Evaluation Manual* says, "Foundation staff should seek to leave an organization stronger in its ability to use evaluation when Kellogg Foundation support ends."

The value of formative evaluation holds true for Kellogg, too, especially with respect to cluster evaluations. Clusters are frequently added to, changed, and merged as program staff, with the help of the evaluations, see other approaches that warrant attention or emerging patterns that call for new combinations.

As clusters of grants mature, cluster evaluations suggest certain additional steps that need to be taken—to affect public policy, for instance. New grants are added to the cluster, representing a move forward in the grantmaking program.

With respect to summative evaluation, Kellogg believes that "the opinions of program staff about projects they have guided through the grant cycle are one of the three data sources for the foundation's approach to program evaluation." The foundation thus places summative staff judgments about grant experience right alongside the formative data sources—project evaluation and cluster evaluation. At the end of a grant, staff opinions are recorded in "closing statements" that describe what was accomplished and what was learned. The project and cluster evaluations are primary sources for these statements, along with site visits and other staff initiatives. "The end result," as the evaluation manual concludes, "is better policymaking by staff and trustees, closing one programming loop but confidently starting another in the foundation's mission to improve the lives of people."

A Case in Point: Evaluation of
the Science Education Program

When the Science Education cluster was first established, in 1989, the grantees consisted of four of Michigan's "science colleges"—Albion, Alma, Hope, and Kalamazoo—together with three other projects—one at Central Michigan University, another a joint program of Lansing Community College and that city's Impression 5 Museum, and a third at the University of Michigan Biological Station at Pellston. The next year, four projects at local school systems in Battle Creek, Benton Harbor, Detroit, and Kalamazoo were added. Most recently, a project of the Michigan Department of Education has been joined to the cluster.

The Program

All twelve projects had been funded by the Kellogg Foundation under its Science Education grantmaking program to advance science learning among Michigan residents, especially school children. National data show low priorities for science in schools, uninspired curriculum development and teacher training in science, subsequent shortages of well-prepared scientists and engineers, and a general lack of scientific literacy throughout the country. In Kellogg's home state, "just 7 percent of Michigan's high school students appear equipped to handle college-level work in science," according to the foundation's announcement of the program. Women and minority students, particularly, "perform at levels which indicate that few of them will be able to successfully enter careers as scientists or as science educators."

Kellogg decided to place most of its grantmaking attention in this program on the upper elementary level, grades four to six. The primary focus was on meeting the needs of teachers and students in these classrooms and cultivating a new generation of teachers accomplished in science education.

The Evaluators

Looking for cluster evaluators whose interests and backgrounds could make them immediate assets to the cluster projects, Kellogg chose the Evaluation Center of Western Michigan University (WMU). James Sanders was associate director of the center at the time. He had been a chemistry major in college, had "spent his whole career in education," and at WMU, had been involved in evaluating science education programs for the National Science Foundation. Zoe A. Barley had just come from the University of Colorado to be chief of staff at the center. She too had been a science major in college and had taught science in elementary school early in her career. As the evaluation began, Mark Jenness joined the team as a graduate assistant, also with a background as a scientist and a science teacher. Kellogg and the center signed a four-year contract in the spring of 1989, soon enough after the first Science Education grants had been made so that the projects were still taking shape. The contract was for $270,000 for the four-year period, with some flexibility for unforeseen costs of extra work that might be agreed upon by the two parties.

When Sanders became evaluation director at the Kellogg Foundation in early 1991, Barley and Jenness took charge of the Science Education cluster evaluation. They worked closely with the grantees, becoming the third corner of the triangle formed for each cluster by the grantees, the foundation, and the cluster evaluators.

Kellogg believes the relationships formed by this triangle are the most crucial aspects of its evaluation program, and it chooses evaluators who will approach their assignments accordingly. Barley and Jenness talk about how they "visit the projects and show a willingness to work with them, learn with them, and adjust to change." Kellogg program staff had anticipated that the grantees in this cluster would need a good deal of help with their project evaluations, so the contract with the WMU center called for providing substantial technical assistance in evaluation.

Alongside this attention to individual projects, however, Barley and Jenness were to collaborate with foundation staff and grantees in building the cluster evaluation process, and in making the concept of being a part of a cluster a working reality among the grantees.

The Evaluation

Cluster evaluation practices vary widely, but the following descriptions of Barley and Jenness's second-year (1990–91) activities, adapted from their annual report to the foundation, give one example of what cluster evaluators for Kellogg do to earn their livings (Barley and Jenness, 1991).

Incorporating New Projects into the Cluster. It has already been mentioned that Kellogg adds new projects to clusters and expects cluster evaluators to help make that happen constructively. New projects were added to the Science Education cluster in the second year, and the fact that Barley and Jenness listed this activity first in their annual report for that year suggests the importance of the task and the time spent on it. They visited the four school systems and the Michigan Department of Education and worked with foundation program staff in getting these new grantees involved in the two networking conferences held during the second year.

The new grantees also needed assistance with their own project evaluations. One needed a whole new evaluation plan, two needed to find and hire evaluation personnel, and all needed help determining what should be included in their annual reports to the foundation.

In addition, as the evaluators' annual report says, "The nature of the five new projects [brought] new dimensions to the cluster." New "contextual and implementation data" were collected and related to what had come from the seven projects already in the cluster. A good deal of the evaluation's first year had been spent working with the seven original grantees to put together a list of sixteen outcomes common to their projects. These outcomes were statements of desired results, each one shared by at least two of the grantees. An example of these statements is: "To encourage interactions among teachers[,] to share learning from inservice experiences and to increase the effectiveness of 'lead' science teachers." Now, Barley and Jenness had to work with the five new grantees, first to match the new projects' intended outcomes with whichever of the sixteen original common cluster outcomes were pertinent and then to identify the new outcomes brought by the new projects. The three new outcomes identified by the new grantees also had to be discussed with the seven original grantees to see if they applied to their projects. Finally, the evaluators drew up a matrix with all nineteen common cluster outcomes down the side and all twelve projects across the top, showing which grantees were addressing which outcomes.

Obtaining Data on Context and Program Strategy from Each Grantee. The projects in the cluster used a variety of programs to serve diverse urban, suburban, and rural communities and their different constituencies. The cluster evaluators continued, in year two, to pull together data on these varying combinations, so that they and the grantees could begin to identify the strategies that seemed to work in many situations, others that worked better under certain conditions, and yet others that did not seem to work at all.

The implementation strategies of the respective grantees were then charted against each of the nineteen cluster outcomes, so that both the cluster evaluators and the grantees had a convenient visual key to who was doing what in order to achieve certain results.

Encouraging Networking and Strengthening Implementation of the Cluster Outcomes. Two networking conferences were held during this second year of the cluster evaluation, with much information exchange and sharing. Notable on the agenda, as far as the cluster evaluation itself was concerned, was a presentation by the seven first year's grantees reporting on the "lessons learned" so far. This list of thirty-five points took a step beyond articulation of cluster outcomes and implementation strategies by joining outcomes and strategies together in tentative conclusions about what seemed to be working. Some lessons were general and predictable but nevertheless essential: for example, "To affect science teaching positively in elementary schools, needs expressed by classroom teachers must be addressed." Others obviously came fresh from the projects' experience to date: for example, "Providing [college] scholarships to [high school] juniors and seniors committed to science education does not aid in recruiting freshmen into science education."

Barley and Jenness also organized two meetings of the project evaluators working for individual grantees, largely to look at the relationships between project and cluster evaluations. There was a need for more evaluation instruments in common, so that the experiences arising from different strategies used to address common goals could be looked at side by side. Moreover, these instruments had to be developed without jeopardizing the uniqueness of the projects and their evaluation designs.

Testing Working Hypotheses. During year two, Barley and Jenness and members of the Kellogg staff continued to carry out the foundation's important questions exercise, articulating what they saw at this stage as the most critical focal points for the cluster evaluation. Considering these questions in the context of the nineteen intended outcomes, Barley and Jenness used the approach mentioned earlier of generating a set of working hypotheses. Each of the nineteen cluster outcomes was to be given special attention in relation to at least one hypothesis and sometimes several. "Some [hypotheses] will eventually be rejected," Barley predicted. "Others will stay with us and become well substantiated as valuable conclusions of this program."

Reviews of project evaluations, together with the cluster evaluators' on-site observations of projects, began producing important data needed to test the hypotheses. Where necessary, Barley and Jenness also began initiating cross-project surveys. One such survey, for instance, was among teachers who had participated in the various in-service training programs produced by some of the grantees. A questionnaire asked them for detailed information about science education in their schools, their needs, their experiences to date with the Kellogg-funded project from which they had received training, and the impact of that experience so far.

On the strength of initial work in testing hypotheses, the cluster evaluators gave the foundation some "preliminary findings," in the form of tentative answers to the important questions. Finally, they offered several recommendations about the future of the Science Education initiative, particularly suggesting where program emphasis might be placed.

As a model, this full year of experience in about the middle of a Kellogg cluster evaluation may seem to have more than its share of lists and paperwork, but in practice there is a flow to the procedure that makes sense and minimizes the piling up of process data; one exercise leads to the next and the first can be left behind. When one talks with Barley and Jenness, it is evident that what is most important to them is their personal contacts with grantees, working with them on project and cluster evaluation tasks. Seeing that the evaluation process helps the projects thrive is obviously their first priority. The lists of desired outcomes, strategies, lessons learned, important questions, and working hypotheses are all useful tools along the way.

There is now another Science Education cluster, made up of five specific school districts to which Kellogg has made grants for special projects. Barley and Jenness are the evaluators for this cluster as well, and it has much the same flavor as the first one. The networking conferences have been especially productive, for everybody. Their fundamental value remains that of bringing people together. When the grantees were asked to rate the various aspects of the first conference, the part with the highest score was "sharing information about individual projects' objectives and activities." At the same time, however, the foundation was able to use the conferences to set the stage for the cluster's grants and strengthen its ties among its grantees. The cluster evaluators — this time appointed before the first conference — were able to use the conference to organize a first draft of the cluster outcomes list. James Sanders says: "If you approach cluster evaluation with the perspective that 'we are all in this together' — grantees, foundation and cluster evaluator — then you get a feeling of camaraderie. It's wonderful; in a meeting or two, you can build a sense of collaboration in a place where there had been none before."

That first conference of the new cluster also promoted cross-cluster sharing of information. Kellogg and the WMU Evaluation Center timed the networking conferences for the two science education clusters so they would overlap, and one afternoon was devoted to a joint meeting.

Evaluation Strengths and Weaknesses

With the first efforts in Kellogg's overall evaluation program still a year away from even initial conclusions, it is too early to pass many judgments about strengths and weaknesses. The observations that follow here, then, suggest some potential hazards in the plan — aspects of Kellogg's design where all involved are still working and living with unresolved questions and issues.

First, however, is an unqualified recognition of a major strength. The evaluation program is exemplary in matching its style to the foundation's convictions about what evaluation should and shouldn't be. Kellogg began its evaluation work with the firm belief that nonprofits have a good deal of skepticism about evaluation, a skepticism the leaders of the foundation shared. They weren't especially interested in research, so it was easy to choose up sides with those nonprofit organizations that saw much of evaluation practice as a burden that manipulates and constricts projects. Coming from that perspective, Kellogg promised from the beginning that the first and foremost purpose of evaluation would be to help their grantees succeed. One early paper about the foundation's evaluation program said: "It is, after all, not outcomes determining 'success' or 'failure' that the foundation seeks, but rather sound, useful information that can be fed back into project and program improvement."

Few evaluation programs show such cautious discipline. In a videotape (Kellogg, 1991) the foundation uses to explain its evaluation philosophy to grantees, staff, and anyone else that is interested, Dan Moore, vice president for program development, comments that he sometimes does not use the word "evaluation." He can be more faithful to what the foundation is trying to do, Moore says, if he talks about "clarity in programs and objectives" and the need to get projects more focused. He says he often asks a grantee on a visit, What's going to be different when I come back? In the same video, Tyrone Baines, a program director in education and youth grantmaking, explains how he avoids evaluation jargon, saying his job is not to mystify. He comments on the need to reassure grantees that "it's all right to change." He feels that what is important is to stay in close touch and keep asking, How's it going? Betty Risely, a consultant who has done a great deal of cluster evaluation work for Kellogg in the health field, talks in the video about how she has to build trust among grantees accustomed to strange and often unfriendly behavior from evaluators representing federal funding agencies. "When people from the foundation say to grantees, 'We want to help you' and 'You learn as much from your mistakes as you do from what you do right,' [the grantees] don't believe it, at first."

It is a very consistent message. Some sample feedback from grantees after networking conferences shows its impact: "Keep up the continued non-threatening approach to support. This is scary stuff and I'll need reinforcement"; and, "It's the most beneficial approach to evaluation I've experienced."

The desire for compatibility within the triangle of foundation, grantee, and cluster evaluator is so strong that some evaluation considerations may not get the attention they deserve. For instance, the competence of grantee personnel has to be a key factor in project performance, yet at least at this early date, the Kellogg evaluation approach doesn't provide much room for looking at personnel competence analytically. When a foundation is trying hard in an evaluation program to be supportive, criticism is difficult. When the foundation insists that the relationships between grantees and a cluster evaluator should be confidential, the evaluator has a difficult time including grantee competence factors in the assessment and reporting what is working and not working. It is not only negative judgments that may be underreported. Evaluator Mark Jenness cites the example of a project that works not so much because of any distinguishing strategy but "mostly because it's run by one or two great people. . . . We need to be able to identify what that means when we compare that project to others." That comparison is hard when the project evaluation process does not encourage candid attention to specific personalities.

Kellogg's Jim Sanders responds to this consideration by pointing out that insights about project performance come to the foundation from several sources. Project evaluators, when they feel independent, have been known to have reported personnel information, favorable or unfavorable. Site visits by foundation staff also yield information about personnel performance, reports from clients can signal performance problems, and the overall quality of project reports and other products is another performance indicator. "We don't miss getting information about project personnel," Sanders explains. "We just don't get it from the cluster evaluators."

Nevertheless, as time goes on, confidentiality may increasingly inhibit documentation. In these early stages of the program, the cluster evaluator's report on the Science Education cluster, for instance, can name names easily because the report concentrates on what types of objectives and activities each project is pursuing. There aren't many judgments to be made yet. However, even the preliminary findings and recommendations in the 1990–91 Science Education report to Kellogg might have been more convincing if the evaluators had felt free to cite examples. As time goes on, it will be increasingly important to document the data on which an evaluator's conclusion is based. At that point, precision will call for specific comparisons and contrasts, yet the promise of confidentiality may prevent those comparisons from being made. Science education evaluators Barley and Jenness and the foundation evaluation director Jim Sanders believe they and the grantees can find ways to overcome the problem.

Looking at the triangle of relationships again, it is inevitable that there will be tensions between, on one hand, the wish to let every grantee in a cluster enjoy autonomy in developing a unique project evaluation ideally suited to its project and, on the other hand, the need for some standardization, so that the cluster as a whole produces valuable information. Barley and Jenness again are confident that they and the grantees in their clusters can understand each other's needs and work to their mutual benefit.

Tensions will also be generated by the issue of whether cluster evaluators should get involved in questions about a grantee's program or stick strictly to evaluation, as the Kellogg guidelines prescribe. It all depends. Noninvolvement cannot be a rigid rule. When an experienced scientist and science teacher such as Mark Jenness is one of the evaluators for a science education cluster, it is difficult to imagine him staying aloof from program content. But he says he knows the limitations of his role in this respect, and he sees to it that he never takes the place of a foundation program staff member.

Kellogg's unwavering emphasis on evaluation methods that affirm and reflect rather than compare and contrast makes it sometimes seem as though only the successful aspects of projects will be evaluated. It raises open questions that can be answered only as experience evolves, and Kellogg's experience with its unusual disciplines should be enlightening. The foundation can play a major role in demonstrating the uses of evaluation work — especially in qualitative evaluation, which is probably the principal approach its noncompetitive emphasis is likely to require. In the nonprofit field, qualitative evaluation is often assumed to be much more informal and less expensive than quantitative, when in fact the opposite can be true. Accurate, in-depth observation and analysis over time, with a focus on qualitative changes in behavior and the significance of program activity in causing such changes, is a challenging task calling for high skills and many hours. Kellogg has the resources to explore the potentials and identify practical ways of realizing them.

W. K. Kellogg is remembered as being the first individual in modern philanthropy to say, "It's been much easier to make money than to spend it wisely," and then to apply that insight to the hard tasks of organizing an effective foundation. He also said early on, "I'll invest my money in people." The evaluation program being developed now, more than sixty years after he established the foundation, is designed to help the foundation spend wisely, and to do so in a way that enhances rather than jeopardizes its relationships with the people in whom it chooses to invest. It will be one of the most interesting initiatives in evaluation for grantees and grantmakers to watch over the next few years, to see how the evaluation program resolves its emerging issues and how it grows in usefulness to the foundation itself and to the important fields the foundation is choosing for its grantmaking.

CONCLUSION

Thirty-Five Keys
to Effective Evaluating

Robert Matthews Johnson

Good case studies raise important issues and ideas. Moreover, when a set of case studies focuses on one certain type of activity, such as evaluation, the case studies display common, recurring elements that are generalizable to other instances of that activity. Although the specifics of the nine cases presented here differ greatly, they nevertheless illustrate thirty-five recurring elements that are keys to effective evaluating. These keys are described in this chapter. To assist the reader, they are grouped into five categories: taking the first steps, engaging in good practices, finding evaluators and working with them, funding, and reporting and dissemination. Where appropriate, the keys are referenced to the cases upon which they are based.

Taking the First Steps

Key 1. Think of evaluation as a management tool that you and your grantees can use to obtain:

- Feedback to improve programs, stimulate good planning, and help you succeed in grantmaking. For example, the

Meyer and Lilly case studies illustrate how evaluation findings can be valuable in developing foundation policies and
practices; the Cities in Schools evaluation revealed what the
program could and could not do, which helped strategic planning; the Gautreaux studies identified special needs that are
now being attended to by the Leadership Council; and the
Technology for Literacy Project, Career/Vocational Exploration Program, and the Winthrop Rockefeller Foundation's
Arkansas public schools program — although very different
from each other — richly define how nonprofit organizations
can benefit from formative evaluation that occurs simultaneously with the programs.

- Essential information to use with outsiders — public policy
people, other agencies, other funders, media, and other constituencies. Cities in Schools and the agencies involved in
the Gautreaux program have made evaluation an indispensable part of their strategies to influence public policy. All
nine cases show that potential. The value of evaluation results
in raising funds for programs is especially clear in the Career/
Vocational Exploration Program and Cities in Schools cases.

Key 2. Develop in-house knowledge about evaluation.
A foundation does not necessarily have to conduct evaluations
in-house, but it needs to be able to establish evaluation arrangements appropriate to each case and then to know how to see
that evaluation results are put to good use. Foundations in the
Meyer, Lilly, Kellogg, Rockefeller, Technology for Literacy,
and Career/Vocational Exploration cases, especially, have developed their knowledge about the evaluation process to the point
where they have confidence in their abilities to work with evaluation and evaluators. Leaders at each foundation began their
education process modestly, by looking at the experiences of
others, reading a book or two (see Annotated Bibliography in
Resource B), and finding people who could help them get started
(see Keys 20 to 28).

**Key 3. Encourage grantees to develop their own abil-
ities to monitor their work and either evaluate it themselves or contract with outside evaluators.** Only then will they

begin to understand what they're doing and be able to capital-ize on that knowledge. The first step in the process is to per-suade grantees to install the good record keeping practices that are so essential to all evaluation. You will then want your grant-ees to find ways to make strong, ongoing evaluation activity a vigorous part of their leadership positions. Foundations have succeeded in encouraging these activities in the Cities in Schools, Rockefeller, and Kellogg programs, and in components of the Technology for Literacy and Career/Vocational Exploration programs.

Key 4. When you do take the initiative in evaluating a program you have funded, find ways to make the grantees partners in the process. Avoid "kill or continue" evaluations — one-on-one confrontations dominated by the issue of renewed funding. Where possible, evaluate a cluster of grants so your approach becomes more comprehensive. Step back and take a broader look at the field. Work with your grantee to make the evaluation belong to and benefit both of you. Start the evalua-tion process early, so grantees can benefit from the findings as they develop their programs. Also, separate the issue of future grantmaking decisions from the evaluation as much as possi-ble. Kellogg shows a special appreciation of its grantees' sensi-tivities on this score. As for the advantages of evaluating clusters, it is probably no accident that seven of the nine cases chosen here have some cluster characteristics.

Key 5. When deciding on which programs to evalu-ate, choose the ones that are really worth it. Consider the following criteria:

- The importance of the ideas involved
- Whether they are innovative
- Whether the programs might affect significant numbers of people — for better or worse
- How much talent and money are at stake
- Whether the evaluation itself has the potential to provide new intelligence

Each of the programs described in the case studies qualifies for evaluation based on at least three or four of these five criteria.

Key 6. Make sure that the people who can make the most use of the evaluation are involved as stakeholders in planning and carrying out the evaluation. In Rockefeller's public school program, school principals and teachers are looked to for leadership in improving education, and they are asked to invent the evaluation questions and be the evaluators. In Philadelphia's Career/Vocational Exploration Program, it has been the grantee agencies and the funders that have taken pride in making the program better and better based on annual evaluation results. In the Technology for Literacy Project, it was the Donor Advisory Board, the school system, and the literacy center itself who have both evaluated and applied the findings. The stakeholders are not just staff, but board members too.

Key 7. Do not be overly impressed with what has already been done or written in the evaluation profession. As the discerning reader of these case studies can attest, there is plenty of room for improvements and new approaches.

Engaging in Good Practices

Key 8. Start early. When evaluation is planned at the same time a program is planned, it can contribute to overall program design, the needed record keeping can be put in place from the beginning, and feedback can start immediately. The practices of the evaluators in the Rockefeller case study show how nothing sharpens program planning better than having to answer evaluation's simplest questions:

- What are you really trying to do in this program?
- What's going to happen that can tell you whether or not you have succeeded?
- How will you know?

Record keeping problems severely limited several of the nine case study evaluations. How much should a grantee have in its initial budget to keep track of the people in its programs? Enough to do it well. Record keeping may seem a low priority to some, but if you don't know who and where the people are that your program has been affecting, you cannot find out whether it's done them any good or not.

Key 9. Get all participants to focus on the essential first question: what is it that is most important for us to find out? Kellogg's "important questions" approach is a good example here. Stakeholders need to sit down, carefully review all the dreams, goals, and objectives of the underlying program, and then reach agreement on what needs to be learned. It is impossible to evaluate every aspect of a program; therefore, decisions about what to evaluate need to be made deliberately. Planning for the Gautreaux evaluation began with a conceptual model that showed everything that could be investigated; then the most important and feasible elements for evaluation were chosen. Each year in the Career/Vocational Exploration Program, new program questions drive the planning for that year's evaluation. A clear statement of how the evaluation is linked to the purposes and open questions of the program to be evaluated should be made part of the evaluation records. Articulating what you chose to evaluate and why becomes in itself an important, revealing part of the process.

Key 10. At the same time, make sure your evaluation plan has built-in flexibility. An evaluation plan must allow for change or expansion in midstream if the evaluation data begin to show an important new direction for inquiry. As the Cities in Schools case study of an evolving program showed, after a time evidence may appear that something is constraining a program and needs to be attended to with the help of evaluation. Or, preliminary findings may show a positive program result that was unexpected — a side effect that may in the end be one of the most important outcomes of the whole program. Such a discovery deserves both program and evaluation attention. The effects of employers paying extra money for additional hours in the Career/Vocational Exploration Program and Gautreaux women finding good jobs in the suburbs are two examples of such side effects.

Key 11. Insist on evaluations that do not count just the hours that shine. Quality evaluations should of course not be hatchet jobs, but neither should they be valentines. The Meyer evaluation, for instance, included substantial criticism of its RFP program. The criticism didn't hurt much, it was used constructively. When the Cities in Schools program scored poorly on an important evaluation question, it turned that experience into a lesson about what its mission was. Evaluations like those carried out by the Skaggs and Rockefeller foundations and the Career/Vocational Exploration Program are on-site and close to the ground so the good and the bad findings can come up side by side. It is important to suspend judgment a little, tolerate both failure and the unpredicted, and reflect, learn, and move ahead.

Key 12. Wherever possible, evaluate at the level of the people who will ultimately be affected by the program. The most valid, useful evaluations are more in touch with the community than with institutions and professions. The Gautreaux, Cities in Schools, Technology for Literacy, and Career/Vocational Exploration programs are good examples of evaluations that were not solely dependent on information from intermediaries. As a result, the foundations and organizations involved could be confident that the evaluations addressed questions important to the program consumers they were trying to help, and that they were getting answers directly from them. The other case study evaluations came close to this goal: Lilly had its eyes and ears tuned more to youthworkers in the field than to officials at national headquarters, Meyer placed great importance on the evaluation team's site visits, Skaggs probed into community experience; Rockefeller in Arkansas kept a student-centered focus in the classrooms; and Kellogg gave high priority to its local grantees' evaluations among their constituents.

Key 13. Wherever possible, ensure that evaluations include a longer-term view. A formal longitudinal study, an annual evaluation, or just a follow-up is important because evaluation over time generally reveals more, and is more credible, than a one-time investigation. It shows change. Gautreaux is using a series of studies over time, including a longitudinal study and follow-ups, and Cities in Schools is developing the same approach. Rockefeller and the Career/Vocational Exploration Program have annual evaluations, with cumulative value added every year. Information provided in Lilly's follow-up evaluation added a great deal to the original study. So did the follow-up surveys of the Technology for Literacy Project, and Meyer is going back to its grantees again for a further look. As long as the program continues, the intelligence of an ongoing evaluation feeds back into a continuous cycle of interaction between programs and their evaluation. In that cycle, first comes program planning, then program experience, evaluation, learning from the evaluation, and then the application of that learning back to program planning. Furthermore, there is always current information to use when a problem or an opportunity to make a point emerges.

Key 14. In planning evaluations, place higher value on finding indications of behavior than on collecting opinions. The most important part of evaluation planning is determining what the indicators of success are to be, and the best indicators are behavioral. Technology for Literacy and Cities in Schools focused on data about student performance and behavioral habits such as attendance. Rockefeller insisted that indicators of success in the public schools be tangible. Gautreaux built a model that showed the discernable causes and effects that needed to be looked at. Lilly asked youthworkers what they had done more than what they thought. The Career/Vocational Exploration Program does the same thing with its working youth. The bottom line at Skaggs was success or failure rather than how the grantees felt about their experiences. A statement that "85 percent said it was a good program" is not an evaluation: it is just a testimonial, and as such, is often debatable.

Key 15. Evaluate not only the merits of a program — whether it's good or not — but also the program's worth. Examine whether it's needed and how it compares to the quality and cost of other existing programs or programs that could be developed. The nine case studies provide little evidence that evaluators had systematically examined how funded programs stacked up against alternatives. The best evaluations see beyond their underlying programs and place them in the context of alternatives. This is an especially critical issue in the evaluation of clusters of grants. It is easy to think of a cluster as the universe — which it rarely is. What else is there? What else could there be? How do the cluster's programs compare? How do they fit in?

Key 16. Have respect for previous work. A good evaluation builds on existing knowledge. Before you begin the evaluation process, learn as much as possible about previous evaluations, research in the field, expert opinions, and unresolved issues. The Lilly and Career/Vocational Exploration Program evaluations took advantage of previous research, Meyer commissioned background papers for their evaluation team, and Technology for Literacy evaluators sought out data from other agencies nationwide.

Key 17. Use a variety of evaluation methods, for different purposes and side by side for verifying or contrasting. Combine quantitative and qualitative evaluation methods; get some numbers and some personal documentary accounts. Most of the evaluations described here used several approaches and benefited. The William Penn Foundation's Richard Cox calls them "cross checks."

Key 18. Squeeze the most you can out of an evaluation. Once the raw data have been accumulated, you have the potential for all kinds of harvesting — breakdowns, attention to variables, comparisons, contrasts. Pursue as many as you can. Leonard Rubinowitz, who evaluated the Gautreaux program, described evaluation findings as patches that can be put together into a patchwork quilt. Although you will never have all the patches, the more you can put into place, the clearer the design will become. Several of the evaluations described limited themselves, for one reason or another, to learning less from their information than they might have.

Key 19. Use evaluation to bring grantees together. The Meyer, Lilly, Kellogg, and Rockefeller cases show the value of using an evaluation as an opportunity for grantees to trade information, share ideas and reactions about their common interests and goals, and make joint plans. If in the process of these collaborations, meetings seem more theirs than yours, you have succeeded.

Finding Evaluators and Working with Them

Key 20. Develop relationships with sources of evaluators — preferably before you need them — and keep scouting around for new and better ones. The Technology for Literacy Project and its funders did this well through the University of Minnesota. The Gautreaux agencies engineered the strategic placement of a good researcher into the right place with the right people at a Northwestern University research center. Though individual foundations may find it advantageous to work alone, the process of scouting around and developing new sources of evaluators for foundations and nonprofits is a good job for a regional association of grantmakers committee.

Key 21. Find evaluators who are disciplined and objective in their approach to the task, yet convivial and tactful in their approach to people. These characteristics need not be mutually exclusive. William Wayson comes to the job in Arkansas as a determined social scientist; he is also warmly received and trusted. Someone once described the best evaluator as being "polite but irreverent."

Key 22. When possible, find an evaluator who has an identifiable personal interest in conducting the evaluation. Hiring an evaluator at a time when he or she has a personal reason for wanting to do the work can give you a better quality job, makes it easier to predict points of view and biases, and often results in lower costs for the time and attention the evaluation gets. The Skaggs, Lilly, Gautreaux, Rockefeller, and Technology for Literacy case studies show five good variations on this theme.

Key 23. Know as much as possible about the professional inclinations and biases of an evaluator before you begin your association. Evaluators all have their favorite ways of doing things, along with motives and points of view that may not be readily apparent. As the Gautreaux researchers explained, the interests of an evaluator can seriously affect the final evaluation. Or, as the case was in the Technology for Literacy Project, the choice of evaluator can make a difference in the evaluation planning process and what you as a client are responsible for. As a matter of practice, good evaluators make it part of their business to identify your prejudices; you can be more confident about the evaluation if you know something about theirs. Before you select an evaluator, ask for and check references, read reports of evaluations they have done, and ask about any specific points in their methods that puzzle you.

Key 24. Be sure that both political and professional issues will be investigated by your evaluator. At least half the evaluators in the case studies, and even some grantors and grantees, tended to believe that delivery of professional services was all that deserved serious evaluating. Yet all the programs ultimately sought to influence other agencies or public policy, and there were important political concerns. If the goals of a program are both to provide services and to make an impact in the field, the ways in which each of these goals is or is not being accomplished must be evaluated. Evaluators who are locked into a service delivery perspective alone have a hard time looking for institutional change.

Key 25. Consider an evaluation team. The foundations involved in the Technology for Literacy, Lilly, Meyer, and Cities in Schools case studies believe they benefited well from the diversity that their teams brought to their evaluations.

Key 26. Be clear with both evaluators and grantees about who is responsible for what in the design, implementation, interpretation, and reporting of evaluations. There were few written contracts or letters of agreement among the evaluations in the case studies. Some important tasks were not done as well as they might have been if a firmer, more comprehensive contract had been jointly prepared and signed. What occurs after the evaluation is as crucial as the evaluation itself. Who owns it? Who is responsible for final reports? Over whose name(s)? With what editing? How and when will they be released? The Gautreaux and Cities in Schools case studies in particular raise these questions. Kellogg's evolving design of relationships among program staff, grantees, and cluster evaluators will be especially interesting as an example of how these questions will be resolved.

Key 27. Make sure that the people who are being interviewed or surveyed are indeed representative of the universe of people the program says is represented. How the evaluators have reached these determinations needs to be clear in the reports. The Technology for Literacy, Gautreaux, and Lilly evaluations show good examples of validating a sample.

Key 28. Insist on comprehensiveness and precision in both quantitative and qualitative evaluations. Vague statements of findings that are not explicitly referenced to the data should be considered suspect. Similarly, interpretations that are not referenced to specific findings suggest that the work to obtain the findings has been wasted. Numbers that don't track well or don't clearly compare with other numbers are worthless. Case studies and other particularistic methods cannot be carried out less carefully or less systematically than methods with lots of numbers; to be authentic and useful, purely qualitative methods need exceptional skills and sensitivity. Although imprecisions in documenting were not detailed in these case studies, significant instances appeared in all of the evaluations described.

Funding

Key 29. Budget adequate funds to do the evaluation. Mediocre evaluations lead to mediocre programs. There is no easy formula for determining how much money to spend on an evaluation. Lilly has established a guideline of 3 percent of annual grants money for evaluation, but determining the amount of money to be spent on each individual program is another question. A modest program that shows strong signs of success, fresh ideas, and potential influence, for instance, may warrant an evaluation that costs much more than the program itself.

Key 30. At the same time, do not let anyone tell you an evaluation cannot be scientific or rigorous unless it costs megabucks. For most foundations, the best evaluator you can hire — inside or outside — is a professional who will tell you and your grantees how to get the results you want with minimum money by looking at such considerations as clever sampling and comparison groups techniques, good ways to get adequate returns on questionnaires, efficient group interview techniques, and qualified people who have personal reasons for wanting to work on your evaluation. The Technology for Literacy, Skaggs, Rockefeller, and Cities in Schools case studies, especially, suggest ways to achieve lower evaluation costs — without jeopardizing evaluation quality.

Key 31. Involve several funders and pool resources. The additional mix of evaluation interests should enhance the results, and the results will receive more attention. The William Penn Foundation leads both the Career/Vocational Exploration Program and its evaluation; but William Penn receives support from others in terms of time and money. The Bruner Foundation (which funded the Cities in Schools case study), may be the only foundation specializing in funding evaluation, but there have to be many others that will try. The Gautreaux case should be inspiring: two local agencies and a university got small grants to enable them to develop their evaluation capacity, and then were able to obtain large grants from three national foundations for the studies themselves.

Reporting and Dissemination

Key 32. Give reporting and dissemination the importance — and the funding — they deserve. Don't accept the evaluation report submitted by your evaluator as a sacred document. Judging from the reports produced for the evaluations in the nine case studies, chances are that your report could be better written and organized, the findings could be presented in a more informative manner, pertinent information has been omitted, and irrelevant information has been included. Different versions of the report — one for the stakeholders and one for other audiences, for instance — may be needed. Perhaps paying a good editor to review and edit the report will give you what you want. But be sure to involve the evaluators in the editing process because the final version must be their professional report. Good evaluation reports become invaluable parts of an ongoing communications program.

Key 33. Use oral reporting opportunities to disseminate information from evaluations. Lilly reported that it communicated best with the executives of its eight national agencies during conferences when evaluation findings were reported by well-prepared field personnel who gave the executives the straight dope from within and around the evaluation itself. At Meyer, the evaluation team's oral report to the trustees became an unusually fine conversation.

Key 34. Keep track of the impact of an evaluation. This includes recording reactions to reports, what happens at meetings where evaluation is planned, reported, critiqued, who asks for and receives copies of the reports, who responds to the reports with a comment or question, who learns about the underlying program by reading an evaluation report, and who takes an action on the basis of a report. One reason for difficulties in raising money for evaluation work may be that the impacts of evaluations are so seldom documented. Jane Quinn's use of the Lilly evaluation added something impressive to the list of worthwhile consequences of the Lilly evaluation; tracking down such instances shows others how evaluations are worth much more than many people give them credit for.

Key 35. Give everyone in philanthropy the opportunity to know what you are learning from evaluation activity.

Inform foundations that you know are interested in the field of a program that is being evaluated, foundations involved in evaluation or thinking about it, regional associations of grantmakers, and the Council on Foundations. All should hear about your evaluations, preferably before and after they happen. This will begin to remedy the current situation in which there is very little trading and discussion of evaluation experiences.

RESOURCE A

Evaluation Approaches
and Methods Defined

Jan Corey Arnett

Evaluations can be objectives-, management-, expertise-, public relations-, or participant-oriented. They can be goal-free or naturalistic. They can look at process, impact, outcome, or costs. They can be conducted during or after a program. And they can analyze numerical, survey, or narrative data. As shown by the case studies, good evaluations make use of a wide variety of approaches and methods—in varying combinations. Evaluations should not, therefore, be thought of in an either/or frame of reference— quantitative or qualitative, formative or summative—because there is no single best path to every evaluation. Rather, the best evaluations are often eclectic—that is, they draw the best from available approaches and methods to strengthen their own work. The essence of successful evaluation, therefore, is knowing when to use a particular approach or method to the greatest benefit.

An evaluation *approach* is virtually synonymous with a *goal,* that is, the orientation or purpose for the activity. An evaluation *method* is the specific tool or technique used to accomplish the task and reach the goal. Thus, for example, an evaluation may be outcome-oriented in approach but use quantitative methods.

Before considering particular approaches and methods, however, it is important to understand the basic standards that should underpin every evaluation. The standards that today's evaluators should adhere to resulted from the work of the Joint Committee on Standards for Educational Evaluation (1980). These important standards are applicable to all evaluations, including those conducted by or for foundations and nonprofit organizations. They fall into four categories:

- Utility: an evaluation must serve the practical information needs of a given audience. Standards under this category cover audience identification, evaluator credibility, clarity in reporting, dissemination, and evaluation impact.
- Feasibility: the evaluation must be realistic and reasonable, not consuming more materials and personnel time than necessary to achieve its purposes. Feasibility takes practical procedures, political viability, and cost effectiveness into consideration.
- Propriety: the rights of persons affected by an evaluation must be protected. These rights extend not just to those involved in the evaluation, but also to those affected by evaluation results. Propriety includes the issues of conflict of interest, disclosure, the public's right to know, privacy, balanced reporting, and fiscal responsibility.
- Accuracy: an evaluation should reveal and convey accurate and adequate information so that judgments can be made about the subject being studied. Accuracy standards cover context analysis, defensible sources of information, data control, analyzing quantitative and qualitative information, and reaching justifiable conclusions.

Selected Approaches

Objectives-Oriented Evaluation

Objectives-oriented evaluations concentrate on the extent to which specific objectives have been achieved by a program or activity. They are carried out in five steps: establish objectives, define them, develop ways to measure them, collect data, and compare actual and anticipated findings. Although the clear delineation of these steps makes them easy to understand and carry out, objectives-oriented evaluations are often criticized because they lack standards for judging the importance of why objectives were or were not reached, they neglect the setting in which the project is occurring, and they ignore outcomes other than those that have been specifically stated. These potential weaknesses result, in part, from how evaluation objectives are set. Objectives may be set too low or too high or established without a clear understanding of what can realistically be achieved within a project's resources. A natural question to work with may very well be: Who established the objectives and what was his or her connection to the program? Still, objectives-oriented evaluations, even with their limitations, are often an adequate means for evaluating small-scale projects that affect small numbers of people and are not likely to be replicated elsewhere.

Goal-Free Evaluation

Goal-free evaluation focuses on the actual, rather than intended outcomes of a program. Goal-free evaluators prefer not to know the stated goals of a program, so that they can remain objective and open to capturing all the effects of the activity without being constrained by or limited to the stated goals. Goal-free evaluations must be conducted by someone external to the program and should supplement and complement objectives-oriented evaluation, which may be done by someone familiar with the program. If conducted in this way, they have the potential for uncovering program impacts that were not intended but that may prove more important than planned outcomes; however, they can also be criticized because evaluations that do not begin with a set of objectives can take longer and be less focused than is acceptable to those who need information from the evaluation.

Goal-free evaluation can be used in a variety of settings. Take, for example, a program for latchkey children and assume that the primary finding of a needs assessment was that children in unsupervised settings experience more in-home injuries

such as burns, cuts, and poisonings. The stated goal of the subsequent latchkey children's program is to reduce in-home injuries by providing a secure, supervised environment during the
hours between the end of the school day and end of the parents'
(or caretaker's) workday. An objectives-oriented evaluation
would look solely at the question of whether injuries were reduced when children were supervised. A goal-free evaluation
would proceed from a simple understanding that this was a program providing supervision for children who would otherwise
be alone for a period of time after their school day. During the
course of evaluation, the goal-free evaluator might discover that
not only did injuries decline, but that the children's in-school
performance improved, their self-esteem levels were raised as
a result of the daily interaction with the attentive adults super-
vising the latchkey program, and their parents and caretakers
reported increased productivity and reduced job absenteeism
(attributable to reduced stress levels) because their children were
now in a secure environment. Objectives-oriented evaluation
would probably have missed many of these important unintended outcomes — outcomes that might have influenced a decision on whether to continue the latchkey program. A weakness
of goal-free evaluation, however, is that its ability to attribute
change to the program is questionable.

The implication here is not that an evaluator can use only
goal-free approaches to learn about outcomes other than those
specifically intended for the project. Quite the contrary. Program officers can ask that other kinds of evaluation, in addition to answering the questions related to the objectives set for
the project, also seek to learn what other things may have oc-
curred as a result of the effort.

Management-Oriented Evaluation

Management-oriented evaluations are geared to meet the needs
of managers who make staffing, equipment, budget, and similar types of decisions. With this form of evaluation, the objectives of the program are not the primary concern. Rather, the
evaluator identifies the decisions the administrator must make

irrespective of the program's goals (for example, Does the facility have space for the program? Is there money in the budget to cover program costs?), and then the evaluator collects data that gives the administrator alternatives for decision making. This approach is commonly used in educational settings as an aid to school administrators. Management-oriented evaluations, because they concentrate the evaluator's work on what the manager wants to know, often ignore the needs of the clients or other stakeholders, when in fact the impact on stakeholders should be one of the prime factors influencing management decisions. Thus, this type of evaluation can be incorrectly focused or incomplete. Several models, such as Daniel Stufflebeam's CIPP model (context, input, process, and product), have been developed to strengthen the management-oriented approach (Stufflebeam and Shinkfield, 1984).

Expertise-Oriented Evaluation

Expertise-oriented evaluations are conducted by an individual or team of professionals with acknowledged expertise in the subject of the evaluation. This approach clearly regards the subjective knowledge of the evaluator as important and desirable. Common forms of this approach include the appointment of blue-ribbon panels, professional or peer review teams, and ad hoc committees — all made up of individuals knowledgeable about the type of program in question. Educational institutions and governmental agencies often use expertise-oriented evaluations to make accreditation and funding decisions. For example, a team of individuals with expertise about the reward systems, curriculum development, and departmental review processes within the university environment may be called upon to evaluate an expanded undergraduate curriculum. The team would be expected to reflect its understanding of the university system in the inquiry and analysis process. If experts are asked to analyze the same program independent of one another, it is good to bring them together (if in no other way than a conference call) to share thoughts and reactions.

Experts can provide a knowledgeable, more efficient, and

perhaps more accurate evaluation than others because they can quickly grasp both the overall picture and the important details of the program being assessed; however, there is always a risk of unintentional bias because an evaluator may concentrate too quickly on what he or she is knowledgeable about, or has experience with, and overlook other program impacts. In addition, the potential exists for an evaluator to be selected based on expertise he or she claims to have but actually lacks, which could result in a shoddy or superficial evaluation.

With the expertise-oriented approach, it is often possible for research projects to be evaluated through document review alone; however, evaluations of service programs generally require observation and interviews with staff and participants and, therefore, almost always necessitate site visits.

Naturalistic, or Participant-Oriented, Evaluation

Although described in a variety of ways, naturalistic evaluations have several universal characteristics. First, they emphasize the human element of an activity, focusing on describing and interpreting what is taking place in the program and its context, rather than on attempting to yield conclusive judgments. Second, they are responsive to the program and its flow, rather than rigidly conforming to predetermined evaluation plans. And third, they allow for differing values or viewpoints to be expressed, rather than holding that any given value is *the* correct one. Naturalistic evaluations employ a number of methods to describe what is being evaluated, including interviews, observations, and document review. They are especially useful in programs where it is important to capture feelings, reactions, and behavioral changes that cannot be easily quantified or measured through scientific testing. Naturalistic evaluation is a very important approach when dealing with personal improvement and self-esteem–building programs. Administrators know they are accountable to funders or other stakeholders, but because they do not know how to translate their perceptions into definitive statements that "prove" impacts, they often — with a mixture of conviction and frustration — can only say, "I *just know* the program is making a difference." When combined with quantitative techniques, naturalistic evaluation can result in a solid, well-rounded report that offers both hard numbers and an understanding of what those numbers mean in human terms.

Naturalistic evaluation would be appropriate, for example, to a program designed to bolster the esteem of women who have low incomes, are displaced homemakers, have suffered abuse, or have low educational levels. Few standardized instruments (such as scales, surveys, and self-measures) measure and assess changes in self-esteem before and after exposure to a program. The naturalistic evaluator would observe the program in operation, interview the women who participate, and review documents (records from counseling sessions or group meetings, for instance) and would note whether the women showed behavioral changes such as having sought employment, having improved their personal appearance, or having made life-change decisions as a result of the program. Naturalistic evaluation results in what is often called "thick description," because in its final form it is a rich narrative.

Critics of naturalistic evaluation suggest that the approach lacks sufficient structure, takes too long, is vulnerable to evaluator partiality, and is difficult to replicate. These criticisms can be valid. Naturalistic evaluations do not render the same kinds of judgments as other approaches, but they do allow a program administrator or evaluation sponsor to make final judgments. Proponents of naturalistic evaluation argue that it has a greater potential than other approaches for learning about a program's effects, because of its openness, flexibility, and sensitivity to human issues. They take the position that evaluation, whatever the approach or method, must always be sensitive to the people and situation involved in what is being evaluated. Evaluation should never interfere with program operation in such a way that it alters normal program flow, antagonizes or intimidates participants, or jeopardizes outcomes.

Public Relations–Oriented Evaluation

Public relations–oriented evaluation requires little explanation. Here, questions for the evaluation derive from a desire to satisfy the interests of a specific audience, generally in a positive way, for purposes of securing project funding, staffing, facilities, or political support. It follows then, that—depending upon who has control of the evaluation—unfavorable aspects of a program may be overlooked or downplayed. Evaluation of this nature unfortunately contributes to the feelings of distrust that some people continue to hold for the field of evaluation in general.

It should be said, however, that societal expectations powerfully influence all evaluation. To reveal one's failings or findings, warts and all, is to risk being denied future funding, acceptance, and approval. Admitting negative outcomes can damage an organization's reputation. What is greatly needed is an attitude of openness and mutual support, an environment in which it is all right to fail as long as there is a sincere attempt to succeed and learn in the process. In such an environment, the rewards result from evaluating and learning, not necessarily from proving program success. Public relations can become public information for the benefit of all, without fear of reprisal.

Process Evaluation

Process evaluation focuses on the processes associated with an activity or program. Its purpose is to analyze elements of program operation (such as management strategies, costs, and other resources used to deliver a program; client interactions; problems encountered; and error rates), so that they can be improved while the program is still underway. Process evaluation can be a component of formative evaluation or a companion of impact or outcome evaluation. Information from process evaluations is valuable both for understanding how program impact and outcome were achieved and for program replication. This type of evaluation is usually undertaken for projects that employ innovative service delivery models, where the technology and feasibility of program implementation are not well known in advance. Examples of process evaluation questions are: What specific interventions were put into place by the program in order to fight the problem being tackled? How many communities were selected for pilot programs and how were they selected? What kinds of problems were encountered? How were the problems resolved?

Impact or Outcome Evaluation

Impact or outcome evaluation seeks to determine how well a program is working or has worked, and whether and how much of a difference the program has made in producing desired changes in a target group. It is generally undertaken to inform decisions about whether a program should be continued or replicated. Sometimes such evaluations seek to demonstrate that outcomes are the results of the program, rather than other factors. To do this, they must overcome the difficult challenge of establishing what might have happened had there been no program. Impact or outcome evaluation is often undertaken when it is important to know how well a grantee's or a foundation's objectives for a program were met, or when a program is an innovative model whose effectiveness has not yet been demonstrated. Impact evaluation questions about a program for smokers, for example, might include: Did the program succeed in helping people to stop smoking? Was the program more successful with certain groups of people than with others? What aspects of the program did participants find of greatest benefit in helping them to stop smoking? Did the program result in a reduced incidence of cancer in the target group?

Process and impact evaluation are brought together in Stufflebeam's CIPP Model. CIPP makes use of four types of evaluation to aid managers with four types of program decisions. The evaluations and their respective types of decisions are context evaluation, which informs planning decisions for the program being developed; input evaluation, which seeks answers to matters such as choosing among available resources or alternative strategies to make the program operational; process evaluation, which helps with decisions related to actually running the program; and product (or impact) evaluation, which aids decisions about what should be done to continue, discontinue, replicate or modify the program once it has been completed. The CIPP Model is used extensively in education.

Cost-Benefit and Cost-Effectiveness Analysis

Cost-benefit analysis and cost-effectiveness analysis are techniques developed by economists to compare program outputs
with program inputs in order to assess the relative efficiencies
of alternative uses of resources. Cost-benefit and cost-effectiveness comparisons are expressed as ratios, typically with cost in
the denominator.

- *Cost-Benefit Analysis:* Costs include both direct monetary program costs and the dollar value of indirect (in-kind or contributed) costs. Benefits are the total positive outcomes of
  the program expressed in monetary terms (dollars). Because
  program benefits typically are experienced in the future, and
  because a dollar received in the future is worth less than a
  dollar expended today, it is necessary to convert the monetary value of these benefits into current dollars. Making this
  conversion is called discounting, and it is an important component of cost-benefit analysis.
- *Cost-Effectiveness Analysis:* Expressing program outcomes in
  monetary units can be difficult, for some outcomes are not
  easily converted into dollars — for instance, what is the value
  of a life saved? Effectiveness, in contrast, uses a non-mon-
  etary measure of program outcomes, typically a measure
  related to the program's objectives, such as the number of
  years of life saved or the gain in mathematics achievement
  test scores. While cost-effectiveness analysis avoids the problem of having to convert outcomes into monetary units, it
  is unable to combine diverse outcomes (for instance, prevent-
  ing teen pregnancy and increasing high school graduation
  rates) into a single measure, as can be done in cost-benefit
  analysis.

Formative and Summative Evaluation

The distinction between formative and summative evaluations
is clear: formative evaluations are carried out during both the
development and operational phases of a program; summative

evaluations occur only at program end. Summative evaluations provide judgments about a program's success or merit, they are not aimed at improving the program unless it is to be continued or replicated in some form. It is for this reason that summative evaluation is frequently associated with the kill-or-continue mode of thinking about evaluation's purposes. Combinations of formative and summative evaluation should be encouraged because decisions made during the operation of a program can improve and strengthen its chances for success. Also, formative evaluation puts a data collection system into motion early on, which can capture information that might not be available at a later date. These formative data, gathered throughout a project's life cycle, help evaluators make summative judgments about what did and did not work — and why.

The difference between formative and summative evaluation and how each is used can be seen in this example. A needs assessment has shown that a specific number of teenage girls are dropping out of school because of pregnancy. The high school develops a new "stay-in-school" program for these pregnant teenagers. It recruits girls (or markets its program) in three ways — through physicians' offices, in-school announcements, and a mailer to the homes of all female students over the age of fifteen. A formative evaluation would raise such questions as, What is the potential number of girls who could be served by this program? How many of those girls are being reached? Of those reached, how many are choosing to stay in or return to school? How many have left school and why? Which approach for reaching students is working most successfully? Can this approach be increased? How can other approaches be modified? Are there students under the age of fifteen who are being overlooked by the program? The answers to these questions would lead to program refinements that could increase the number of girls reached and, thereby, improve the chances for the success of the program while it is still in its first phase.

A summative evaluation that has not been preceded by a formative evaluation would raise similar questions, but with two distinct differences. First, the questions could only be asked retrospectively: How many girls were served? Which approach for reaching them was most successful? Second, because the project would be nearing or at its conclusion at the time the summative evaluation is initiated, some questions would be impossible to answer because no system had been put into place early on to answer them. Why? Because no one would have anticipated the questions! And even if the question could be answered summatively, it would be too late to make use of the information unless the program was to be continued or replicated. If the program did not work very well (because no refinements were made as it evolved), chances are it would not be considered for replication or continuation anyway. If this sounds like a plea for formative evaluation, it is. Formative evaluation, by providing immediate feedback about what works, what does not work and why, can strengthen operating programs and provide essential data for successful summative evaluations.

Selected Methods

The broad range of evaluation approaches and goals reviewed in the previous section requires the use of an equally diverse array of research designs and methods. The following discussion offers a brief introduction to some of these strategies and techniques and should not be regarded as a comprehensive overview. This section differentiates between quantitative and qualitative evaluation methods, identifies the general types of evaluation research designs, and describes commonly used data-gathering techniques. It concludes with a discussion of the eclectic nature of most evaluation efforts.

Quantitative and Qualitative

Quantitative and qualitative evaluation reflect two ways of collecting and reporting information. Quantitative evaluation involves producing — through experimentation, testing, and statistical methods — numbers that reflect the changes introduced by a program or project and their effects on organizations and/or individuals. Qualitative evaluation produces narrative descriptions of activities, processes, and outcomes, which are generally based on observation and interviewing, and both of which can bring the evaluator's own style and values into play. In the words of evaluator Michael Quinn Patton (1990a), "While quantitative approaches tend to produce uniformity of measures, which has the advantage of facilitating direct comparisons among programs, qualitative methods permit documentation of program differences, idiosyncrasies, and uniquenesses" (p. 104).

Historically, quantitative and qualitative methods have been considered to be in opposition to one another; however, today, more and more evaluators see the value in combining the two methods to respond to different needs. For example, administrators of a health-care institution may want to know whether to continue delivering care at several city clinics. Their questions might include whether certain or all of the clinics should remain open, what services are in greatest demand, whether staffing is adequate to meet those demands, and what are the costs and associated benefits of different decisions. In this case, a quantitative evaluation would present data on numbers of patients served and the costs for those services, and it would render comparisons among the clinics. A qualitative evaluation would add information — in a narrative description — on patient satisfaction with the delivery of services and would consider differences among clinics based on client opinion. Thus, a quantitative evaluation would not address the human aspect of programs in the same way as would a qualitative evaluation.

Case Studies

Case studies are closely associated with qualitative methods for evaluation. They involve an in-depth study of a representative activity of a program or a group of its participants. Their intent is to draw some conclusions about the whole from this careful, detailed treatment. Case studies are usually based on interview data, observational data, quantitative data, documents such as clinical records, life history profiles, data accumulated over time, and program reports. All available and possible sources of data are tapped, the data are compiled and organized into manageable chunks. From this, the case study is written to create a holistic portrayal of a person or program. Case studies are sometimes referred to as descriptive analyses. When completed, they are often viewed as the evaluation report itself. For more information on case studies see Patton (1990a) and Yin (1989).

Sampling

Sampling is the process of drawing information from a representative portion of a total population to make judgments about the whole. Sampling techniques are employed to reduce the time and cost of an evaluation, as well as to keep it manageable. Samples are of two general types: *random probability samples,* in which every person, household, or organization of concern to the researcher has an equal chance of being included, and *quota samples,* in which observations (either persons or organizations) are selected purposefully according to their characteristics. The objective is to obtain a sample that in total corresponds to the population of interest for the evaluation. However, such samples are difficult to construct because there are so many characteristics that may be relevant; a random sample overcomes such problems naturally. Sampling is associated with the survey technique, though it also may be used to select observations from a compilation of records on the whole population of interest (for instance, all health insurance claims submitted within a year). For additional information on sampling see Jaeger (1984) and Worthen and Sanders (1987).

Survey

A survey is a series of questions specifically tailored to evaluate a program, which are asked of program participants or other program stakeholders. A survey may involve a face-to-face or telephone interview or it may use a self-administered questionnaire. Face-to-face or telephone surveys are more costly and time consuming than self-administered questionnaires, but they offer the greatest opportunity for getting the most useful information. Among the many sources of information about interviews and survey methods are Gorden (1987), Fowler (1989), and Dillman (1978).

Randomized Designs

Randomized designs involve comparing at least two groups that are considered to be alike — members of each group are assigned randomly to one of the groups. In its simplest form, a randomized design entails a single treatment group and a single control group; however, it may also involve several groups receiving varying types of treatment. When properly applied, randomized designs can be the most rigorous and exacting form of quantitative evaluation; however, their use is limited by the nature of the program being evaluated. They are best used to test services that can be readily transferred to other agencies or when small sample groups are adequate for making evaluative judgments. They are not useful when a program reaches 80 percent or more of its target population, when it is unlikely that the treatment and control groups can be regarded as reasonably similar overall before one group receives the treatment program or product, or when there is a likelihood that the control group will be "contaminated." Contamination occurs when the control group is exposed in some way to whatever is being administered to the treatment group, whether it is tangible — as in a drug versus placebo test — or intangible — such as becoming aware of what others are learning in a specific educational program. The use of control groups is usually costly and time-consuming. Rossi and Freeman (1989) and Fitz-Gibbon and Morris (1987) provide useful information on this evaluation method.

Quasi-Experimental Designs

In quasi-experimental designs, the comparison group is carefully selected to be as similar as possible to the group(s) that will receive the treatment (for instance, students in similar high schools or residents of adjacent counties). Quasi-experimental designs are subject to the same flaws as randomized designs in that their usefulness depends on the accuracy (honesty, perhaps) of the match between groups and the care taken in administering treatments, controlling for contamination, and assessing impacts. For example, if the project involves teaching children arithmetic in a new way, the intervention group will be taught using the new approach, while the comparison group will learn through traditional methods. Comparisons of the effectiveness of the one method versus the other can then be made through testing and observation. Sometimes the treatment group itself can serve as its own comparison group by making careful pre- and posttreatment assessments. This method is generally prone to error, however, because factors external to the program could be partly or entirely responsible for changes that occur. The success of the design is largely dependent on the nature of the program. See Rossi and Freeman (1989) and Fitz-Gibbon and Morris (1987) for further information.

Longitudinal Designs

Longitudinal designs involve collecting data to assess change at intervals before and during a program and after it ends. This method may involve the designation of a panel, from whom data are collected over the period. Longitudinal evaluation, however, can also refer to simply continuing an evaluation for some period of time beyond the program's conclusion in order to determine whether the program's benefits persist over the longer term. Longitudinal evaluations are also useful when it is likely that the impacts of a program will not be immediately evident. For example, it may take years before youth who participate in a leadership development program become community leaders, receive recognition in their fields of endeavor, or earn leadership roles in the business world. Fitz-Gibbon and Morris (1987) provide further detail on this approach.

Interview

An interview is a means for conducting a survey that requires personal contact, either face-to-face or by telephone. If inter-

views are used as part of an evaluation, it is essential that the
interviewer be trained in the process because the manner in
which he or she asks questions, listens to an interviewee, and
records responses, as well as his or her personal behavior and
appearance, can affect both the quality and validity of an interview. A few tips for interviewing are: start the interview slowly
and in a relaxed manner to establish rapport; never interject
personal opinions and avoid the use of leading words, questions,
or inflections; and allow interviewees the opportunity to clarify
answers and probe beyond what is given on questionnaires. Interviews may be structured in such a way that the interviewer
moves through the interview in a prescribed manner, asking
questions in a preplanned sequence within a controlled environment such as a specific interview room, but interviews may also
be unstructured or informal, in which case a general set of questions is asked of the persons interviewed but not necessarily in
a given order. Informal interviews may take place in a variety
of settings, such as the homes or offices of the people being interviewed. For more information, in addition to those sources
noted under the survey and questionnaire methods in this resource, see Fowler and Mangione (1990) and Patton (1990a).

Questionnaire

A questionnaire is a self-administered survey instrument that
consists of a set of written questions to which the recipient is
asked to respond in writing. Questionnaires may be distributed
through the mail or administered in a group setting, such as
a classroom. All questionnaires (indeed, all interview instruments) should be pilot tested within a small group of people before they are administered to the full group. This provides an
opportunity to make corrections before going to the time and
expense of administering the questionnaire broadly and assessing results. Helpful hints for questionnaire development include:
keep it as short as possible, provide very clear directions on how
it is to be completed, prominently display the date by which
it is to be returned both at the start and at the end of the document, allow plenty of white space to keep it attractive, use easy-

to-read print, and guard against asking leading questions. The use of written questionnaires to survey transient populations, neighborhoods where multiple languages may be spoken, or individuals whose illiteracy or poor comprehension rates are likely to be high is not recommended. Additional detail on questionnaires can be found in Berdie and Anderson (1974) and the sources cited in this resource for the interview method.

Testing

A test is a collection of items designed to measure individuals' educational, health, or psychological status. It is among the most frequently used methods for conducting an evaluation, particularly within educational settings and learning-related programs. A common method for attempting to measure changes that can be attributed to the effects of an educational program is to test both before program implementation (pretest) and after (posttest). Other types of testing include norm-referenced, criterion-referenced, objectives-referenced, and domain-referenced. Because of the chance for error in this sensitive evaluation method, an individual who is trained in testing methods and procedures should assist whenever an evaluation incorporates testing. Resources for testing procedures include Hopkins and Stanley (1981), Fitz-Gibbon and Morris (1987), and Morris, Fitz-Gibbon, and Lindheim (1987). Commercially available tests are listed in *Tests in Print* and reviewed in the *Mental Measurements Yearbook,* which is published by the Buros Institute at the University of Nebraska. The Educational Testing Service in Princeton, New Jersey, is another source for information on testing.

Attitude Scale

Attitude scales are employed to learn how individuals feel about other people, programs, or institutions. They may be used to measure social or psychological, occupational or political attitudes. Although many such scales have been developed, most require adaptation to the particular program for which they are to be used. Defined in simplistic terms, most attitude scales are sets of statements with which respondents can agree or disagree. Construction of a sound scale that will result in valid data is not an easy task. Statements must be very carefully written and the list of do's and don'ts in their construction is long. For example, they should not be interpretable as fact, should be fewer than twenty words, should express only one thought per statement, and should avoid double negatives. Attitude scales are nearly always used with other evaluation methods and are analyzed using statistical methods. See Shaw and Wright (1967), Henerson, Morris, and Fitz-Gibbon (1987), and the sources noted for the testing method.

Observation

Observation methods — the means by which one sees and acknowledges what happens — can be quantitative or qualitative, structured or unstructured, and obtrusive or unobtrusive, as need dictates. Quantitative measures of observation include checklists and structured means for counting and categorizing items or behaviors. Qualitative means of observation include keeping a diary or log about what is happening during the course of an activity, watching a person or activity periodically and recording behaviors — especially as those behaviors change — and completing questionnaires as the observer rather than as the subject of the program being evaluated.

Obtrusive and unobtrusive refer to carrying out evaluation in ways that directly or indirectly involve others, usually the participants in the program being evaluated. Obtrusive methods include interviewing program participants while they are taking part in program activities, conducting surveys that participants are asked to complete, and in other ways making it obvious that an evaluation is being done.

Unobtrusive methods are less obvious (or more indirect). They include using concealed devices, such as tape recorders, for gathering data; examining physical traces, such as campus areas where the grass is worn away from students shortcutting between buildings; and reviewing archival records. Unobtrusive observation measures that can contribute to an evaluation generally consist of noting whether physical items (such as books, exhibits, and locations) are being used, or recording people's actions through note-taking or video or audio recording. A longstanding resource on unobtrusive measures is Webb, Campbell,

Schwartz, and Sechrest (1966). Also see Patton (1990a). Program participants generally are not openly asked to do anything related to the evaluation and may not even be aware an evaluation is occurring in some cases. Unobtrusive measures should always be cross-checked with other sources of data.

Document Analysis

Document analysis typically involves repeated review of a series of similar documents to note trends and changes over time, for example coverage in a local newspaper of a community issue. It is more than simply reading periodic reports compiled by a program that is being evaluated — although these actions are part of the process. The utility of program reports as a source of evaluation data is increased when guidelines on what is expected in the way of report content are specified at a program's onset. These guidelines should not be prescriptive to the point of constraining the report; however, the program administrator should stay focused on objectives and on the major questions being pursued about program activities and accomplishments. See Budd (1967) for additional information on document analysis.

Site Visits

Site visits — an overarching activity within which a series of evaluation methods is employed (for example, observation, document analysis, and interviews) — are a useful method both for formative and summative evaluation purposes. Site visits may take a variety of forms depending upon the personal style of the evaluator and the client for whom the evaluation work is being done. For example, site visits to a program may be unannounced, so that the program may be seen as it really operates day in and day out. However, care should be taken not to create the feeling in the program administrator or staff that evaluation done this way is for purposes of "checking up on them." There is no quicker way to feed the fires of distrust. Site visits may also be carefully structured, with the evaluator providing the program to be visited with specific advance instructions on when the visit will take place and what will be expected. The most important tip for conducting site visits is to answer these questions in advance: What information will be sought? Who will questions be directed to? What sources for information will be needed? Will more than one individual be needed at the site visit to allow for comparisons? Also important to the success of the site visit is that the person making the visit conduct him- or herself in a nonthreatening, nonjudgmental manner, demonstrating a sincere desire to learn from others. For a discussion about site visits see Worthen and White (1986).

Eclectic Evaluations

Just as an evaluation can be planned to incorporate more than one approach, that is, to address questions related both to program impacts and management, it also is likely to include a variety of methods. The evaluation's design plan is based on the important questions identified by evaluator, client, and other customers of the evaluation. Once the questions have been identified, appropriate means for answering each question are selected. Most evaluations are eclectic in nature in order to meet the informational needs of stakeholders. Most of the evaluations in the case studies presented in this text could be called eclectic. The use of a variety of methods and approaches is not only acceptable but practical and is preferred in most settings today, particularly those known to the world of foundation grantmaking and nonprofit human services (see Worthen and Sanders, 1987).

Interviews and questionnaires are two of the most common elements to the evaluations described in this book and to most evaluations of service-oriented programs, as are document analysis and site visits, when possible. Less common are pre- and posttesting and the use of control groups—although examples of both are found among the evaluations described here. What this reaffirms is that evaluation planning is not a simple process of "if this" is the program "then that" is the evaluation process. Although such precision might make evaluation far less complicated, it would also make it far less interesting in results. Each evaluation is idiosyncratic to the program it evaluates.

RESOURCE B

Annotated
Bibliography

Jan Corey Arnett

This bibliography contains annotations on four types of materials, plus lists of selected articles and journals, that are helpful to foundation or nonprofit managers who are looking for both general and specific information about evaluation. These four types of materials are:

- *Evaluation texts* that have been recommended by members of the Council on Foundations' Evaluation Handbook Advisory Committee. Some focus on specialized evaluation approaches or methods, others contain forms and working documents that have been developed by organizations to meet specific needs.
- *Evaluation manuals* that have been developed by foundations and are, therefore, tailored to the foundations' philosophical, cultural, and programming perspectives. These manuals can be obtained from the respective foundations.
- *Evaluation reports or surveys* that have been authored by foundations themselves or foundation grantees and can be obtained from the authors.

- *Perspectives on evaluation* that provide food for thought as an organization considers program or project evaluation.
- *Articles and journals.*

Evaluation Texts

Berk, R. A., and Rossi, P. H. *Thinking About Program Evaluation.* Newbury Park, Calif.: Sage, 1990. A primer to evaluation research that introduces the reader to evaluation fundamentals and provides concrete examples of how researchers set evaluation goals and the methods they employ to achieve those goals. The authors emphasize that the research methods depend on the empirical question being asked and the evolution of the program under evaluation. The appendix is an excellent guide to evaluation literature and to professional associations and organizations engaged in evaluation and social policy research in the United States.

Brandt, R. S., and Mondrak, N. (ed.). *Applied Strategies for Curriculum Evaluation.* Alexandria, Va.: Association for Supervision and Curriculum Development, 1981. Nine evaluation "gurus" describe their different approaches to evaluating the same middle school humanities program, including evaluation needs identification, establishment of priorities, data collection and analysis, and the formulation of recommendations. Each author states his or her value position. This variety of evaluation approaches provides alternative models for school program planners.

Brinkerhoff, R. O., Brethower, D. M., Hluchyj, T., and Ridings Mowakowski, J. *Program Evaluation: A Practitioner's Guide for Trainers and Educators: Sourcebook* and *Program Evaluation: A Design Manual.* Boston: Kluwer-Nijhoff Publishers, 1983. Written for those who work with special and regular education clients and students, this guide and accompanying spiral-bound manual are intended for use in training, teacher education, and professional development programs and projects in local schools, state agencies, higher education, and similar settings. The guide includes case examples, and poses and answers questions critical for effective evaluations. The manual includes evaluation worksheets and checklists.

Campbell, P. B. *Evaluating Youth Participation, A Guide for Program Operators.* Boston: Institute for Responsive Education (formerly National Commission on Resources for Youth, Inc.), 1982. A discussion of the yearlong effort of the Chicago Idea Exchange (composed of eleven youth agencies, three foundations, and the Chicago Mayor's Office of Employment and Training) to evaluate the effectiveness of projects with a strong youth participation emphasis. The evaluation was undertaken because the involved agencies and funders believed a clearer picture of youth participation project accomplishments was needed. The booklet's premise is that effective, useful evaluation results more from applied common sense than from technical training or professional expertise. Thus, commonsense terms are employed to discuss how an evaluation should look, what questions should be asked, and how to determine who should do the evaluation, as well as budgeting and reporting. Lists of the rights of a client in an evaluation, sample data collection instruments, and basic evaluation vocabulary are also included.

DeRoche, E. E. *An Administrator's Guide for Evaluating Programs and Personnel.* (2nd ed.) Needham Heights, Mass.: Allyn & Bacon, 1987. A guide to evaluation within school settings, including evaluations of classroom climate, office systems, facilities, instructional leadership, teachers, student activities programs, and more. Each chapter includes guidelines for evaluating the given area, special considerations, specific instruments that might be used, and selected references.

Evaluation Research Society Standards Committee. "Evaluation Research Society Standards for Program Evaluation." In P. H. Rossi (ed.), *Standards for Evaluation Practice.* New Directions for Program Evaluation, no. 15. San Francisco: Jossey-Bass, 1982. Fifty-five standards for evaluations, organized into six sections—formulation and negotiation, structure and design, data collection and preparation, data analysis and interpretation, communication and disclosure, and utilization—are presented as simple admonitory statements that should be useful to those who commission, conduct, and employ the results of program evaluation.

Feuerstein, M. T. *Partners in Evaluation: Evaluating Development and Community Programmes with Participants.* London: Macmillan, 1986. A book about participatory evaluation involving people of vastly differing educational levels, which grew from community development field experience in several regions of the world, including Southeast Asia, Africa, and South and Central America. Written in words that can be easily translated, it covers evaluation tools and such issues as planning an evaluation, using existing resources, reporting results, and using evaluation to strengthen programs. Sections of this book have been used to train people in community development projects worldwide. Dozens of helpful illustrations are included and users are permitted to copy the book as needed.

Fink, A., and Kosecoff, J. *An Evaluation Primer.* Sacramento, Calif.: Capitol, 1978. A hands-on text of basic procedures for evaluating existing social action programs, rather than a discussion of the theories, politics, or ethics of evaluation. It describes how to formulate evaluation questions, construct designs, and manage an evaluation in terms of budget and staff. Examples are provided throughout the text and its two workbooks: *Practical Exercises for Educators* and *Practical Exercises for Health Professionals.*

Herman, J. L. (ed.). *Program Evaluation Kit.* (2nd ed.) Newbury Park, Calif.: Sage, 1987. A nine-volume kit of "how-to" books on evaluation. *The Evaluator's Handbook* (vol. 1) provides a broad overview of evaluation planning complete with a practical guide to designing and managing evaluations and a directory to the other eight volumes. *How to Focus an Evaluation* (vol. 2) provides advice on planning an evaluation and discusses three elements in the focusing process and five perspectives on the evaluation process. *How to Design a Program Evaluation* (vol. 3) addresses the logic of quantitative research designs, provides an in-depth examination of six designs, and gives instructions on how to construct random samples. *How to Use Qualitative Methods in Evaluation* (vol. 4) explains the basic assumptions of qualitative procedures and guides the reader through proper procedures in data gathering and analysis. *How to Assess Program Implementation* (vol. 5) looks at the role and importance of implementation evaluation and includes step-by-step guides for handling program records, observations, and reports. *How to Measure Attitudes* (vol. 6) addresses means for selecting — or designing — credible evaluation instruments for measuring attitudes, and supplies precise instructions for developing questionnaires. *How to Measure Performance and Use Tests* (vol. 7) offers an overview of various approaches for measuring performance outcomes and selecting the instruments best suited to achieve an evaluation's specific goals. *How to Analyze Data* (vol. 8) deals with the functions of quantitative analysis and discusses meta-analysis techniques. *How to Communicate Evaluation Findings* (vol. 9) suggests ways to convey findings to various audiences and describes how to prepare outlines, written and oral reports, and tables and graphs.

House, E. R. *Evaluating with Validity.* Newbury Park, Calif.: Sage, 1980. A book intended for evaluators and others interested in extending their understanding of evaluation beyond methods and approaches to political and moral principles. It aims to bring a stronger sense of moral responsibility to the field of evaluation. Social and federal programs are frequently cited as examples.

Levin, H. M. *Cost-Effectiveness: A Primer.* Newbury Park, Calif.: Sage, 1983. An informal self-study tool or formal course text intended as a first course of study for educational evaluators and administrators. Topics include concepts, uses, and applications of cost-effectiveness analysis within a decision-oriented context. Exercises at the end of each chapter test the reader's understanding of the topic covered.

Love, A. J. *Internal Evaluation: Building Organizations from Within.* Newbury Park, Calif.: Sage, 1991. A discussion of the ways internal evaluation fits with other aspects of organizational life, the essential steps of the internal evaluation process, and the most frequent methods of accomplishing internal evaluations. How management's and evaluators' perceptions of each other affect their ability to work together and how political and organizational realities confront the internal evaluator are among the issues covered. Examples, and exercises at the end of each section provide an opportunity to explore key concepts in real world settings. Valuable to those involved in internal evaluation, but also very useful to foundation staff who evaluate projects and programs.

Madaus, G. F., Haney, W., and Kreitzer, A. *Testing and Education: Learning from the Projects We Fund.* New York: Council for Aid to Education, 1992. A brief primer for corporate contributions administrators, describing how to actively, purposefully, and usefully initiate, monitor, and apply the results of *independent* evaluations of educational projects and programs. It covers such topics as the three major approaches to educational evaluation; evaluation budgeting, tasks, tools, and questions; the role and choices of testing in evaluation; and what can be learned from funded projects. Includes a glossary of evaluation terms.

Owens, T. R., and Evans, W. *Program Evaluation Skills for Busy Administrators.* Portland, Ore.: Northwest Regional Educational Laboratory, 1977. A brief, easy-to-read guide to the mechanics of program evaluation that describes the purposes of evaluation, how to establish evaluation guidelines, how to prepare and carry out an evaluation plan, and how to report on evaluation results. Includes checklists and charts that are handy aids for the working administrator.

Patton, M. Q. *Qualitative Evaluation and Research Methods.* (2nd ed.) Newbury Park, Calif.: Sage, 1990. A thoughtful, candid, in-depth analysis of qualitative methods, presented in an enjoyable and often humorous manner, rather than as a "how-to" list of formulas. The reader learns, for example, that interviewing involves various kinds of questions — experience/behavior, opinion/value, feeling, and so on — before learning ways those questions should be framed and delivered as part of a well-constructed evaluation.

Patton, M. Q. *Practical Evaluation.* Newbury Park, Calif.: Sage, 1982. An exploration of the practical implications of conducting evaluation in relation to theories. Building on the work of the Joint Committee on Standards for Educational Evaluation, the Evaluation Network (currently the American Evaluation Association), and the Evaluation Research Society, this book provides grounding in evaluation fundamentals within the framework of utilization-focused evaluation. Goal setting, interviewing, surveys, data analysis, creative designs for evaluation, and managing information systems are all covered.

Patton, M. Q. *Utilization-Focused Evaluation.* (2nd ed.) Newbury Park, Calif.: Sage, 1986. A work based on the premise that underutilization is both a major problem in evaluation and a crisis in institutional arrangements. To address the question of how to enhance the value and use of evaluation research, the author presents an overall framework within which individuals can develop an evaluation design appropriate to their organization's unique circumstances. Appropriate both as a handbook for experienced evaluators and as a textbook for beginners.

Rossi, P. H., Freeman, H. E., and Sandefur, G. D. *Evaluation: A Systematic Approach* (with corresponding workbook). (4th ed.) Newbury Park, Calif.: Sage, 1989. A comprehensive review of evaluation, from key concepts to program tailoring, program monitoring, assessing impact, and measuring efficiency. Both randomized and nonrandomized designs for conducting impact assessment are discussed, as is the social context in which evaluation occurs. Examples and case studies illustrate major points. The workbook summarizes the book chapters and provides exercises for reviewing key points. Most useful for the student.

Scriven, M. *Evaluation Thesaurus.* (4th ed.) Newbury Park, Calif.: Sage, 1991. A wide-ranging description of terminology, models, techniques, and positions in evaluation. It provides practical checklists, ideas, and procedures not available elsewhere and pinpoints ways to correct the flaws and limitations of existing models of program evaluation. It presents a radically different concept of evaluation as a "transdisciplinary" field related to "value-free social science" — a concept believed to be free from the limitations and flaws of existing models. Includes a quick overview of major concepts, positions, acronyms, processes, and checklists in the field of evaluation.

Shadish, W. R., Cook, T. D., and Leviton, L. C. *Foundations of Program Evaluation.* Newbury Park, Calif.: Sage, 1991. A careful and incisive reexamination of the field of program evaluation, including the field's origins, the accumulated experience of evaluators, and the many underpinnings that have profoundly influenced development of the field. The work of the seven major theorists of program evaluation is reviewed, compared, and contrasted. A concluding chapter summarizes areas of agreement and disagreement among these influential theorists and suggests future directions for a new theory of program evaluation.

Shortell, S. M., and Richardson, W. C. *Health Program Evaluation.* St. Louis, Mo.: Mosby, 1978. The essentials of health program design, analysis, and evaluation. This text keys on means to bridge the diverse worlds of technical evaluation and political reality, and reminds the reader that researchers must understand the political and administrative environment in which research and health services evaluation are likely to occur.

Stufflebeam, D. L., and Shinkfield, A. J. *Systematic Evaluation.* Boston: Kluwer-Nijhoff, 1984. A thorough treatment of approaches to evaluation in easily-readable form, including Suchman's scientific approach, Stufflebeam's improvement-oriented model, and Scriven's consumer-oriented approach. Each chapter describes an approach and concludes with questions to measure comprehension of the concepts presented. Provides an informative introductory chapter on the history of evaluation and an analysis of the pros and cons of various evaluation approaches.

Worthen, B. R. and Sanders, J. R. *Educational Evaluation: Alternative Approaches and Practical Guidelines.* White Plains, N.Y.: Longman, 1987. An easy-to-read text that leaves no stone unturned in its description of evaluation. Some of the topics covered are the various approaches to evaluation, including strengths, weaknesses, and cautions about employing them; when an evaluation is appropriate and how an evaluator should be selected;

how resources should be committed to the process; how evaluation questions should be identified; and how to develop the evaluation plan, contend with political questions, gather and analyze data, and report findings.

Yin, R. K. *Case Study Research: Design and Methods.* Newbury Park, Calif.: Sage, 1989. A description of the distinctive characteristics of case studies — design, analysis, and reporting. Although long stereotyped as a weak sibling, the case study is a valid method of doing social science research, and this book helps the reader make choices about when and how the case study might best be used.

Foundation Evaluation Manuals

Henry J. Kaiser Family Foundation. *Strategic Plan for Evaluation.* Menlo Park, Calif.: Henry J. Kaiser Family Foundation, 1989. A systematic approach for guiding foundation evaluation activities to "ensure that evaluation is incorporated routinely into [the foundation's] operations." The text discusses reasons why a foundation should do evaluation, considerations in planning, various evaluation methods, the principles that guide the Kaiser Family Foundation's own program, components of Kaiser's monitoring system, ways to determine when monitoring is enough or when a more extensive evaluation is warranted, and budgeting issues. Includes an appendix of evaluation terminology.

W. K. Kellogg Foundation. *Program Evaluation Manual* and *Evaluation Resources Handbook.* Battle Creek, Mich.: W. K. Kellogg Foundation, 1989. The manual details a framework for focusing evaluation on both individual projects and clusters of similar projects, and it guides program staff through specific aspects of their evaluation work, including proposal review, interaction with grantees, requiring annual reports from grantees, conducting evaluation conferences, and preparing reports to the foundation's board of trustees. The manual also describes the historical context for evaluation at this foundation and the foundation's belief that evaluation should be used to "see problems more clearly and discover new avenues for growth." The companion handbook provides some professional evaluators' names, qualifications, and references. Although the handbook is an internal document, copies of the materials used in its development are available.

The Lilly Endowment, Inc. *Evaluation Notebook.* Indianapolis, Ind.: The Lilly Endowment, Inc., 1989. A statement of foundation procedures for evaluation and a discussion of focusing evaluation work, designing the plan, obtaining information, analyzing and reporting results, and interpreting and remembering what has been learned. Lilly views evaluation as a form of continuing education that provides opportunities for critical thinking, gaining an informed perspective, and meeting accountability requirements. Contains discrete sections that can be copied as needed, several appendices of checklists and guidelines that Lilly uses to aid its work, and a discussion of the endowment's "context and commitment" for grantmaking.

Pew Charitable Trusts. *A Manual for Evaluation.* Philadelphia, Pa.: Pew Charitable Trusts, June 1989. A manual of guidelines and procedures for evaluation of the trust's projects, and information on how to select grants to be evaluated, the kinds of evaluation that are most appropriate, how to organize an evaluation study, "quality assurance" in evaluation, and how to use evaluation findings.

Rockefeller Foundation. *Program Evaluation at the Rockefeller Foundation: An Overview.* New York: Rockefeller Foundation, 1990. A white paper describing the Rockefeller Foundation program evaluation system developed in 1990 and pilot tested as a "set of working hypotheses" in 1991. It sets forth the system's assumptions, goals, and principles; points out the many dimensions of the evaluation of the foundation's major programs — such as intervention strategy, context, cost, levels of impact, and sustainability; and concludes with charts that define general evaluation activities and corresponding staff responsibilities. Includes observations from a 1989 survey of three philanthropic organizations and two development agencies regarding evaluation.

The Saint Paul Foundation, Inc. *Evaluating Foundation Programs & Projects*. Little Canada, Minn.: The Minnesota Curriculum Services Center, 1989. A handbook to help grant recipients learn more about the value of evaluation and also learn how to develop evaluation plans, collect and analyze information, and use findings to report on and improve programs. It is one part of a comprehensive evaluation plan, initiated by The Saint Paul Foundation and its client foundations, the F. R. Bigelow Foundation and Mardag Foundation, to improve the information available to them on the effects of past and current grantmaking programs; to inform future grantmaking decisions, and to increase the effectiveness of programs to which grants are made.

The San Francisco Foundation. *An Evaluation Primer*. San Francisco: The San Francisco Foundation, 1984. A manual of evaluation approaches for the foundation as intermediary, venture capitalist, change agent, and community citizen. The manual also defines the evaluation principles of the San Francisco Foundation. It suggests that a foundation use evaluation primarily as a learning tool, to help the foundation do better work, rather than as a tool for decision making. Concepts to be considered in testing hypotheses about projects, seven levels at which to evaluate projects, questions to be asked for selecting projects for evaluation, and means for developing evaluation criteria and for reviewing an evaluation plan are listed. Standards for reports submitted to the San Francisco Foundation by evaluation consultants are defined. Includes a bibliography of texts and articles on evaluation.

Evaluation Reports/Surveys

Center for the Study of Family Policy. *Basics of Evaluation*, Workshop for Council on Foundations Annual Conference, Apr. 1990. A packet of materials developed for use in a 1990 Council on Foundations workshop for foundation representatives. It contains examples of evaluation-related forms, letters, and reports used by the Edna McConnell Clark Foundation, the San Francisco Foundation, and the National Charities Information

Bureau. Contact: Center for the Study of Family Policy, Hunter College, City University of New York, Room 1420 East, 695 Park Avenue, New York, NY 10021.

The Forbes Trust. *Evaluation in the Voluntary Sector.* London: The Forbes Trust, 1988. A package of information (comprising a series of booklets, a book, and a wall poster) resulting from ten seminars about the current state of evaluation practice in the United Kingdom's voluntary sector. The seminars were part of the process to create Charities Evaluation Services (CES), a registered charity whose main function is to provide an evaluation advisory service to voluntary organizations. The book presents practical tips for carrying out an evaluation. The wall poster ("How Good a Job Are You Doing? Evaluation Is a Way to Find Out") poses common questions and offers suggestions on evaluation. Contact: Charities Evaluation Services, Forbes House, 9 Artillery Lane, London, U.K. E1 7LP.

Henry J. Kaiser Family Foundation. *Survey of Evaluation Strategies in Private Foundations.* Menlo Park, Calif.: Henry J. Kaiser Family Foundation, July 1989. A survey initiated by the Kaiser Family Foundation and conducted in collaboration with Social Research Applications, Inc., to learn about, and from, the evaluation strategies of other foundations before Kaiser developed its own evaluation processes. Fourteen foundations participated in some way and outcomes are reported on the issues of monitoring, self-evaluation, evaluation of individual grants, and the many ways in which evaluation can be used. Includes the survey instrument employed for the study. Contact: Kaiser Family Foundation, Quadras, 2400 Sand Hill Road, Menlo Park, CA 94025.

Kehrer, B. H., Bonjean, C., Meyerson, D. C., and Johnson, R. M. *Grantmaking Basics: Evaluation.* Workshop for the Council on Foundations Annual Conference, 1991. Audio Cassette. A ninety-minute taped discussion among panelists and audience members at the 1991 workshop. The discussion focuses on some of the most common evaluation concerns among foundation staff: how evaluation can be done within small, minimally staffed foundations, the difference between evaluation and monitoring, overcoming the fear of evaluation, evaluation costs, and where to find good evaluators. Contact: Audio Archives International, Inc., 3043 Foothill Boulevard, Suite 2, La Crescenta, CA 91214. Audio cassette order no.: i10422-480.

The Pew Charitable Trusts. *A Survey of Evaluation Practice in Peer Institutions.* Philadelphia, Pa.: The Pew Charitable Trusts, Dec. 1988. A report on the findings of a three-part telephone survey to learn about the evaluation, monitoring, and audit practices of sixteen foundations, including seven of the ten largest foundations in this country and nine other foundations with grant monitoring/evaluation systems. Contact: The Pew Charitable Trusts, One Commerce Square, 2005 Market Street, Suite 1700, Philadelphia, PA 19103.

United Seniors Health Cooperative. *Mistakes Can Lead to Success.* Washington, D.C.: United Seniors Health Cooperative, 1989. A fifteen-page booklet that succinctly cites the "ten biggest mistakes" the United Seniors Health Cooperative made during its start-up phase. Cooperative president James P. Firman notes, "By learning from our experiences, we not only survived, we are thriving. Our successes are built on our failures." Contact: United Seniors Health Cooperative, 1334 G Street, N.W., Suite 500, Washington, D.C. 20005.

Sumariwalla, R. D., and Taylor, M. E. *The Application of Program Evaluation in the Management of the Nonprofit Sector: An Exploratory Study.* Alexandria, Va.: United Way of America, 1991. A report, prepared for the 1991 Spring Research Forum of the Independent Sector, containing the results of a 1990 survey of a sample of foundations, United Way agencies, national social service agencies, and other national member organizations of the Independent Sector. The survey determined the types of evaluation being conducted, the kinds of technical assistance being provided, the staff resources dedicated to evaluation, and the practices regarding the sharing of evaluation findings. The report presents conclusions, recommendations, and notes that "funders and national organizations should work together to design outcome measures and instruments . . . so that funder expectations and available techniques will be compatible." It further states, "Funders must work with their grantees to develop program evaluation strategies that make sense and can be implemented by providers." Contact: United Way of America, 701 North Fairfax Street, Alexandria, VA 22314-2045.

Perspectives on Evaluation

The Foundation Center (ed.). *Conducting Evaluations: Three Perspectives.* New York: The Foundation Center, 1980. A volume of three papers commissioned for a 1980 workshop sponsored by three foundations to discuss evaluation in foundations: Marvin Alkin, "A User Focused Approach"; Robert Bothwell, "A Grantee Perspective"; and Marilyn Levy, "Documenting the Grantmaking Process." Each paper takes a different perspective, and the three views provide a starting point for the discussion of evaluation policy and strategy. Includes an annotated bibliography on evaluation by Peggy Sweitzer. Contact: The Foundation Center, 888 Seventh Avenue, New York, NY 10106.

The Lilly Endowment, Inc. *Annual Report 1990.* Indianapolis, Ind.: The Lilly Endowment, Inc., 1990. A report that focuses on the endowment's 1990 evaluation program, calling it "one of our most important tools for the cultivation of both prudence and creativity." Includes an executive message ("Coping with Growth Against a Backdrop of Realism"), an evaluation essay ("Learning Begins at Home"), and a discussion of endowment activities that illustrate how evaluation provides direction for future programming. Contact: The Lilly Endowment, Inc., 2801 North Meridian Street, P.O. Box 88068, Indianapolis, IN 46208.

White, S. *Evaluation of Foundation Activities.* An occasional paper. New York: Alfred P. Sloan Foundation, June 1970. A paper in which Stephen White of the Sloan Foundation poses several questions that guide the grantmaking process: for example, are the formal procedures of grantmaking being efficiently and effectively carried out, so that foundation activities constitute the optimum use of foundation resources? And, What did the grant accomplish? Suggests issues that should be considered when an evaluation is undertaken to answer these questions. Contact: The Alfred P. Sloan Foundation, 630 Fifth Avenue, New York, NY 10020.

Articles

Magat, R. "Decisions, Decisions" (pregrant assessment). *Foundation News,* March/April 1983, pp. 24–31.

Butt, M. G. "Getting to Know You" (postgrant evaluation). *Foundation News,* July/August 1985, pp. 26–35.

"New Perspectives on Evaluation." *Grassroots Development Journal of the Interamerican Foundation,* 1990, *14*(1).

The 1, 2, 3 of Evaluation, an Introduction to Three Basic Tools. The National Charities Information Bureau, 1989.

"Should More Grants Fail?" *Chronicle of Philanthropy,* 1990, *2*(21).

Journals

Educational Evaluation and Policy Analysis, quarterly publication of the American Educational Research Association, Washington, D.C.

Evaluation Practice, tri-annual publication sponsored by the American Evaluation Association and published by JAI Press, Greenwich, Conn.

Evaluation Review: A Journal of Applied Social Research, published six times annually by Sage Publications, Newbury Park, Calif.

New Directions for Program Evaluation, publication of the American Evaluation Association, published quarterly as part of the Jossey-Bass Education Series by Jossey-Bass, San Francisco, Calif.

References

Barley, Z., and Jenness, M. "Cluster Evaluation for the W. K. Kellogg Foundation Science Education Initiative." Annual Report 1990–91. Kalamazoo, Mich.: The Evaluation Center, Western Michigan University, June 1991.

Berdie, D., and Anderson, J. *Questionnaires*. Metuchen, N.J.: Scarecrow Press, 1974.

Bruner Foundation and Primerica Foundation. "Final Report: Evaluation of New York Cities in Schools." Unpublished monograph. New York: Bruner Foundation and Primerica Foundation, January 1988.

Budd, R. W., and others. *Content Analysis of Communication*. New York: Macmillan, 1967.

Corder-Bolz, J. "Report on National Youthworker Education Project." Unpublished monograph. Indianapolis, Ind.: Lilly Endowment, 1979.

Corder-Bolz, J., and Wisely, D. S. "An Evaluation of the National Youthworker Education Project — A Summary Report." Unpublished monograph. Indianapolis, Ind.: Lilly Endowment, September 1980.

305

Council on Foundations. *Grantmakers for Children and Youth Report.* Washington, D.C.: Council on Foundations, September 1988.

Dillman, D. A. *Mail and Telephone Surveys: The Total Design Method.* New York: Wiley, 1978.

Erickson, J. *A Follow-up Study of the National Youthworker Education Project, 1975–1980.* St. Paul: Center for Youth Development and Research, University of Minnesota, 1986.

Fitz-Gibbon, C. T., and Morris, L. L. *How to Design a Program Evaluation.* Vol. 3 of J. L. Herman (ed.), *Program Evaluation Kit.* (2d ed.) Newbury Park, Calif.: Sage, 1987.

Foundation Collaborative. "Creating Opportunities: A Report on the First Five Years of Operation of the Summer Youth Employment Career/Vocational Exploration Program." Philadelphia: William Penn Foundation, December 1987.

Foundation Collaborative. "The 1990 Summer Youth Employment Career/Vocational Exploration Project." Final Report. Philadelphia: William Penn Foundation, November 8, 1990.

Fowler, F. J., Jr. *Survey Research Methods.* (2nd ed.). Newbury Park, Calif.: Sage, 1989.

Fowler, F. J., Jr., and Mangione, T. W. *Standardized Survey Interviewing: Minimizing Interviewer-Related Error.* Newbury Park, Calif.: Sage, 1990.

Gorden, R. L. *Interviewing: Strategy, Techniques, and Tactics.* Belmont, Calif.: Dorsey Press, 1987.

Green, L. W., and Lewis, F. M. *Measurement and Evaluation in Health Education and Health Promotion.* Palo Alto, Calif.: Mayfield, 1986.

Hegstrom, L. T. "Evaluation Report, Fred Meyer Charitable Trust Aging and Independence Program." Unpublished monograph. Portland, Oreg.: Meyer Memorial Trust, 1988.

Henerson, M. E., Morris, L. L., and Fitz-Gibbon, C. T. *How to Measure Attitudes.* Vol. 6 of J. L. Herman (ed.), *Program Evaluation Kit.* (2nd ed.) Newbury Park, Calif.: Sage, 1987.

Hopkins, K. D., and Stanley, J. C. *Educational and Psychological Measurement and Evaluation.* Englewood Cliffs, N.J.: Prentice-Hall, 1981.

Jaeger, R. M. *Sampling in Education and the Social Sciences.* White Plains, N.Y.: Longman, 1984.

Joint Committee on Standards for Educational Evaluation. *Standards for Evaluations of Educational Programs, Projects, and Materials.* New York: McGraw-Hill, 1980.

W. K. Kellogg Foundation. *Program Evaluation Manual.* Battle Creek, Mich.: W. K. Kellogg Foundation, 1989.

W. K. Kellogg Foundation. *Evaluation at the W. K. Kellogg Foundation.* Battle Creek, Mich.: W. K. Kellogg Foundation, 1991. Videotape.

Klein, M. R. "Enhancing the Impact of Grantmaking." Unpublished monograph. Portland, Oreg.: Meyer Memorial Trust, 1988.

Konopka, G. *Young Girls: A Portrait of Adolescence.* New York: Simon & Schuster, 1976.

Krasney, M. "The James Irvine Foundation's 1991 Evaluation: A Summary Report." Unpublished monograph. San Francisco: The James Irvine Foundation, 1991.

Landy, L., and Prior, E. K. "'The Millionaire' Revisited: Lessons from a Nonprofit Venture Capital Program." Unpublished monograph, May 1989.

The Lilly Endowment, Inc. *Evaluation Notebook.* Indianapolis, Ind.: The Lilly Endowment, Inc., 1989.

Miles, M. B. *Innovations in Education.* New York: Columbia University Press, 1964.

Morris, L. L., Fitz-Gibbon, C. T., and Lindheim, E. *How to Measure Performance and Use Tests.* Vol. 7 of J. L. Herman (ed.), *Program Evaluation Kit.* (2nd ed.) Newbury Park, Calif.: Sage, 1987.

Nason, J. W. *Foundation Trusteeship: Service in the Public Interest.* New York: The Foundation Center, 1989.

Nelson, L. M., "Recommendations to Trustees of the Fred Meyer Charitable Trust." Memorandum. Portland, Oreg.: Meyer Memorial Trust, April 6, 1988.

Patton, M. Q. *Utilization-Focused Evaluation.* (2nd ed.) Newbury Park, Calif.: Sage, 1986.

Patton, M. Q. *Qualitative Evaluation and Research Methods.* (2nd ed.) Newbury Park, Calif.: Sage, 1990a.

Patton, M. Q. "Taking Mission Seriously: An Evaluation of the Mission and Accomplishments of the Northwest Area Foundation, 1986–1990." Unpublished monograph. Saint Paul, Minn.: Northwest Area Foundation, 1990b.

Peterson, P. E., and Jencks, C. (eds.). *The Urban Underclass.* Washington, D.C.: Brookings Institution, 1991.

Polikoff, A. *Housing the Poor: The Case for Heroism.* New York: Harper Business, 1978.

Rosenbaum, J. E., and Popkin, S. J. *Economic and Social Impacts of Housing Integration.* Evanston, Ill.: Center for Urban Affairs and Policy Research, Northwestern University, March 1990.

Rosenbaum, J. E., Rubinowitz, L. S., and Kulieke, M. J. *Low-Income Black Children in White Suburban Schools.* Evanston, Ill.: Center for Urban Affairs and Policy Research, Northwestern University, February 1986.

Rossi, P. H., Freeman, H. E., and Sandefur, G. D. *Evaluation: A Systematic Approach.* (4th ed.) Newbury Park, Calif.: Sage, 1989.

Shaw, M. R., and Wright, J. M. *Scales for the Measurement of Attitudes.* New York: McGraw-Hill, 1967.

Stake, R. E. *Quieting Reform.* Chicago: University of Illinois Press, 1986.

Stockdill, S. H. *The Technology for Literacy Evaluation Report.* St. Paul: EnSearch, August 1988. (ED 321 003)

Stufflebeam, D. L., and Shinkfield, A. J. *Systematic Evaluation.* Boston: Kluwer-Nijhoff, 1984.

Turner, T. C. and Stockdill, S. H. (eds.). *The Technology for Literacy Project Evaluation.* St. Paul: The Saint Paul Foundation, December 1987. (ED 295 028)

Webb, E. J., Campbell, D. T., Schwartz, R. D., and Sechrest, L. *Unobtrusive Measures: Nonreactive Research in the Social Sciences.* Skokie, Ill.: Rand McNally, 1966.

Worthen, B. R., and Sanders, J. R. *Educational Evaluation: Alternative Approaches and Practical Guidelines.* White Plains, N.Y.: Longman, 1987.

Worthen, B. R., and White, K. R. *Evaluating Educational and Social Programs: Guidelines for Proposal Review, Site Evaluation, Evaluation Contracts, and Technical Assistance.* Boston: Kluwer-Nijhoff, 1986.

Yin, R. K. *Case Study Research: Design and Methods.* Newbury Park, Calif.: Sage, 1989.

Index

Participant observers, at TLC, 134, 136–137
Participant-oriented evaluation, 272–273
Particularistic evaluation, for CIS, 111, 115–117, 126–127
Patton, M. Q., 15, 29, 130, 137–140, 141–144, 146, 152, 153, 154, 279, 280, 283, 286, 294–295
Pennsylvania. *See* Career/Vocational Exploration Program
Peterson, P. E., 225
Pew Charitable Trusts, 298, 301
Pfizer Foundation, 107
Philadelphia, Career/Vocational Exploration Program in, 182–198
Philadelphia Urban Coalition, 193, 197
Planning: evaluation for, 6–7, 8, 232; for evaluation, 255–256
Polikoff, A., 201, 202, 203, 224, 225, 229
Popkin, S. J., 215
Postgrant assessments, forms of, 22–23
Pratt, C., 52, 56, 60–61, 63, 65, 66, 69
Pre-post design: and choices, 14; for TLC, 130
Primerica (Inc.) Foundation, and CIS program, 103, 104, 107, 111, 117
Prior, E. K., 78, 79, 80, 81, 83–86, 88–89
Priorities, clarifying, at CIS, 119–120
Private Industry Council, 193
Process evaluation: applications of, 27, 28, 31; for Career/Vocational Exploration, 183; concept of, 274–275; by Meyer, 52; questions of, 12; of Skaggs grants, 78, 82
Program quality or impact, evaluation to assess, 6, 8, 129, 156, 232
Programs: criteria for evaluating, 254–255; types of, and evaluation, 25–29; worth of, 258–259
Project Girl, 159, 160, 163, 165, 171, 180
Proposals: evaluation of, 21; for outside evaluators, 39–40; request for, 51–76

Public relations-oriented evaluation, 273–274

Q

Qualitative methods: and choices, 15, 278–279; by Kellogg, 233
Quantitative methods, and choices, 14–15, 278–279
Quasi-experimental designs, 14, 281–282
Questionnaires: on Career/Vocational Exploration, 183, 187–188, 190; for CIS, 104, 110–111, 113–114; concept of, 283–284; and confidentiality, 110–111, 166, 188; for Gautreaux program, 200; for TLC, 130; for youthworker project, 157, 165–168
Quinn, J., 179, 181, 264

R

Randomized controlled experiment, 14, 281
Reagan administration, 78
Records analysis: for CIS, 104, 108, 111–113; for Rockefeller, 93
Report cards, for school programs, 96–97, 99–100
Request-for-proposals, case study assessing, 51–76
Research and evaluation grants, approaches for, 26
Richards, R., 234
Richardson, W. C., 296
Riddings Mowakowski, J., 290
Risely, B., 248
Rockefeller Foundation, 298. *See also* Winthrop Rockefeller Foundation
Rooks, C. S., 53, 55–56, 60, 61, 66, 67–69, 70, 71, 72, 76
Rosenbaum, J. E., 199, 203, 206, 207, 209n, 211, 214, 215, 217, 220, 221, 224, 225–226, 228, 229
Rossi, P. H., 281, 282, 290, 295
Rubinowitz, L. S., 199, 203, 204, 206, 207, 209n, 211, 213, 214, 225, 227–228, 259